Killer Bodies

Killer Bodies

The Rise and Fall of "Bad Girl" Comics

JOSEPH CRAWFORD

Rutgers University Press
New Brunswick, Camden, and Newark, New Jersey
London

Rutgers University Press is a department of Rutgers, The State University of New Jersey, one of the leading public research universities in the nation. By publishing worldwide, it furthers the University's mission of dedication to excellence in teaching, scholarship, research, and clinical care.

Library of Congress Cataloging-in-Publication Data

Names: Crawford, Joseph, 1982– author
Title: Killer bodies : the rise and fall of "bad girl" comics / Joseph Crawford.
Description: New Brunswick : Rutgers University Press, 2025. |
Includes bibliographical references and index.
Identifiers: LCCN 2025013085 | ISBN 9781978841963 paperback |
ISBN 9781978841970 hardcover
Subjects: LCSH: Comic books, strips, etc.—United States—History and criticism |
Comic books, strips, etc.—20th century—History and criticism | Women
superheroes in comics | LCGFT: Comics criticism
Classification: LCC PN6725 .C73 2025
LC record available at https://lccn.loc.gov/2025013085

A British Cataloging-in-Publication record for this book is available from the British Library.

∞ The paper used in this publication meets the requirements of the American National Standard for Information Sciences—Permanence of Paper for Printed Library Materials, ANSI Z39.48-1992.

rutgersuniversitypress.org

This book is dedicated,
with great affection,
to my colleague of eleven years, Paul Williams,
who failed to stop me
while he still had the chance.

Contents

Killer Bodies

Introduction

This book is a history of the "bad girl" subgenre of American superhero comics, which flourished roughly from 1992 to 2000. The "bad girl" craze was characterized by a glut of titles starring violent and aggressively sexualized superheroines, marketed primarily to young male readers. Time has not been kind to these titles, and most writers on comics have been happy to consign the genre to history. Within comics scholarship they are generally regarded as an embarrassment, an example of American comics culture at its worst. Every other phase of comics history has its defenders, but no one seems to want to talk about the "bad girls" at all.

This book aims not to rehabilitate the genre, which for the most part I found to thoroughly live down to its reputation, but simply to map it, and to explore what it reveals about the way that third-wave feminism and postfeminism interacted with American popular culture. Despite the retrospective shame with which they are now viewed, in their day these comics were extremely popular, on a scale which makes them useful barometers of cultural change within their sociocultural microclimates. They clearly tapped into something important in the 1990s zeitgeist, and the sword-swinging, semi-naked "bad girl" heroine, simultaneously liberated and objectified, is a vivid symbol for the often-conflicted attitudes that their readers and creators held toward ideas of female empowerment and changing gender roles. If the era during which they thrived is now remembered within comics history for landmark graphic novels such as *Maus*, *Sandman*, and *Persepolis*, which demonstrated that comics could be used to address serious issues relating to politics, violence, gender, and sexuality, then "bad girl" comics constituted their low-culture shadow, addressing similar themes in a cruder and more exploitative fashion (Beaty and Woo 5). They, too, were interested in pushing the boundaries of what could be done in comics, even if their motives were commercial rather than artistic or ideological: Indeed, it is their very commercialism that makes them useful to the cultural historian, as they lived and died by their ability to reflect the shifting preferences of their target audience. If an artistic triumph like *Maus* reveals what was happening at the cutting edge of early 1990s comics culture, then a commercial triumph like *Lady Death* is equally revealing of what was happening in the median comic shop, where the median comic book reader continued to buy his median selection of "bad girl" titles month after month after month.

I was a child of the '90s, but I did not grow up reading comics. As a straight(-ish), white(-ish), middle-class teenage boy, I was squarely in the target market for the works discussed in this book, but at the time they passed me by: In the neopagan, Goth-adjacent circles I then moved in, the only comic to be seen with was Neil Gaiman's *Sandman*. It was not until years later that I read anything more mainstream, and when I did it was in the form of the black-and-white *Marvel Essentials* line, through which I became acquainted with the foundational work of Jack Kirby and Steve Ditko. Nothing past their 1960s heyday held much interest for me, and when I glanced through the mainstream comics first published during my own adolescence I saw little that seemed worthy of attention.

Exposure to the wider discourse around American superhero comics soon taught me that my opinions were widely shared, and that the 1990s were generally seen as a dark age for the genre, characterized by embarrassing sexism, rampant commercialism, and meaningless violence (Beaty and Woo 74). The "bad girl" comics were usually cited as the worst of the worst, exemplifying everything wrong with 1990s comic-book culture: bad writing, incoherent plotting, pornographic art, and a crude reliance on sex and bloodshed to sell comics to an audience of hormonal adolescent boys. In the academic scholarship on comic books, their status was, if anything, even lower: They were what Bart Beaty and Benjamin Woo described as "implausible objects of study," doomed to be found wanting by academic writers trained to value "literariness, seriousness, or difficulty" (13, 84). If graphic novels such as Alison Bechdel's *Fun Home* were cited as proof that comics could be serious works of literary art, then 1990s "bad girl" titles functioned rhetorically as their despised antitypes, embodying everything they were not: They were dismissed as sexist, racist, immature, derivative, and crassly commercial (25, 32–33). Understandably, scholars eager to prove to a skeptical academy that comics had more to offer than wish-fulfillment fantasies for straight white men had little sympathy for works which confirmed on every page that the straight white male gaze was the only one they had any interest in. It is thus unsurprising that the genre has never yet been seriously studied, and is mentioned primarily to establish the merits of other works by showing that they form their absolute antithesis.

Academic discussion of "bad girl" comics is thin on the ground, and no scholar has yet studied the genre in any detail. In *Tough Girls* (1999), Sherrie Inness notes that "recent comic books . . . contain many supposedly tough women who actually are little more than overly endowed caricatures with large guns and skimpy costumes," but her analysis of the genre is limited to a very small number of titles (145–146). Jeffrey Brown's *Dangerous Curves* (2011) accurately describes the "bad girl" trend as being comprised of "female characters that dominated the struggling comics industry in the mid-nineties," characterized by what he calls "an odd combination of toughness and sexiness" and exaggerated anatomy that "amount to an almost hysterical mask of femininity," but his discussion of them is very brief, used mostly as a springboard for his analysis of the 1996 film *Barb Wire* (53–55). The same "odd combination" is noted by Christopher Hayton in his 2014 article "Evolving Sub-Texts in the Visual Exploitation of the Female Form":

> Bad Girls would frequently take on the role and form of a dominatrix, combining ultra-feminine seductiveness with masculine toughness. . . . Interpretation of Bad Girl comics is difficult, however, because, on the one hand, they feature powerful, assertive females. Then again, Bad Girl comics tend to undermine any progress towards sexual equality by maintaining, and indeed intensifying the use of female bodies as sexual objects, despite the sexual power attributed to them. . . . Sexual objectification and opportunity for fantasy are intensified, yet Bad Girl scripts still tend to present mixed messages that include feminist stances. Lady Death, for instance, seems not to yield to any male character, yet she is depicted in extreme ways that are clearly intended for consumption by the male gaze.

Mike Madrid's superheroine history *The Supergirls* (2009) devotes just two pages to the "bad girl" trend and its rapid descent into self-parody, while Carolyn Cocca's *Superwomen* (2016) skips over the 1990s almost entirely, describing it as a dark age characterized by exclusionary white male fan cultures, exaggerated gender binaries, and hostility to women (Madrid 96–97; Cocca, *Superwomen* 10–12). In *Superwomen*, the trend is described as a mere interregnum between more worthwhile epochs, one that was thankfully ended by the rise of the internet and the diversification of the audience for American comic books (14).

Cocca's two other articles on "bad girl" comics, "Negotiating the Third Wave of Feminism in *Wonder Woman*" (2014) and "The 'Broke Back Test': A Quantitative and Qualitative Analysis of Portrayals of Women in Mainstream Superhero Comics, 1993–2013" (2014), likewise position the 1990s as a nadir for female representation in comics, from which subsequent developments have only partially redeemed them. These articles do important work in drawing attention to the connections between "bad girl" aesthetics and third-wave feminism, and "The 'Broke Back Test'" remains the only scholarly work to date that systematically examines a corpus of "bad girl" comics rather than relying on generalizations.

Due to the constraints of the article form, however, the number of "bad girl" titles it surveys is relatively small: just thirty-six issues from the 1990s, and another thirty-six from the early 2000s (413).

An excellent example of the ways in which comics scholarship has struggled with "bad girl" comics can be seen in Hope Nicholson's *The Spectacular Sisterhood of Superwomen* (2017). Nicholson's knowledge of comics history is immense, and she perceptively discusses comic book heroines from the 1930s right up to the 2010s. When she comes to the 1990s, she offers a succinct summary of the "bad girl" aesthetic:

> In the 1990s the bad girl reigned supreme. Of course, pinup girls in scandalous clothing weren't exactly new to comics. In fact, as we saw from Sally the Sleuth, they've been with us since the very beginning. But girls who were on the ambiguous side of good and evil, who fought monsters viciously and with a savage joy, those characters are particular to the '90s. Also unique to the decade were the particular aesthetics of the bad girl character, all of whom were fairly interchangeable. Big boobs, big butts, long, long slender legs, pouty lips, tiny noses, and catlike eyes with arched brows were the hallmarks. Along with clothing that somehow always managed to just cover the nipple and vulva, though rarely much more. (179–180)

However, when Nicholson comes to discuss a specific "bad girl" comic, *American Woman*, she expresses confusion at its incoherent plot, its incongruous combination of heartfelt speeches and pinup imagery, and above all at the way that it breaks off mid-story after only two issues. "It's hard to really know what this comic is all about," Nicholson writes, clearly rather bewildered by what she has just read. "Could this T&A comic be a biting social commentary and work of dystopian fiction? Why not? It's certainly able to be considered as more than just a story of a sexy lady-girl with superpowers" (158–160).

As anyone familiar with "bad girl" comics will know, two issues of confusing fight scenes between barely dressed women followed by an unresolved cliffhanger and a series cancellation is pretty much the quintessential "bad girl" reading experience. "Bad girl" titles were notorious for their nonsensical storylines, and few were published for long enough to reach any kind of satisfying conclusion: Many were canceled after just a handful of issues, and in some cases after just one. The fact that fans of the genre kept buying them anyway strongly suggests that these traits were not seen as deal-breakers, at least by their target audience, and indeed the entire trend makes more sense once it is understood that most of these comics existed primarily as a delivery system for variant covers and images of sexualized violence rather than as narratives in any traditional sense. But while describing *American Woman* as "a biting social commentary" is a stretch, Nicholson is correct to note that the comic "[can] be considered as more than just a story of a sexy lady-girl with superpowers." Despite, or sometimes because of, their aggressive incoherence, these works frequently reflected a whole range of larger cultural issues.

As Martha McCaughey and Neal King argue in *Reel Knockouts*, it is often "the lowest genres" which most clearly reveal "the subconscious of our popular culture" (20). In this context, I find it highly suggestive that Brown, Hayton, and Nicholson all describe the genre as an essentially *confusing* one: They describe it as "odd," find "interpretation . . . is difficult," and conclude that "it's hard to really know what [it's] all about" (Brown 55; Hayton np; Nicholson 160). If these comics are confusing, I would suggest that it is because they themselves were fundamentally *confused*. They were torn between their loyalties toward incompatible ideals, and their confusion can tell us something valuable about the contradictions of the cultural moment which gave rise to them.

My analysis of these works is not informed by nostalgia: I never set foot inside a 1990s comic shop, and would probably not have felt welcome if I did. Yet the more I learned about the "bad girl" craze, the more intrigued I became. Many of these comics were initially written with clear feminist intent: It is easy to critique titles like *Ghost* and *Witchblade* and *Catwoman*, and indeed this book shall do so at some length, but it is nonetheless obvious that their creators initially aimed, however imperfectly, to communicate messages of female empowerment and antipatriarchal resistance. They were early adopters of manga styles, and their pages are marked by cross-cultural exchanges between Japanese and American comic book traditions. Their art was sometimes boldly experimental, their storylines addressed everything from trans metaphors (*Mantra*) to Japanese nationalism (*Kabuki*) to the abuse of women within the psychiatric system (*Elektra: Assassin*), and for a while they enjoyed considerable commercial success. So how is it that a genre which began as an attempt to introduce some much-needed feminist ideology and cultural diversity into American superhero comics ended up degenerating, within just a few years, into something little better than pornography, a byword for all that was worst in comic book culture, even as their creators continued to insist that their stories were meant to empower women rather than degrade them? Why had almost all the titles that sold so well in 1994 been canceled by 2000?

This book is my attempt to make sense of the rise and fall of "bad girl" comics. It is the story of how a group of men persuaded themselves, and each other, that they were the ideal people to act as spokesmen for female experience, and the ways that their attempts to do so crashed and burned. It is a story of good intentions, unacknowledged privilege, terrible business decisions, and appalling fashion sense. And ninjas. Many, *many* ninjas.

When I began my research, I created a spreadsheet to keep track of the comics I had read. At the time of writing, I am up to 2,371: It is distressingly possible that I have read more "bad girl" comics than anyone else who has ever lived. As I assembled my research corpus I acquired physical copies, first by ones and twos, then by dozens, and finally by hundreds: cheap lots, for the most part, purchased online for a fraction of their original cover price. As they accumulated, most of them still bagged and boarded and in pristine condition, I felt the powerful sense that I was heaping up the wreckage of other people's faded dreams. These were clearly comics whose original owners had preserved them carefully because they believed they would one day be worth something, convinced that their chromium covers or red foil lettering would make them valuable collector's items, or that future fans would pay dearly to own the issues in which once-popular characters like Witchblade first appeared. Their hopes came to nothing: Their values crashed in the late nineties and have carried on falling ever since. Unsalable "bad girl" back issues clog the catalogues of every online comic retailer. I even own a copy of the *Shi / Lady Death* issue 0 crossover with a novelty cover of printed canvas, whose original price was an eye-watering $100—well over $150 in today's money. In 2022 I bought one on eBay for ten euros.

The collapse in the monetary value of these comics vividly illustrates the extent of their fall. Works that once seemed novel and exciting have come to seem merely embarrassing, with none of the classic status that attaches itself to comics of older eras. Nor is their decline much to be mourned, as I have no doubt that they collectively contributed to a cultural climate in which women were habitually objectified, exploited, silenced, and abused. But among the parade of girls and gore I found some works of genuine interest, and I believe that even those that were exactly as bad as I expected remain worthy of study, both for what they reveal about their original cultural context and for the lasting impact they have had upon the depiction of gender in American comic books and popular culture. It is this analysis that forms the subject of this book.

Good Girls Gone Bad: Defining "Bad Girl" Comics

Before proceeding, it is important to clarify what was distinctive about the "bad girl" comics of the 1990s. As Nicholson notes, superhero comics starring physically capable, highly sexualized female characters are hardly new: Examples can be found as far back as the 1930s (179). The term "good girl art" was coined in the mid-twentieth century to describe comic book art styles that traded on sexualized depictions of women, often partially nude or dressed in revealing costumes (Gabilliet 35; Madrid 23; Hayton). This tradition was particularly associated with early comics such as *Torchy* (1949–1950) and *Sheena* (1942–1952), but it never really went away, though it went into brief abeyance after the institution of the Comics Code in 1954. Retro 1940s-style "good girl" comics even enjoyed a resurgence in the late 1980s, right on the threshold of the "bad girl" craze, in titles such as *Nightveil* (1984–1987, 1989–1991), *FemForce* (1985–2021), *Good Girl Art Quarterly* (1985–1995), and the rebooted *Torchy* (1990–1992) (Voger 40). So if a knife-wielding, scantily dressed 1940s superheroine like Sheena was classed as "good girl art," what made a knife-wielding, scantily dressed 1990s superheroine like Razor an example of "bad girl art" instead?

The key distinction between the two styles was essentially one of *innocence*. "Good girl" heroines might try to make themselves look stylish or glamorous, but they were not shown as consciously attempting to sexualize themselves in order to ensure that they remained sexually unthreatening for their target audience. The illusion would be spoiled if they seemed to be deliberately aiming for overt sex appeal: Thus classic "good girl" characters like Torchy were forever *accidentally* finding themselves in what Jean-Paul Gabilliet describes as "risqué situations where their figures were particularly highlighted" (35). Such comics made liberal use of shower scenes, accidental nudity, and similar situations that gave their heroines "legitimate" excuses to appear in states of undress, and were infamous for their use of bondage scenarios in which the bodies of heroines were exposed against their will—a trend that ran right through the "good girl" genre, from *Wonder Woman* and *Sally the Sleuth* in the 1940s to *Spider-Woman* in the late 1970s. (See, for example, *Spider-Woman* vol. 1, nos. 4–6.) The costumes of superheroines drawn in "good girl" styles tended to be modeled on swimwear rather than lingerie, and when "good girl" characters such as Sue Storm or Spider Woman appeared in formfitting costumes it was supposedly for practical adventuring reasons rather than because they wanted to show off their bodies.

While totally objectified, "good girl" heroines were traditionally depicted as being unaware of their own objectification. Indeed, this lack of awareness was an important part of the overall "good girl" aesthetic, as it implied innocence and an absence of sexual agency. *Deliberate* sex appeal was for female villains like Catwoman or Emma Frost, and when superheroines were turned evil by external mind control—when Jean Grey became the Black Queen, for example, or when Sue Storm became Malice—the outward symbol of their change was often the adoption of a more revealing and fetishistic costume. It would not be quite accurate to say that these costumes were *more* sexualized, as their everyday supersuits already ensured that their bodies were perpetually on display, but their "evil" costumes lacked the plausible deniability of their "good girl" equivalents. When Jean Grey, in her Black Queen persona, dressed herself in high-heeled boots and a corset, it was obviously because she *wanted* to look sexy, which the comics depicted as a clear sign that her mind had been consumed by evil (*X-Men* vol. 1, nos. 130–133).

The "bad girl" aesthetic represented a redeployment of this visual vocabulary, previously reserved for female supervillains, to heroic (or at least antiheroic) female characters. If "good girl" femininity combined sex appeal with innocence, moral purity, and a willingness to defend the status quo, "bad girl" femininity was aligned with sexual aggression, violence, and rebellion. "Bad girl" costumes were overtly sexualized, and often inspired by bondage gear, fetish wear, or countercultural street fashion styles such as goth and punk. As well as being dressed differently, "bad girl" heroines were often drawn differently to their "good girl" predecessors, with bigger breasts and longer legs: In some comics this was taken to hyperbolic levels, resulting in bizarrely drawn characters with breasts bigger than their heads and legs making up over two-thirds of their total height. They were posed differently, often with their backs arched to thrust out their breasts and/or buttocks, or twisted to display buttocks and breasts simultaneously, sometimes to such an extent that their spines appeared to be broken. Improbably, they were often drawn adopting these poses even during combat, thus aligning their physical and sexual aggression.

Because the conventions of American comics meant that explicit sex was considered much more transgressive than explicit violence, most "bad girl" comics used violence in lieu of sex, implying that the heroine's bloodlust was matched by (or symbolic of) her sexual appetites. Whereas "good girl" superheroines used nonlethal attacks and had codes against killing, "bad girl" heroines fought using lethal weapons such as guns and swords, and generally had no qualms about slaughtering their enemies: Indeed, they often displayed an orgasmic delight in bloodshed. Their character designs traded on the juxtaposition of exaggerated weapons (hard, cold, masculine, violent) with exaggerated bosoms (soft, warm, feminine, sexual): Matthew Pustz summarized the whole genre as "powerful women with gravity-defying breasts doing horrific things to victims" (5). Paired blades or guns were commonplace, frequently held on either side of the heroine's chest to emphasize the doubling of weapons and breasts as almost interchangeable implements of physical and sexual power. Claudia Herbst's description of the "bad girl"–inspired video game heroine Lara Croft could be applied to almost all of them: "At the site of her body an ongoing exchange takes place between sex and violence, one leading to and allowing for an amplification of the other" (28).

When I write about "bad girl" comics, then, I mean action-adventure comics (including, but not limited to, superhero comics) whose protagonists are violent, aggressive, hypersexualized, and female. They are not necessarily actually *bad*, and indeed most of the leading "bad girl" heroines were much less antisocial than their character designs implied: Areala was a nun, Avengelyne was an angel, Razor was a crime-fighting vigilante, Shi was an honorable warrior (and a good Catholic), Witchblade was a police detective, Vampirella was a dogged foe of evil, and even Lady Death usually fought against people much worse than she was. This mismatch was noticed at the time: In a 1996 issue of *Gen13*, the protagonists meet Shi as part of a cavalcade of "bad girls" and ask her if she's bad too. She replies, as so many other "bad girl" heroines could have done, by quoting *Who Framed Roger Rabbit*: "I'm not really *bad* . . . I'm just *drawn* that way" (*Gen13* vol. 2, no. 13C).

Around these four key traits of violence, aggression, hypersexualization, and femininity clustered a constellation of related tropes, such as horror imagery, urban settings, revenge plots, borrowings from Japanese shonen manga, and a prurient fascination with female homosexuality. As ever, some works fit more neatly into the genre than others: The murderous lesbian vampire queen Purgatori was very obviously a "bad girl" character, whereas the happy-go-lucky brawler

Angel Fire was right on the edge of the genre, linked to it mainly by her sexualized character design and the fact she once teamed up with Shi. Collectively, however, these comics form a distinctive and easily identifiable trend which became popular in the early 1990s, peaked in 1994–1996, and mostly faded out over the course of the 2000s.

The "bad girl" aesthetic did not appear out of nowhere. It had several clear predecessors in American comics, including the skimpily dressed vampire heroine of *Vampirella* (1969), the chainmail-bikini-wearing barbarian Red Sonja (whose first appearance was in 1973, and whose first solo series dates from 1977), the ninja assassin Elektra in *Daredevil* (1981), the mutant heroine Storm's adoption of punk stylings in *Uncanny X-Men* (1983), and the female mercenary Silver Sable with her guns and her skintight bodysuit in *Spider-Man* (1985). Many of these characters became fan favorites, pointing the way to things to come, and Elektra and Silver Sable soon graduated from their initial roles as antagonists to male superheroes to become the protagonists of their own comic books. (One of the original comic-book "bad girls," Catwoman, made the same jump at much the same time.) It was in the early 1990s, however, that all these elements came together to form a cohesive subgenre, associated not just with a specific style of costume but a specific mood (dark, angry cynicism), a specific kind of story (violent revenge plots), a specific setting (urban decay), specific character types (vampires, cyborgs, criminals, ninjas), specific clothes (thigh-high boots, lingerie, opera gloves), and even specific colors (red, white, and black).

Responding to then-contemporary anxieties over American urban blight, "bad girl" stories were often set in crime-ridden cityscapes inspired by Frank Miller's *Daredevil* (1979–1983) and *Sin City* (1991–2000) and James O'Barr's *The Crow* (1989), settings in which the innocence of traditional "good girl" heroines seemed out of place in ways that the hyperviolent, hypersexual "bad girl" heroines were not. One "bad girl" comic can stand for many in this regard. The *Razor and Shi Special* (1994) opens with a full-page image of a beautiful young woman, drawn in classic "good girl" style, accompanied by a caption: "A young starry-eyed beauty leaves home for the big city—with big dreams . . . but big trouble is all this runaway is about to find." Having foolishly wandered into this blighted urban domain, she is set upon by a street gang called, appropriately enough, the Balls. "These streets belong to *the Balls*," they tell her, proclaiming that this is an urban space ruled by testosterone-fueled masculine violence, within which a "good girl" like her can only ever appear as a victim. Before they can assault her, they are themselves ambushed by the "bad girl" heroine Razor, who cuts her way through several men before finally being overwhelmed; Razor is then saved by the intervention of a *second* "bad girl" heroine, Shi, who kills even more of them. Razor and Shi proceed to massacre the remaining Balls in an almost wordless four-page sequence packed with bloody amputations and beheadings before going their separate ways. The comic closes with Razor musing, "For the first time I can remember I'm not alone . . . because somewhere out there . . . is a friend," the two heroines evidently having bonded through their shared capacity for vigilante violence. The "good girl" victim, meanwhile, runs away on page 3 and is never mentioned again. Razor would probably find the idea of being *her* friend risible.

As this comic suggests, the "bad girl" heroine acts as a physical and sexual apex predator. She is a woman who has responded to the threat of male sexual violence by becoming even more violent than the men who threaten her: They may hunt other women, but *she* hunts *them*. Bluntly, she has nothing to fear because she is the one with the biggest phallus, just as Shi's katana dwarfs the knives brandished by the Balls. (This "phallic woman" imagery reached its logical conclusion in the manga adaptation of *Witchblade*, whose heroine, when threatened with rape by demons, draws an enchanted sword *from her own vagina* and uses it to bloodily dismember them [*Witchblade Takeru Manga* vol 1.].) As the *Razor and Shi Special* indicates with almost comical directness, these heroines thus act as agents of symbolic (and sometimes literal) castration. Razor is the knife that cuts off "the Balls," and it is only fitting that she first became popular in the same year that Lorena Bobbitt became a feminist folk heroine for amputating her abusive husband's penis (Marcus 282; Yarrow 231).

These comics demonstrate the influence of second-wave feminism in three key ways: They recognize the pervasive threat of male violence toward women, they endorse the importance of female solidarity in the face of that violence (Razor's plaintive "I'm not alone . . ."), and they accept the possibility that women can and should save *themselves* from such threats, without the need of male protection. But their feminism is deeply individualist, a kind of parody of 1990s liberal feminism, celebrating only those exceptional individual women who can transcend their status as potential victims through sheer strength and determination (Whelehan 36). Cristina Stasia summarizes the message of much 1990s postfeminist media as being "we are always already equal, it is just a matter of exercising one's girl power," but as Susan Hopkins notes of 1990s media heroines, "Girl Power is not equally open to everyone" (Stasia 240; Hopkins 7). To the real-world woman afraid of the gang of men loitering on her street corner, "practice martial arts until you can kill them all single-handedly" is unlikely to seem like practical advice. The same attitudes suffuse their approach to sex: Razor can dress however she likes because she, unlike the woman she saves, is strong enough to maim anyone foolish enough to interpret her revealing clothes as a sexual invitation, and her ability to wear ultrasexualized costumes in violent urban environments and remain unmolested thus acts as a badge of her prowess in battle. The sexual agency of such characters is underwritten by their access to violence, without which they would be reduced to the unenviable position of the helpless "good girl" victim.

The conflicting meanings which were originally attached to this "bad girl" aesthetic are clearly visible in a *Fantastic Four* plotline published from 1992 to 1994, the very years in which the "bad girl" trend was gaining momentum. Sue

FIGURE 1 The archetypal "bad girl" plot, summarized in a single page. Bad men threaten the "good girl" with sexual violence, and the "bad girl" punishes them with physical violence, her blades violently penetrating the body of the would-be rapist. From *Razor and Shi Special* (1994), written and penciled by William Tucci, inks by Bobby Rae.

Storm, the team's token woman, had always acted as an exemplar of ultrarespectable comic book femininity: First introduced in 1961, she married her teammate Reed Richards in 1965, and gave birth to their first child in 1968. For the next twenty-five years Sue was characterized primarily as a wife and mother, as comic-book time meant that her son never grew up, leaving her stuck forever as a young mother with a small child to look after at home: She did not even graduate from "Invisible Girl" to "Invisible Woman" until 1986. In 1992, however, Sue began to change: She designed an extremely revealing, "bad girl"–style costume ("I was starting to feel like an old *frump* in that tedious, outdated jumpsuit!"), started to become more aggressive in her interactions with her husband ("*You inattentive, inconsiderate, self-absorbed, rattleheaded jerk!*"), and became more forceful in combat, using her powers to attack as well as defend (*Fantastic Four* vol. 1, no. 371). Other characters were swift to notice that her change in clothing was accompanied by a change in personality, noting, "She's become so *aggressive* lately—and downright *nasty*" (*Fantastic Four* vol. 1, no. 374).

At last Sue's nanny, the witch Agatha Harkness, diagnoses the problem: Sue was being possessed by her evil alternate personality, Malice. As Agatha explains: "*Malice* is a temporary identity which you once assumed . . . a creature of *total darkness* . . . and *naked aggression!* She has obviously *returned* . . . and now *controls* you! It's the only explanation for your recent *unruly behavior!*" Sue, however, did not share Agatha's assessment of the situation: "I was never as *sweet* and *delicate* as I appeared, Agatha! Malice was *always* an integral part of me . . . a part that I used to struggle to keep *repressed! NO MORE!*" (*Fantastic Four* vol. 1, no. 376).

The 1980s comics in which Malice first appeared endorsed Agatha's interpretation: The *real* Sue Storm was the "good girl" wife and mother she had always appeared to be, and her physically and sexually aggressive "Malice" persona was a pathological aberration to be expunged. In 1985 Sue had accepted this explanation, but by 1993—perhaps after listening to Bikini Kill on the radio—she was claiming something different: That "Malice" was merely the angry, assertive, sexually aggressive side of herself that she had been forced to repress in order to play her socially approved role as wife and mother. Her "unruly behavior" was not the result of a mental breakdown or demonic possession: She was just tired of repressing herself all the time. Her "bad girl" makeover thus symbolized her rejection of the restrictive, repressive "good girl" role she'd been locked into since 1961, which forbade her from expressing any kind of aggression or frustration with her lot. There were also strong implications that Sue was sexually unsatisfied by her long-term marriage with Reed—she complains that "you wouldn't notice if I were dancing *naked* in Macy's window!"—and that her provocative costumes and angry outbursts were motivated partly by a desire to push him into recognizing and addressing this fact (*Fantastic Four* vol. 1, no. 371).

Sue's change of character was controversial even at the time, and an editorial in the comics magazine *Wizard* complained, in characteristically misogynistic terms, that she had previously been "an exemplar of how a strong female character needn't be a bitch or an ice queen" but was now "just another bimbo showing too much flesh" (*Wizard* no. 30, 28). Her rebellion was short-lived, and it was not long before she was apologizing to her husband for "acting like a *total witch*." (The Comics Code forbade Marvel from using the word "bitch.") But the reason she gave for her behavior is highly significant: "The *Fantastic Four* has been pretty static for the past few years . . . while the world has *changed* . . . and grown considerably *darker* around us! I guess I'm just trying to *catch up* all at once . . . and I'm not handling it well!" (*Fantastic Four* vol. 1, no. 377).

This is Sue talking to Reed, but it's clearly also the writer talking to the reader, explaining why Sue's traditional "good girl" femininity had come to seem anachronistic, and apologizing for the clumsiness with which it had been updated. A few issues later Sue's time-traveling son entered her mind and forced Malice out of it, declaring, "You don't *belong* here! My mother has been your innocent victim all along!," and shortly afterward Sue abandoned her "bad girl" costume for good (*Fantastic Four* vol. 1, no. 384). Today Sue's "bad girl" look is usually viewed as her worst costume, and the whole episode is generally derided by fans as an example of the inappropriate oversexualization of superheroines characteristic of 1990s comics culture (Elfring). In context, however, this attempt to give Sue an aggressive "bad girl" persona was clearly not *only* an exercise in sexist fan service: It was also part of a bid, however flawed, to depict her as a more empowered and liberated character, very much of a piece with other portrayals of feminism in early 1990s popular culture. Sue ultimately had all the Malice driven out of her psyche, but the other "bad girls" of the era did not: In fact, "*unruly behavior*," "*naked aggression*," and "acting like a *total witch*" is a pretty fair summary of most "bad girl" comics, which often combined objectifying, male gaze–oriented visuals with stories about the necessity of violent resistance to patriarchal authority. After so many years of dutiful self-repression, it's easy to understand why Sue, like so many other superheroines, might have wanted a chance to be a bit of a bad girl, too.

Action Heroines in Feminist Scholarship

Although "bad girl" comics themselves have been the subject of very little scholarly criticism, 1990s action heroines more broadly have been considered in numerous critical works. Studies of comic book superheroines include Trina Robbins's *The Great Women Superheroes* (1996) and *From Girls to Grrrlz* (1999), Madrid's *The Supergirls* (2009), Cocca's *Superwomen* (2016), and Nicholson's *The Spectacular Sisterhood of Superwomen* (2017), while studies of action heroines include Yvonne Tasker's *Spectacular Bodies* (1993), Elizabeth Hills's "From Figurative Males to Action Heroines" (1999), Hopkins's *Girl Heroes* (1999), Inness's *Tough Girls* (1999) and *Action Chicks* (2004), McCaughey and King's *Reel Knockouts* (2001), Frances Early and Kathleen Kennedy's *Athena's Daughters* (2003),

Rikke Schubart's *Femme Fatalities* (2004) and *Super Bitches and Action Babes* (2007), Susan Owen, Sarah Stein, and Leah Vande Berg's *Bad Girls* (2007), and Brown's *Dangerous Curves* (2011) and *Beyond Bombshells* (2015). The fact that many of these studies were published during the same 1992–2004 period that forms the focus of this book reflects the extent to which the media of this era was recognized as taking a new approach to the depiction of violent women, prompting much scholarly discussion over whether the figure of the action heroine should be viewed as progressive or regressive in character.

Writing in 1993, Tasker pointed out that female-led 1970s action media such as *Charlie's Angels*, *Wonder Woman*, and *Policewoman* had depicted women as powerful but still required them to be both conventionally glamorous and loyal to male authority structures (19). Subsequent films such as *Aliens* moved away from this to some degree, but Tasker noted that feminist critics still generally took a negative view of action cinema, seeing it as glorifying patriarchal ideals of strength and violence even when its protagonists were female (134). Elizabeth Hills took a more positive view of cinematic action heroines, arguing that when feminist film critics condemned characters like Ripley in *Alien* as "pseudo males" because of their mastery of violence and technology, they risked entrenching a paradigm whereby femininity was understood as fundamentally incompatible with action and power (38, 42). She thus interpreted Ripley optimistically as a Deleuzian "body without organs," which "exceeds the limits of the binary and essentializing system of gender identities to become something beyond both" (48). Inness, meanwhile, acknowledged that such action media often had real appeal to female audiences, but argued that its visions of female empowerment were always softened by keeping its heroines "sexualized and feminine," thereby attempting to soothe "the very real societal uneasiness about Second Wave feminism." As she puts it, "the threat posed by the killer woman is mitigated in part because she is commonly portrayed as very sexually appealing to men," thus "demonstrating that their tough attitudes and actions fail to interfere with their primary role as sex objects for men" (37, 41, 47, 69–70).

The essays in *Action Chicks*, which Inness edited, communicate a similarly complex response to the figure of the action heroine. Herbst expressed alarm at the popularity of the *Tomb Raider* franchise, whose glorification and sexualization of violence she saw as essentially fascistic (31, 41). Charlene Tung reported that her female students were divided in their responses to cinematic depictions of violent women, with some reporting that such scenes made them feel powerful, while others found violence objectionable regardless of the gender of its perpetrator (102–105). Tung also noted that the violence of then-popular action heroines such as Buffy and Nikita was rendered more palatable to its target audiences by aligning it with whiteness and heterosexuality, while their victims were coded as threatening racial "Others" (97, 107). This analysis was shared by David Greven, who argued that the *Witchblade* TV show positioned its violent heroine as a punisher of nonnormative sexuality, softening the spectacle of a woman policing and punishing men by coding the action heroine as straight and her victims as queer (126, 136–138, 149). Meanwhile, in *Girl Heroes*, Hopkins offered a more optimistic view of action heroines as products of a postfeminist media landscape in which young women increasingly saw femininity as a source of power as well as vulnerability (35–36, 108–109).

In *Reel Knockouts*, McCaughey and King summarized the objections that feminist critics made to violent women in media, who were critiqued both as "uselessly unrealistic" (and thus not useful as role models to real women) and as imitations of "silly male fantasies" (and thus not "really" female at all) (12). They noted that such characters had been critiqued for being oversexualized and overemotional, and for their alignment with male authority systems (17–18). Despite this, they argued, "There must be more to analysis than condemnation, the perpetual unmasking of violent women as frauds," and that going through each work to sort out which parts were and were not "resistant" to hegemonic gender ideologies was unhelpfully reductive, ignoring the complex ways in which such media was interpreted in real life (15–16). As they wrote:

> This book cannot possibly decide whether the movies studied are hegemonic (bad) or subversive (good). We take it for granted that they're all both all the time in ways that undercut the moralistic distinctions. We like morals, of course, and wouldn't produce books like these if we didn't think that they, and the movies they study, could do some good. But we'd rather grant from the outset that one's victorious fantasy will send another away unsatisfied in a manner unlikely to be captured by intensive interpretation. (19)

The essays in their collection repeatedly affirm this duality, finding redemptive, pro-feminist content in popular media ranging from martial arts films to vampire stripper films to women-in-prison movies, while also noting that such media was usually deeply sexist and exploitative at the same time, and that the reactions of female audiences to violent women in film remained highly conflicted (Arons 34; Brown, "Looks" 56–73; Vares 229; Walters 115, 122).

The most nuanced and insightful analysis of the action heroine was that offered by Schubart in her study *Super Bitches and Action Babes: The Female Hero in Popular Cinema*. Less optimistic than Elizabeth Hills about the heroine's capacity to transcend normative gender categories, she argued that "as she breaks society's gender expectations she also confirms them," and that "rather than unite two genders she is in-between, a position that may only last as long as the plot but which creates fascination and unease, ambivalent responses and conflicted interpretations" (6, 2). Schubart saw the division between positive and negative readings of such characters as replicating the split between feminist and postfeminist perspectives: "From a feminist perspective, she is a victim of patriarchy. From a postfeminist perspective, she represents female agency" (2). She also warned against dismissing the radical potential of such media, arguing that "we tend to overlook alternative images because we do not expect to find them and when we find them, we are unable to determine their significance" (184). "I will not claim that the female hero is a progressive role model, or a feminist, or that she subverts patriarchy. It is for an audience to decide how to read her. But neither will I deny her the potential for feminist critique and postfeminist action" (23).

By the time Brown argued in *Dangerous Curves* that the action heroine's combination of physical strength and normative attractiveness meant that "to understand these figures as simply *either* good and empowering—*or* as bad and disempowering, is to miss the complex range of issues their current popularity raises," he was articulating what had by then become a critical orthodoxy (Brown, *Dangerous Curves* 9–10).

These arguments, which were mostly based on films released during the same years as the comics studied in this book, have informed my reading of "bad girl" comics and associated media. Like Inness, McCaughey, King, Schubart, and Brown, I accept that these comics were often both "good and empowering" and "bad and disempowering" simultaneously: They can be read as either or both, and different readers could interpret the same works in very different ways. As Cocca notes in her account of the "bad girl" trend: "Some readers did not distinguish what they saw as the sexiness of the female subjects from their sexualization as objects. Others saw the objectification, then read around it and against it; still others stopped reading these comics. Some loved the images and dismissed the complaints. All four reactions among fans, artists and editors are evident in interviews and letter columns" ("Reproducing Inequality" ch. 1).

My own interest is thus less in trying to ascertain whether the positive aspects of these works outweighed the negative—though I strongly suspect that they did not—and more in exploring what their publication and reception history reveals about the relationship among gender, feminism, and popular culture in the 1990s. The insights of Hopkins and Schubart that the 1990s action heroine is a deeply *postfeminist* figure is crucial here, as is Cocca's point that such characters grew out of the tensions that existed within third-wave feminist ideology, as many of these comics are clearly products of the same postfeminist moment reflected by other media forms such as cinematic action heroines, rom-coms, and chick lit (Cocca, "Negotiating" 99). Counterintuitive though it may seem, I believe real cultural parallels can be drawn between a rom-com like *Four Weddings and a Funeral* and a "bad girl" comic like *Lady Death*, both of which were, in their respective fields, among the surprise breakout hits of 1994. Both are concerned with simultaneously celebrating and containing sexually disruptive women, and Carrie (with her list of thirty-three previous sexual partners) is to the traditional rom-com heroine what Lady Death (with her sword and bikini and army of demons) is to the traditional comic-book superheroine. It is no accident that Andie MacDowell, who played Carrie in *Four Weddings and a Funeral*, was picked by *Wizard* magazine as the ideal actor to play the "bad girl" antiheroine Typhoid Mary in a hypothetical *Daredevil* film (*Wizard* no. 56, 34).

The contradictions of these "bad girl" heroines reflect the deep ambivalence that their creators and audiences clearly felt about the idea of female empowerment. In these comics, male hopes that female sexual liberation might translate directly into female sexual availability mingled with fears of castrating, phallic women, sometimes combining into feverish fantasies of female sexual dominance and masochistic male submission. Many "bad girl" comics had a pronounced femdom edge: A poster on the cover of the first *Razor Annual* reads, "BITCH GODDESS LETS YOU LICK HER LEATHER," right next to an image of Razor wearing black leather boots and not much else. As Inness suggests, the hyperbolic (even parodic) femininity of these heroines can be read as a defensive gesture to ward off the anxieties such figures might otherwise provoke (38).

In this study, I aim to situate these comics in relation to the shifting gender ideologies of the 1990s, and to explore how these cultural currents rippled outward through American popular culture. Precisely because 1990s comic shops were such male-dominated spaces—what the comics scholar Anne Rubenstein described in 1997 as "appalling little shrines to overextended male adolescence"—it is highly significant that feminist and postfeminist discourses were able to reach them at all, even if they tended to mutate there into forms that were often grotesque and sometimes virtually unrecognizable (98). Before proceeding further, it is thus important to briefly outline the history of American feminism in the 1990s, and the impact it had on the popular culture of the era.

Cultural Context: Feminism, Postfeminism, and Popular Culture, 1985–2000

As the 2020 drama *Mrs. America* made clear, the 1970s have come to be remembered as the heroic age of American feminism. There were giants in the earth in those days: Barbara Smith, Betty Friedan, Kate Millett, Gloria Steinem, Shulamith Firestone, Germaine Greer. By the 1980s, many of the legal obstacles to gender equity in the United States had been dismantled, and what remained was a more diffuse struggle against the persistent economic and cultural imbalances that continued to perpetuate gendered inequalities in practice, despite the legal equalities that now existed in theory (Lotz 72).

The triumphs of 1970s feminism left a powerful mark on American popular culture, and despite Susan Faludi's description of the 1980s as a "backlash decade" in which American media demonized independent women, there were widespread signs of change (ch. 4–6). In film and TV, women began to appear in roles previously reserved for men, such as scientists and police detectives. Action heroines began to be taken more seriously, evolving from the tongue-in-cheek camp of *Charlie's Angels* (1976–1981) to the muscular heroism of Sigourney Weaver in *Aliens* (1986) and Linda Hamilton in *Terminator 2* (1991). In popular music, performers such as Madonna, Debbie Harry, Joan Jett, Annie Lennox, and Siouxsie Sioux exemplified new styles of confrontational and sexually confident female-led pop, rock, and post-punk. Women's popular fiction moved away from the bodice rippers and Gothic romances of the 1970s, which fetishized female innocence, and toward the "bonkbusters" of Jackie Collins, Jilly Cooper, and Danielle Steele, whose heroines devoted themselves to the pursuit of wealth, sex, and power. The success of franchises such as Collins's best-selling Santangelo series (1981–2013), which chronicled the adventures of the mafia "Lady Boss" Lucky Santangelo, demonstrated that by the 1980s, female characters could be depicted as unapologetically ambitious, aggressive, and sexually empowered without alienating their target audience.

Within the American feminist movement itself, however, the late 1980s were years of division, triggered by what Imelda Whelehan describes as "the recognition that political feminism had gone into such rapid decline" in the face of opposition from the Reaganite "New Right" (Whelehan 126; Faludi ch. 9–11). "Many women sense that women's collective progress has stalled," wrote Naomi Wolf in 1990: "Compared with the heady momentum of earlier days, there is a dispiriting climate of confusion, division, cynicism, and above all, exhaustion" (*Beauty Myth* 10). Different strands of American feminism disagreed strongly on the best means by which to advance their cause, and the feminist literature of the period was marked by intense and frequently acrimonious debates between liberal, radical, and Marxist feminists, between "sex-positive" feminists and antipornography activists (the so-called feminist sex wars), between feminists inside and outside the academy, and between feminists who embraced postmodern theory and those who regarded it with deep suspicion (Healey passim; Whelehan 100–101, ch. 6). The antipornography campaigns headed by Andrea Dworkin and Catharine MacKinnon encountered strong opposition from other feminists such as Susie Bright, who opposed what they saw as attempts to constrain the range of female sexual expression, and queried their tactical alliances with the religious right: The very title of MacKinnon's *Feminism Unmodified* (1987) testified to her concern that feminism *was* being modified, in directions that she saw as antithetical to its true purpose (Whelehan 78; Modleski 158–160). The works of Camille Paglia, Naomi Wolf, and Katie Roiphe, all written in the early 1990s by women who declared themselves to be feminists while simultaneously rejecting what they saw as the disempowering "victim feminism" of the previous generation, were enormously controversial in feminist circles, leading to angry exchanges between them and other feminist writers (Henry 101; Whelehan 140–143, 234–235; Zeisler 156–157, 182; Snyder 176). Other examples of the feminist literature of controversy to which this period gave rise include Lynne Segal's *Is the Future Female? Troubled Thoughts on Contemporary Feminism* (1987), Gail Chester and Julienne Dickey's *Feminism and Censorship* (1988), Sheila Jeffreys's *Anticlimax* (1990), and Christina Sommers's *Who Stole Feminism? How Women Have Betrayed Women* (1995), all written by avowedly feminist authors as critiques of other sections of the feminist movement. All agreed that the fight for gender equality was far from over, but consensus on a unifying program of action proved elusive.

It was in this context that the word "postfeminist" started to be used in the media (Gamble ch. 4; Tasker and Negra 8–9; Zeisler 144; Henry 18–19). While some academics used the word in different ways, Amanda Lotz notes that "postfeminism had primarily been used in the popular press to suggest the current era was 'after feminism' in a manner that at least implicitly suggested that feminism's goals had been achieved and activism was no longer necessary": It was in this sense that Wolf described postfeminism as a "pernicious fib" (Lotz 74; Wolf, *Beauty Myth* 281). Feminism was thus consigned to the past, leaving women free to pursue their own interests and desires without reference to a feminist ideology that was now represented as obsolete—a position sometimes described as "choice" postfeminism due to its emphasis on the idea that women were now free to choose any life path they desired, including those that might previously have been viewed as disempowering from traditional feminist perspectives (Schubart 300; Lotz 79).

Within this paradigm, traditional femininity and radical empowerment were no longer viewed as an either-or proposition. With their fundamental freedoms supposedly secure, postfeminist women were encouraged to playfully adopt "girlie" styles and behaviors without worrying over whether doing so might weaken their economic or political position (Owen, Stein, and Vande Berg 8, 114; Snyder 179). As Lotz points out, such attitudes risked "[the] depoliticisation and reduction of 'feminism' to a justification for lifestyle and commodification" (Lotz 76, 79; Hopkins 23; Modleski ix, 3). Astrid Henry noted in 2004 that the number of women identifying as feminists dropped over the course of the 1990s, as "many young women today define themselves as postfeminist" (21). As the decade progressed, a succession of postfeminist icons such as Bridget Jones (1996), the Spice Girls (1996), Ally McBeal (1997), and the protagonists of *Sex and the City* (1998) combined the trappings of feminist liberation with those of "girlie" culture to such effect that *Time* magazine famously published an issue on 29 June 1998 with Ally McBeal's face on its cover over the question: "Is Feminism Dead?" (Gorton 212; Owen, Stein, and Vande Berg 93–98; Hopkins 2, 11–12).

Third-wave feminism, which emerged from the outrage over the 1991 Anita Hill hearings and overlapped with the Riot Grrrl feminist punk subculture, frequently struggled to fully distinguish itself from postfeminism (Henry 30; Lotz 75–76; Marcus 113; Zeisler 151). One of its key points of differentiation from second-wave feminism was its assertion that, as R. C. Snyder writes, "'femininity' is not opposed to feminism, but is positioned as central to a politics of agency, confidence and resistance." As the first issue of the *Bikini Kill* Riot Grrrl zine succinctly stated, "Being a sexy and powerful female is one of the most subversive projects of all" (Snyder 179; Marcus 145; Munford 274; Owen, Stein, and Vande Berg 106–107; Whelehan 142–143). As Wolf wrote in 1990, "To look however we want to look—and to be heard as we deserve to be heard—we will need no less than a feminist third wave" (*Beauty Myth* 274). However, as critics of the movement pointed out, in seeking to articulate a more radically inclusive vision of feminist ideology, third-wave feminism risked collapsing into an effectively postfeminist position that, as Snyder puts it, "legitimizes potentially everything a woman chooses to do as feminist" (Stasia 239; Snyder 189). Sara Marcus reports that one contribution to the 1992 zine *What Is Riot Grrrl, Anyway?* read simply, "Riot Grrrl is whatever *I* want it to be. It's whatever *you* want it to be"—a statement so all-encompassing that it risked becoming virtually meaningless (223).

Compared with previous waves of feminist activism, third-wave feminism was much more concerned with popular culture, giving rise to media-focused feminist publications such as *Bust* (1993–present) and *Bitch: Feminist Response to Pop Culture* (1996–2022) (Henry 31; Snyder 177–178; Zeisler ix). While swift to call out examples of media sexism, the fact that *Bust* and *Bitch*—like third-wave feminism more generally—defaulted to a "sex-positive" stance meant that their responses to sexualized depictions of female empowerment in media were often much more conflicted. Faced with highly sexualized and conventionally attractive women wielding power in popular media such as *Batman Returns* (1992), they frequently argued that such depictions modeled forms of liberated female sexuality which their viewers would do well to emulate (Rosenfeld). Indeed, superheroines—especially Wonder Woman—were a recurrent element of third-wave feminist and postfeminist iconography, invoked by everyone from Riot Grrrls to the Spice Girls (Marcus 17, 281; Hopkins 19).

Feminism itself was seen to suffer from something of an image problem during the 1990s. Many women did not describe themselves as feminists, Wolf noted in 1990, because "feminism is not considered sexy" (*Beauty Myth* 283). Writing in 1991, Jackie Brookner lamented, "Too often women will fight for [feminist] causes, yet not want to identify with feminism itself," and that "many young women fear that feminists are women who don't like men, can't get men, or simply want to be men" (11–12). Rebecca Munford quotes the explanation given by the Spice Girls for why they advocated "girl power" rather than "feminism": "Feminism has become a dirty word. Girl Power is just a nineties way of saying it" (267). As Tania Modleski noted in 1991, young feminists complained that the previous generation of feminist critics had deprived them of the enjoyment of popular culture (ix). Much third-wave feminist rhetoric was consequently aimed at establishing distance from a second-wave movement that was perceived to be characterized by "ideological rigidity," and as "antimale, antisex, antifemininity, and antifun" (Snyder 176, 179).

Much postfeminist media of the period was preoccupied with the question of how its heroines could retain the gains of feminism—legal equality, economic independence, sexual liberation—while still signaling that they were not aligned with the traditional feminist movement. As a university-educated woman with a professional career, the archetypal 1990s chick lit heroine Bridget Jones lives a life made possible by the achievements of the women's movement, but she guiltily admits to not having read Faludi's *Backlash*: She's too preoccupied with looking for a boyfriend (Fielding 14). Confronted by a feminist caricature who orders her to "start dropping that skinny whiny emotional slut thing," Ally McBeal insists that she has no desire to be anyone's role model (Owen, Stein, and Vande Berg 109–110). In *Miss Congeniality* (2000), the FBI agent Gracie Hart learns to stop worrying and love the beauty pageant, while in *Legally Blonde* (2001) Elle Woods achieves success at Harvard Law School without relinquishing her hyperbolically feminine sorority girl style (Stasia 243). Postfeminist action film series such as *Lara Croft* (2001, 2003) and *Charlie's Angels* (2000, 2003) were similarly concerned with demonstrating that women could be tough and capable without ceasing to be glamorous or conventionally feminine (Schubart 291–300; Stasia 238). Thus Schubart quotes Drew Barrymore, one of the stars of the *Charlie's Angels* films, as saying: "I'm not a torch-carrying feminist, but I love women . . . I think what's great is if you can have intelligence and capability as your foundation and be fun and sexy on top of it" (300).

In this sense, the "bad girl" comics with which this book is concerned were quintessential examples of postfeminist media. Their foundational assumption was that there was no tension between a female character being empowered to pursue her own goals and being sexualized for the male gaze: In fact, the two were depicted as complementary, with the weaponized sex appeal of the "bad girl" heroine simply providing her with another form of power that she could use to get what she wanted, just like the sexual power attributed to the female pop stars and supermodels of the same era (Hopkins 31, 60–61, 75–79). As Frida Beckman has shown, some early "bad girl" titles such as *Kabuki* explored these ideas seriously and critically (39–54). However, later "bad girl" authors tended to merely draw opportunistically upon popularized versions of postfeminist and third-wave sex-positive feminist rhetoric to argue that, far from being sexist, their works were in fact contributions to female liberation, demonstrating that hyperbolic femininity was not irreconcilable with female agency or the pursuit of power. In this, they were very much of a piece with the 1990s "raunch culture" of magazines such as *Maxim*, *FHM*, and *Playboy*, which depicted themselves not as instruments of sexist repression but as champions of female empowerment (Yarrow 300; Levy). The rhetorical cover provided by these claims was often extremely thin, and one might plausibly question the extent to which the creators of a comic such as *Jade Warriors* (1999), which consisted mostly of women in stripper costumes getting embroiled in contrived bondage scenarios, can really have believed their own claims to be depicting women "center stage, taking command" (*Jade Warriors* vol. 1, no. 3). But the fact they felt the need to make such claims in the first place testifies to the mainstreaming of feminist and postfeminist ideology during the period—and the fact that they thought it remotely plausible that such objectified and hypersexualized characters might still be read as "taking command" bears witness to the success of third-wave and postfeminist rhetoric in maintaining that female empowerment did not have to be incompatible with either traditional femininity or heteronormative sexuality. The relationship between 1990s comic book culture and popular feminist discourses thus forms one of the key topics of this book.

Methodology and Structure

This book is based on a survey of over 2,000 "bad girl" comics, the vast majority of which were published in the United States between 1985 and 2005. Because the "bad girl" craze was a commercial, mass-market phenomenon, it would be misleading to try to analyze it based only on close readings of specific works: The impact of the trend was felt not through any single comic book but through the cumulative weight of hundreds, all using the same character designs, art styles, and plot devices. This study thus makes use of the kind of "distant" readings described by Franco Moretti in his essays on world literature, surveying large numbers of titles to draw out their common features and changing patterns over time ("Conjectures" 57–58). That said, certain works were clearly pivotal to the development of the genre, and I thus devote special attention to those titles which were most successful and widely imitated, such as *Catwoman*, *Witchblade*, and *Shi*.

To gauge reader responses to these works, I have made use of both qualitative data from letter columns and quantitative data from the sales ranks provided by the Diamond, Capital City, and Heroes World comics distribution companies and aggregated online by Comichron. I am aware that letter columns are hardly objective sources. As Pustz notes, "Editors decide which letters to publish and which to ignore," and they thus reflect "the self image of the comic," which may not be identical to the ways it was actually read (166, 177). Given how controversial the "bad girl" trend was at the time, however, letter columns constituted crucial spaces in which their creators could offer defenses of their artistic practices, and the letters they published from fans and critics alike thus provide valuable insights into the nature of these debates.

Information from *Wizard* magazine's "Top 10 comics," "Market Watch," and "Comic Book Price Guide" has also been used, but with greater caution. The inflated valuations offered by *Wizard* played a crucial role in stoking the "bad girl" craze, but its business model relied upon persuading its readers that the value of their comics was rising on a monthly basis, and it thus cannot be straightforwardly trusted as a guide to the secondary comics market during this period (Gearino 133; Gabilliet 149). Much more reliable evidence can be derived from the simple fact of which comics were launched, continued, and canceled, and when these events took place. Moretti's account of the "Darwinian feature of literary history" has seldom been more true than in the 1990s American comics industry, which spent most of the decade in a state of perpetual crisis ("Slaughterhouse"

215). Underperforming titles were routinely scrapped at very short notice, so the simple fact that some of these comics ran for over one hundred issues while others never made it to issue 2 is, itself, strong proof of which titles were and were not giving their audience what it wanted to see.

This book is organized into five chapters. Chapter 1 surveys the rise of the "bad girl" trend, from its 1980s origins to its takeoff in the early 1990s, and discusses how the ninja heroines of 1980s comics like *Elektra*, *Shuriken*, *Samuree*, and *Scimidar* laid the groundwork for the genre's subsequent development. Chapter 2 explores the relationship between the "bad girl" genre and the wider trends within the 1990s comic book market, including the influence of manga, the rise of graphic novels "for mature readers," the changing art styles ushered in by the launch of Image Comics, and the economic consequences of the direct distribution system. Chapter 3 examines early "bad girl" comics in relation to the rise of third-wave feminism, discussing the ways in which works such as Kurt Busiek's *Vampirella*, Mindy Newell's *Her Sister's Keeper*, Mike Barr's *Mantra*, and Eric Luke's *Ghost* engaged with the feminist thought of the early 1990s. Chapter 4 explores how the genre pivoted toward postfeminist action-heroics during the years of its greatest popularity, showing how titles such as *Catwoman*, *Wonder Woman*, and *Elektra* were aggressively rewritten and reimagined in the mid-1990s to match the postfeminist politics of successful "bad girl" comics such as *Witchblade*. Finally, chapter 5 charts the genre's rapid decline following the comics industry crash of 1996–1997, before discussing the surprisingly extensive history of "bad girl" comics since their supposed demise in the early 2000s, including the unexpected online resurgence that they have experienced in recent years.

Historians of American comics have generally characterized the "bad girl" trend as sexist and regressive, and nothing I found during my survey has led me to question this overall conclusion. But digging into the genre revealed it to be stranger and more varied than I had expected, and it is this strangeness and variety that I hope to communicate. Since their decline, "bad girl" comics have become so very unfashionable as to condemn almost every title associated with the trend to obscurity, but some bad girls were badder than others, and some were sufficiently interesting, or sufficiently important, or just sufficiently *odd*, as not to deserve to be so soon forgotten. For better or worse, this book aims to lift them once more into the light.

1

Secret Origins

The Birth of the "Bad Girl" Genre

Before the Bad Girls

For as long as there have been superheroes, there have been superheroines. Cú Chulainn was taught by the female warrior Scáthach. Achilles fought the Amazon queen Penthesilea outside the walls of Troy. The knightly heroes of early modern chivalric epics included women among their number: Bradamante in Ariosto, Clorinda in Tasso, Britomart in Spenser. It is thus unsurprising that the first modern superhero comic—*Action Comics*, no. 1 starring Superman, published April 1938—was rapidly followed by comics featuring superheroines such as Fantomah (1940), Wonder Woman (1941), and Miss Fury (1941). Indeed, depending on one's definition of superhero comic, it could be argued that superheroines came *first*, as both Olga Mesmer (September 1937) and the jungle heroine Sheena (January 1938) made their debuts before Superman's first appearance (Nicholson 16, 20). As Hope Nicholson points out, many of the superhero comics published during World War II were written and drawn by women because so many male artists were away on military service—a fact that may help to account for the relatively large number of female protagonists in the comics of this era (20).

The prominent role accorded to women in comics and the suggestive costumes in which they often appeared were among the things that made Frederic Wertham suspicious of the form. In his famous attack on the American comics industry *Seduction of the Innocent* (1954), Wertham argued that comic books depicted women as overly sexualized and insufficiently moral, claiming that Wonder Woman represented "a morbid ideal," and asserting: "In these stories there are practically no decent, attractive, successful women. A typical female character is the Catwoman, who is vicious and uses a whip" (191, 193). Wertham's critiques helped bring about the 1954 congressional inquiry that led to the formation of the Comics Code, which strictly regulated the content of American comics (Uslan 5; Gabilliet 41–43; Peppard, "Introduction" 2). Coupled with waning sales, the code contributed to the withering of many comic book genres, such as crime and horror, which proved difficult to reconcile with its strictures against sex, violence, and immorality. In their place came the dominance of superhero comics, whose moral simplicity and bloodless mayhem better fitted the code's requirements (Madrid 26–27). The code also led to the decline of "good girl" art, a fetish-adjacent comic book art style popular in the 1940s, through which female characters—including many of the original superheroines—had been marketed to male audiences via copious use of partial nudity and bondage imagery (Gabilliet 43; Madrid 23; Hayton). Catwoman, whom Wertham had called out by name, disappeared from DC Comics in 1954 and did not return until 1966.

These changes had significant consequences for the industry. The mid-century comics market appealed to a wide variety of readers, offering everything from comics for young girls (e.g., *Little Lulu*) to teen comics (e.g., *Archie Comics*) to romance comics (e.g., *Young Romance*) to "spicy" crime comics for adult men (e.g., *Spicy Detective*) (Gabilliet 31–33). However, the shift toward superheroics led to comics being primarily marketed to young male audiences who were assumed to have no interest in stories about women: As Gabilliet writes, "Young male readers would ostracize any magazine 'for girls'" (Gabilliet 31; Robbins 45). DC Comics even adopted an official policy of keeping appearances by female characters to a minimum, making clear that superhero narratives were homosocial spaces within which women had no legitimate place. As the DC Editorial Policy Code declared: "The inclusion of females in stories is specifically discouraged. Women, when used in plot structure, should be secondary in importance, and should be drawn realistically, without exaggeration of feminine physical qualities" (Uslan 5).

The result of these trends was an almost total segregation of male and female comics readers. Describing her childhood, the feminist theorist Shulamith Firestone recalled her lack of interest in her brother's "room-size collection of comic books," and how alienated she was by his collections of war comics and *Superman* (180–181). Although several notable superheroines such as Barbara Gordon (Batgirl), Janet Van Dyne (Wasp), Jean Grey (Marvel Girl), and Sue Storm (Invisible Girl) premiered during the 1960s, only Wonder Woman had her own title: The rest appeared as part of larger superhero teams, within which they usually played the role of "token woman." The exception that proved the rule was

Superman's Girl Friend, Lois Lane (1958–1974), which ran for 137 issues, but always subordinated the adventures of its heroine to those of her superpowered boyfriend. Lacking superpowers of her own, Lois Lane didn't even get top billing in the title of her own comic book. Rather than being "Lois Lane, Superman's Girl Friend," she was merely "Superman's Girl Friend, Lois Lane."

In 1964, Warren Comics began to experiment with non-code-approved publications by printing black-and-white horror comics in their horror magazines *Creepy* (1964–1983) and *Eerie* (1966–1983). As magazines marketed (notionally) to adults rather than comic books marketed to children, *Creepy* and *Eerie* were not bound by the code, and in 1969 they were joined by a third horror title, *Vampirella* (1969–1983). *Vampirella* chronicled the adventures of a heroic female alien vampire, traded heavily on sex appeal, and ran for an extraordinary 112 issues. (The fact that her incredibly skimpy costume was designed by the feminist comics artist and historian Trina Robbins was very much a sign of the times: In the 1960s, women being permitted to freely display their bodies was still primarily associated with women's liberation rather than exploitative sexism [Madrid 55–56; Nicholson 93].) The success of *Vampirella* emphasized how tightly bound together sex, violence, and female protagonists were in the comic-book culture of the period, and helps to explain why when the Comics Code eliminated the first and second categories, the third largely disappeared as well. The formula that made *Vampirella* an outlier in 1969—a powerful, highly sexualized, barely dressed female protagonist moving through horror-themed stories—would go on to become the industry standard in the 1990s during the waning days of the Comics Code, leading Nicholson to identify her as an important forerunner of the "bad girl" aesthetic (Nicholson 95).

In the 1970s and early 1980s, Marvel experimented with code-approved, female-led comics as part of an attempt to attract more female readers, publishing titles such as *Night Nurse* (1972), *Shanna the She-Devil* (1972–1973), *Ms. Marvel* (1977–1979), *Red Sonja* (1977–1979, 1983–1986), *Spider-Woman* (1978–1983), *She-Hulk* (1980–1982), and *Dakota North* (1986–1987) (Peppard, "This Female" 110–112). The most important of these was *Red Sonja*, whose portrayal of an invincible female warrior in a chainmail bikini was later described by the *Elfquest* author Wendy Pini—who worked as a Red Sonja cosplay model in the late 1970s—as delivering "a powerful feminist message with a spoonful of ale-soaked sugar" (Gearino 39–40, 51). Pini explained that her performances as Red Sonja gave her "a socially acceptable way of getting a lot of anger out," while Nancy Collins, whose influential *Sonja Blue* action-horror novels (1989–2002) encoded an obvious reference to Red Sonja in their title, recalled "how excited I was when I plucked *Conan the Barbarian* #23 off the spinner rack as a kid, all those years ago, and finally saw a female hero capable of dishing it out with the best of them" (Licari-Guillaume, "Delayed Recognition" 32; *Dejah Thoris and the Green Men of Mars*, no. 6). The feminist comics writer Gail Simone—who wrote her own *Red Sonja* series in 2013–2014—described her surprise at discovering that other women shared her love of the character:

> I really thought, once again, that I was the freak, I was the outsider, the only female who loved Red Sonja outright. So I had this idea to ask the top female artists in the industry to do the covers and Dynamite ran with it beyond my dreams . . . but I thought it would take some convincing. Not only did all the artists we asked immediately agree, they all confessed their secret love for Sonja. They adore her! (*Dejah Thoris and the Green Men of Mars*, no. 4)

However, despite the subsequent significance of characters such as Red Sonja, none of Marvel's female-led titles proved durable. The longest-lived was *Spider-Woman*, which lasted fifty issues primarily by pandering to its male audience with skintight costumes, shower scenes, and bondage imagery. At DC the situation was even starker: *Supergirl* had a short-lived series from 1972 to 1974 and another from 1982 to 1984, while *Isis* (1976–1978) lasted for only eight issues. It was also during this era that comics publishers once again began trading heavily on overt sex appeal in their female-led titles, uneasily combining empowered heroines with hypersexualized costume designs (Cocca, *Superwomen* 33; Madrid 57–58, 61–62). The fact that so many prominent comic-book storylines of this era dealt with superheroines being abused, traumatized, depowered, or losing control of their abilities suggests the ongoing discomfort that many comics authors clearly felt about powerful female characters, and these authors' reflexive tendency to write narratives that undermined and disempowered them (Madrid 62–64, 77–78).

Probably the most successful female-led superhero comic of this era was Marvel's disco-themed title *Dazzler* (1981–1986), which lasted for forty-two issues and retains a substantial queer and female fan base to this day (Nicholson 135–138; Johnson 103–128). In second place was DC's *Amethyst, Princess of Gemworld* (1983–1988), edited by Karen Berger, who was open about her desire to see "comic book publishers producing more female-oriented magazines" and would later play an important role in making DC's "Vertigo" imprint more friendly to female readers and writers (*Wonder Woman* vol. 2, no. 2; Nicholson 158; Groth, "Vertigo" 54; Licari-Guillaume, *Vertigo* 50). *Amethyst*'s story of a teenage girl discovering that she was actually a magical princess represented an unusual example of a comic aimed primarily at girls rather than boys, at least until its swerve into fantasy-horror in 1987–1988 (Kashtan 324–325). But *Dazzler* and *Amethyst* were atypical, and as late as the early 1990s the prevailing wisdom within the industry was still that "girl books don't sell" (*Wizard* no. 38, 43; Kashtan 329). Just as the DC editorial code had declared decades earlier, superhero comic creators understood themselves to be in the market of creating power fantasies for adolescent boys, within which women were only ever "secondary in importance."

Within American media culture more generally, however, the action heroine was slowly becoming a more familiar figure. Films such as *Alien* (1979), *Red Sonja* (1985), *Aliens* (1986), *La Femme Nikita* (1990), and *Terminator 2* (1991) gradually established a precedent that leading action roles could be played by women, while even action films in which the main protagonist was a man, such as the *Star Wars* trilogy (1977–1983), *Mad Max 2* (1981), *Conan the Barbarian* (1982), and *Willow* (1988), often included physically capable female characters as allies or love interests. The same years saw a growing number of Americans becoming familiar with the traditions of Japanese manga and Hong Kong martial arts cinema, both of which made extensive use of action heroines: Influential manga examples include *Lady Snowblood* (1972–1973), *Nausicaa* (1982–1994), *Bubblegum Crisis* (1987–1991) and *Ghost in the Shell* (1989–1991), while examples from Hong Kong include the extensive filmographies of Angela Mao Ying (1970–1992), Michelle Yeoh (1984–present), and Cynthia Rothrock (1985–1997), all of whom built careers on their legendary abilities to do their own martial arts stunt work (Schubart 125–144; Tasker 23–24). Even the growing popularity of Japanese video games contributed to this trend, introducing American audiences to Japanese video game action heroines such as Samus Aran (*Metroid*, 1986), Tyris Flare (*Golden Axe*, 1989), and Chun Li (*Street Fighter 2*, 1991).

It was in this context that Marvel and DC began, once again, to experiment with giving female characters their own titles: first *Elektra* (1986–1987, 1990), then *Huntress* (1989–1990, 1994), *Catwoman* (1989, 1992), *She-Hulk* (1989–1994), *Black Canary* (1991–1993), and *Silver Sable* (1992–1995). Other publishers also began to move into the same space: Eclipse had *Ms. Tree* (1983–1993) and *Dirty Pair* (1988–1991, subsequently published by Dark Horse from 1993 to 1995), Victory had *Shuriken* (1985–1987, subsequently published by Eternity from 1987 to 1991), First had *Whisper* (1986–1990), Continuity released *Samuree* (1987–1995) and *Ms. Mystic* (1987–1994), Eternity had *Scimidar* (1988–1992), Dark Horse had *Martha Washington* (1990–1991, 1994, 1997–1998), and Harris began a new series of *Vampirella* (1991–1997). Even Aircel Publishing, which primarily published pornographic comics, began a fantasy series about a female warrior called *Sapphire* (1990), although unsurprisingly she spent most of her time stumbling between various sexual misadventures. These comics collectively formed a prelude to the "bad girl" trend, and the first and most important of them was Frank Miller's *Elektra*.

"Leave Nothing Alive": Elektra

Frank Miller has been described as the single most influential man in superhero comics since Stan Lee, even though his shift toward militant xenophobia after 9/11 alienated many of his former admirers (Wright 266; Young 225–226). His initial run on *Daredevil* (1979–1983) did a huge amount to set the agenda for the next two decades of superhero comics, and one of its most significant legacies was Elektra: a character who grew out of Miller's teenage frustrations with what he called "the helpless-female types [that] have cluttered up comics for so long," and who became the prototype for every "bad girl" superheroine who followed her (Young 103–104). As Paul Young argues, "There had never been a superhero comics character like her before," and her success became one that "the rest of the comics industry scrambled to emulate" (104). Describing Elektra as "the comic book 'It' girl of 1981," Mike Madrid writes:

> Unlike the earlier heroines who strove to find love, Elektra eliminated emotions from her life to shield herself from the tragedies she had endured. What was left was a grim, emotionally crippled, but incredibly sexy murderer—the ultimate *belle dame sans merci*. Brandishing her deadly daggers, Elektra cut an impressive figure with her long black hair, asymmetrically cut costume, and strap festooned limbs, ushering Ninja Chic into the world of comic books. Her debut came at a time when comics from Japan, as well as fashion, were starting to make a big impact in America. Elektra became a sensation, and made the comic book anti-heroine the style du jour. (78–79)

Elektra initially appeared in *Daredevil* as a tragic love interest for the hero, Matt Murdock, who saved her from being murdered but was unable to save her father (*Daredevil* vol. 1, no. 168). This bereavement drove them apart, and when she next appeared it was as a vengeful ninja assassin. Her character design became the template for dozens of "bad girl" heroines over the next twenty years: skimpy, skintight costumes, long, flowing hair, long legs, bladed weapons, and large breasts (Young 109). Her balletic fighting style gave artists numerous opportunities for drawing her with her body stretched out on display for the assumed male gaze of the reader, but at the same time her signature weapon, the sai, allowed her to function symbolically as a castrating "phallic woman": When she encountered male adversaries, it was they rather than she who ended up being violently penetrated (112). (The roles were reversed only once, in Elektra's shocking death-by-stabbing in *Daredevil* issue 181, which Miller himself identified as a scene of symbolic rape [198].) This combination of traits meant that Elektra played a double role in *Daredevil*: From the perspective of its *characters* she was a terrifying embodiment of female rage and power and violence, but from the perspective of the *readers* she was utterly objectified, her sexualized body safely available to be ogled at will. It was a combination that would be repeated endlessly over the years to come.

Like her classical namesake, Elektra's story was largely defined by men. In the *Oresteia* of Aeschylus, Elektra helps her brother, Orestes, to murder her mother, Clytemnestra, in revenge for the death of their father, Agamemnon—a narrative which led Jung to choose "Electra complex" as the name of the female equivalent of Freud's more famous "Oedipus complex" (Jung 69). Within the Electra complex, Jung claimed, "Typical affection for the father develops, with a correspondingly jealous attitude towards the mother" (69). Miller, who would later explicitly reference Jung, clearly had this theory in mind when he wrote Elektra's story, as she was written from the first as a woman entirely devoted to her father's memory. In traditional romance fiction the death of the father frees the heroine to seek out a male lover to replace him, marking the end of childhood and the beginning of sexual maturity. So strong is the hold of Elektra's Electra complex, however, that her father's death marks the end rather than the beginning of her relationship with Murdock. With the father dead, there is nothing left to desire.

Elektra's subsequent history was told in *Daredevil* issue 190. Having turned her back on sexuality, Elektra is taught the arts of violence by a mentor with the hyperbolically phallic name of Stick, who leads a mystic order called the Chaste. The Chaste are ascetics, who dress in virginal white and live among ice and snow. Their doctrine deals with the repression of libidinous phallic energies, symbolized by the fact that Stick had to leave his wife to join them: Stick can only join the Chaste if he swears his "stick" (phallus) to chastity. Stick becomes Elektra's second father figure, but he is one with whom her Electra complex can never be consummated, and her unresolved traumas force her to leave him. (As her sensei explains to her, "It was your *father*, Elektra. You loved him too *dearly*. And he held you too *closely*.") She thus abandons the Chaste to join the demon-ninja cult of the Hand, which becomes her third father figure, signifying a shift from repression to the tactile pleasures of sex and violence: As a member of the Chaste remarks, sounding rather like an antimasturbation campaigner, "Contact with the *Hand* made her a *twisted* soul." Finally she becomes a freelance assassin, but after dying in battle she is reanimated by the Hand, in a resurrection ceremony whose language evokes sexual submission and impending orgasm. ("Empty your *souls* to Elektra . . . Your *blood* is hers . . . Your *lives*—your *flesh*—hers . . . Ah . . . She is *close* . . .") At the last moment, however, the Hand are thwarted by Murdock and the risen Elektra disappears, implicitly to rejoin the Chaste. This concludes her original story arc.

Elektra's alternation between the Chaste ("good girl," white costumes, virginal, obedient to father figures, using violence only when necessary for prosocial reasons) and the Hand ("bad girl," red costumes, hypersexual, rebellious against father figures, using violence freely for antisocial pleasure and profit) sketches out in miniature the conceptual space that the comic-book heroines of the 1990s would occupy. On the side of the Chaste were all the female knights, battle nuns, warrior angels, samurai girls, and similar character types: Women who were depicted as sexy without being sexually threatening, who served larger organizations and higher ideals, and who used violence in defense of the status quo. On the side of the Hand were the vampire girls, demonesses, ninja assassins, and their ilk: Women whose sex appeal was rooted in their sexual aggression, whose objectives were personal and selfish rather than institutional or idealistic, and who used extreme and amoral violence to achieve their ends. Elektra held both in tension, her subsequent stories oscillating endlessly between the two poles: between her socially approved desire for her Good Father (Stick) to discipline her, and her perverse, socially deviant desire for her Bad Father (Hand) to pleasure her. The Hand plays the symbolic role of abusive father in her stories, never letting her go, constantly trying to drag her back into its incestuous embrace. Stick, by contrast, functions as pure phallic superego, the Freudian "voice of the father," constantly criticizing her for failing to live up to the ideals of the Chaste: In later stories Stick literally manifests as an endlessly critical voice inside her head, making his role as an embodiment of Elektra's superego even clearer (*Elektra* no. 1; Young 81). Her Electra complex is never resolved, and compared to the grip of these mythic father figures her notional love interest, Matt Murdock, never stands a chance.

That Miller was highly self-conscious in his use of Elektra as an incarnation of the Electra complex is made clear by his sequel *Elektra: Assassin* (1986), which he cocreated with Bill Sienkiewicz, and which explicitly made reference to Jungian psychology. Compared to Miller's other works of the period, *Elektra: Assassin* has received little critical attention: Jean-Paul Gabilliet describes it as having been "a commercial failure" whose "excessively confusing story" was "too esoteric in form and style" (93). It is a surreal and daringly experimental work, which made use of nonrealist painted art and fragmented, nonlinear, stream-of-consciousness storytelling to communicate the mental state of its protagonists. In a genre obsessed with what women like Elektra look like from the outside, *Elektra: Assassin* stands out for its determination to communicate what being Elektra feels like from within, with art styles that shift depending on her mental state: line art with flat block colors for childhood memories, blurred watercolors when she has been drugged, pencil sketches for romantic fantasies, and panels that fragment into pieces or dissolve into the white of the gutters at moments of mental crisis. It is consequently the work which goes deepest into what Elektra *means* both as a character and an idea, and thus lays out with considerable precision the symbolic logic that would go on to underlie the "bad girl" heroines of the 1990s.

The most crucial step taken by *Elektra: Assassin* was to spell out explicitly what Miller's original comics only hinted at obliquely, in their references to Elektra's father having "held [her] too *closely*": That Elektra was abused by her father at the age of five, just the age when Jungian theory predicts that she would be developing her Electra complex. When she reports this, however, she is disbelieved and medicated into denial: "The *pills* and the long, long *talks* your friends gave me—they show me I am *wrong*. They show me I *made that up*. You never . . . They tell me I *wanted* you to" (*Elektra: Assassin* no. 1). Her father's "friends" here are clearly psychiatrists, well versed in Freudian and Jungian theory, and hence well equipped to dismiss reports of actual child abuse as merely oedipal fantasies.

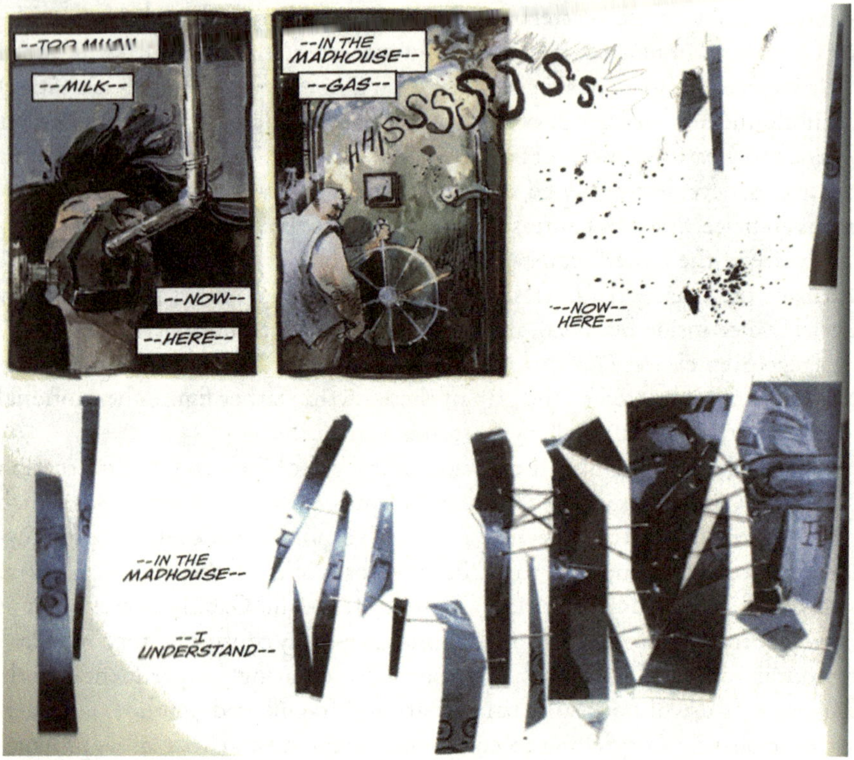

FIGURE 2 Elektra stitches her fragmented memories back together, in *Elektra: Assassin* issue 1. Written by Frank Miller, art by Bill Sienkiewicz. Epic Comics, 1986.

(This suggests that as well as being aware of Jung, Miller and Sienkiewicz may have been aware of Florence Rush's then-recent arguments in *Freud and the Sexual Abuse of Children* [1977], which critiqued the Oedipus and Electra complexes as enabling the psychoanalytic cover-up of widespread child abuse.) *Elektra: Assassin* also clarifies the status of the Hand as a metaphor for Elektra's abusive father: They worship a demon called the Beast, which Elektra instantly identifies with him (*Elektra: Assassin* no. 1). The incarnate Beast is almost never depicted directly on the page: At most we see a claw, or a mouth, or a cloud of darkness. It thus serves as a visual representation of the unresolved trauma of Elektra's childhood abuse, abuse that she cannot look at directly because she has been taught to deny it even to herself. Naturally, when she is subsequently examined by a (male) psychiatrist, he identifies the Beast not as a manifestation of real trauma but as "a mythic, even Jungian figure," and asserts that Elektra's "fantasy life is rich in oedipal imagery" which "fits the pattern of infantile delusion of 'good parent' replaced by 'bad parent,'" in which "sexual imagery throughout again fits classic pattern of Oedipal dilema [*sic*]." The injuries that she has sustained in her struggle with the Beast are dismissed as "presumably self-inflicted," and even the violence of her "fantasies" is interpreted as proof of her "restricted sexual urges" rather than evidence of real abuse (*Elektra: Assassin* no. 3).

Elektra: Assassin begins with Elektra imprisoned in an asylum—a decision which draws on the long history of asylums appearing in feminist fiction as exemplary spaces of male oppression and female resistance, from Mary Wollstonecraft's *Maria: or, The Wrongs of Woman* (1798) to Sylvia Plath's *The Bell Jar* (1963). In a series of nightmarish scenes she is drugged, abused, and almost lobotomized by the doctors, whose misuse of patriarchal power marks them out to her as agents of the Beast, before finally escaping, leaving a trail of corpses behind her. Once she escapes from the asylum, and hence from the system of patriarchal control it represents, the narrative begins to fragment, and "Elektra" starts to function less as a person than as a dream, or a delusion, or a psychic infection—one might even call her "a complex." At multiple points in the series different female characters change into Elektra and then back into themselves, as though to emphasize that "being Elektra" is less a stable identity than a state of mind. For most of the series her primary antagonist seems to be the fictional covert agency SHIELD, which appears here not as the noble force it was previously depicted as being in Marvel Comics but as a massively morally compromised organization modeled on the real-world CIA. But it ultimately becomes clear that SHIELD, and by extension the whole system of military and political coercion that it represents, has no real power over Elektra, and never did. What SHIELD took to be their hard-fought battle with Elektra was merely her manipulating them for her own ends: Her true battle was only ever with the Beast, and is fought on a higher psychic plane over which SHIELD has no authority.

For the male SHIELD agents who pursue her Elektra manifests as an obsessive fantasy, endlessly desirable and entirely unobtainable. Frequently they themselves are uncertain if they want to love her or kill her, but the question is moot, as she exceeds their power to grasp or control. As the SHIELD agent Garrett remarks, in a moment of clarity: "She's run the show from the *start*. She's run my *mind*. And she's *in* my mind. All the *time*" (*Elektra: Assassin* no. 4). They repeatedly fantasize about killing or raping Elektra, but she always controls the sexual script. At one point she appears to masochistically offer herself to Garrett, speaking inside his mind to ventriloquize his fantasies: "I *give* myself to your every *cruelty* . . . You *humiliate* me—*punish* me—I *beg* you—not to *stop*—" (*Elektra: Assassin* no. 3). But his desire for her gives her access to his mind, allowing her to control his actions, leading up to a feverish, dreamlike sequence in which she mentally holds Garrett immobile while she bathes naked in front of him, mocking his thwarted desires. Finally she straps a leash and collar around Garrett's neck and subjects him to extended sadomasochistic abuse, amid which he parrots her own words back to her: "You *punish* me—*humiliate* me—I *beg* you—not to *stop*—" (*Elektra: Assassin* no. 6).

Tellingly, the moment when Elektra comes closest to losing her battle with the Beast (symbolically, the unresolved trauma memory of her abuse at the hands of her father) is when she hides herself inside the identity of "Sandy," a sweet, ultrafeminine teenager with a head full of romantic fantasies (*Elektra: Assassin* no. 4). Elektra tries to use this performance of normative femininity as protective camouflage, but this turns out to be a trap: The agents of the Beast are waiting, in the form of a blandly handsome suitor named Brad, who seems to be modeled on Elektra's memories of Matt Murdock. Brad's interactions with Sandy/Elektra are experienced by Sandy as courtship, marriage, and initiation into true femininity ("he makes a *woman* of me"), identified here with motherhood and submissive sexuality. However, these same interactions are simultaneously experienced by Elektra as an ordeal of abduction, captivity, and near death, from which she is saved only by the intervention of Garrett, whom she has kept "under *psychic domination*" (*Elektra: Assassin* no. 5). Within the traditional Jungian scheme, in which a girl's acceptance of heterosexuality is the way for her to resolve her Electra complex, "Elektra" becoming "Sandy" should have been her path to a happy ending. But Miller and Sienkiewicz depict this instead as a mere capitulation to the Beast, an exchange of one abusive father figure for another, suggesting that normative femininity is so psychically dangerous that even adopting it temporarily and strategically risks total ego death. It is only her violent, manipulative femme fatale identity as Elektra, which explicitly rejects any kind of conventional morality ("no one is innocent"), that gives her a chance at victory (*Elektra: Assassin* no. 5).

The other major female character in *Elektra: Assassin* is the SHIELD agent Chastity McBride, who—as her name suggests—represents the "good girl" femininity that Elektra rejects, defined by the sexual self-discipline of the chaste bride. The patronymic "Mc" suggests her subordination to patriarchal authority, embodied here by the head of SHIELD, Nick Fury: Chastity serves Fury dutifully throughout the series, and when she finally goes to confront the Beast at the end of the story she is literally dressed as a nun (*Elektra: Assassin* no. 8). That Chastity is, in some sense, another version of Elektra—her "Chaste" self, the version of herself she was with Stick—is suggested by the parallels other characters spot between the two of them ("she's as crazy as *you* are"), as well as by a surreal sequence in which Elektra somehow imprints Chastity with her identity, leading to Chastity being captured by SHIELD in the mistaken belief that she is actually Elektra (*Elektra: Assassin* no. 5). If Sandy represents one possible way out of Elektra's psychological dilemma, by maturing into normative heterosexuality and leaving the Bad Father behind, then Chastity represents another: complete submission to the superego, the internalized voice of the idealized Good Father, in whose name she ultimately goes into battle against the Beast riding on top of a tank. (Chastity, having subordinated herself to the patriarchal order, still uses the trappings of the military-industrial complex such as tanks and helicopters—trappings that Elektra transcends, and which she

FIGURE 3 Elektra's "bad girl" assassin-persona kills her "good girl" persona, Sandy, in *Elektra: Assassin* issue 4 (1986). Written by Frank Miller, art by Bill Sienkiewicz.

destroys whenever they are deployed against her.) But Chastity, with all her guns, cannot destroy the Beast: Deep down, the Good Father and the Bad Father are the same person, and the master's tools (patriarchal authority, military hardware) will never dismantle the master's house. Only Elektra—bad girl, escaped lunatic, mental infection—can do that, transposing the Beast's soul into the body of a dying man, reducing it from a mythic, unconfrontable embodiment of childhood trauma to mere fallible flesh and blood.

Miller wrote a final coda to Elektra in *Elektra Lives Again* (1990), another surreal, hallucinatory narrative in which Elektra appears more as a dream or a haunting than a flesh-and-blood character. Murdock, who is tormented with nightmares about Elektra being hunted and killed, has a final ambiguous encounter with a woman dressed in white, nunlike garments, who may or may not be real, and may or may not be the resurrected Elektra. The comic ends with a wordless image of Elektra in white, standing in the snow, implying that she has once again joined the Chaste—but this may be only another of Murdock's dreams, showing that he is now at peace with her memory rather than tormented by it. Elektra herself never speaks in *Elektra Lives Again*, and it remains deeply unclear whether she is actually alive anywhere except in Murdock's memory.

Young notes that this story initially implies that Elektra is haunting Murdock, but ultimately makes clear that in fact the reverse is true: "*he is haunting her*" (116). As Young writes:

> Elektra is not an independent subject but Daredevil's projection of himself, the insatiable avenger of the violent crime that enforcers of the law committed against the father. So much of the saga is hooked to Matt's perspective that we cannot tell for certain whether we know her primarily by her own lights or whether what we have come to know as "Elektra" has actually been a representation of Matt's relationship to her as seen by him and only him. The real Elektra, if there is one, wants to be free to pursue something she can never have in Matt's presence: her own life, of which she is the author, and her own death. (116)

Murdock's nightmares tell us something about *him*, but nothing about Elektra: They merely reflect the obsessions that he has projected onto her. Elektra herself eludes his grasp, just as she eludes the grasp of the many men who pursue her through the pages of *Elektra: Assassin*, only to realize too late that what they took to be the woman herself was only ever a phantom of their own making.

Collectively, Elektra's appearances in the comics that Miller wrote between 1981 and 1990 formed a potent template for later "bad girl" heroines, an emblem of violent, eroticized female vengeance against a world that seems determined to inflict pain on women like her. What set her apart from her imitators is that Miller seems to have understood much more clearly than most of his followers that "Elektra" isn't exactly a real woman: She's a dream, a nightmare, a fantasy, and the person having that fantasy is *always a man*. Both the "Chaste" and "Hand" versions of Elektra are essentially male illusions, each combining a fantasy with an anxiety: the former of a woman shaped by the Good Father to be socially disciplined but sexually inaccessible, the latter of a woman shaped by the Bad Father to be sexually available but morally unbound. Elektra herself, who wears these fantasies like red and white garments, slips through the gap between the two. She vanishes like a dream and leaves only (male) corpses in her wake.

This, perhaps, was the original sin of the "bad girls": In copying Elektra, they read her literally rather than metaphorically, in ways that radically shifted her meaning as a character. If Elektra is read as a *fantasy* (which she mostly seems to be in *Elektra: Assassin* and *Elektra Lives Again*), then her objectification can be read as a commentary on the nature of that fantasy—but if she is simply a character like any other then that same objectification becomes simply objectionable, clearly at odds with her role as a symbol of female empowerment and defiance. Young laments that the way American comics changed in the 1990s was "fueled by a fundamental misreading of Miller's success," which too many writers understood as merely "a matter of telling 'gritty' stories," full of gratuitous sex and violence (6). One symptom of this misreading was the way that the bad girl comics of the same era emulated the superficial elements of Elektra's character—especially her appearance, memorably described by Larry Rodman as that of a "psychotic swimsuit model"—without any real engagement with the character's underlying symbolic logic (104). So thoroughly did these imitations come to obscure their original that when Marvel finally relaunched *Elektra* in 1996, several years into the "bad girl" craze, she was reduced to an imitation of an imitation. No longer a dream or a nightmare, she was now just another martial arts superheroine with too many weapons and not enough clothes.

Elektra's Daughters: Ninja Heroines of the 1980s

In the early 1980s, American popular culture was infested with ninjas. If *Enter the Dragon* (1973) had helped to popularize East Asian martial arts culture more generally, then Eric Van Lustbader's best-selling novel *The Ninja* (1980) fixed the figure of the Japanese ninja assassin in the American popular imagination as the ultimate practitioners of martial arts, beginning a craze for ninjitsu that lasted well into the 1990s. Films such as *Enter the Ninja* (1981), *Revenge of the Ninja* (1983), *The Ninja Mission* (1984), and *American Ninja* (1985) swiftly codified the genre, and soon ninjas began appearing in great numbers in American comics.

As with so much else, Miller's run on *Daredevil* was an influential forerunner of this trend. Miller was hugely impressed by his first encounter with manga, in the form of Koike and Kojima's *Lone Wolf and Cub* (1970–1976): He later described the series as "perfect storytelling," and his own manga-style series *Ronin* (1983–1984) was written as an homage to it (Cremins 107–108). Its influence can also be seen in *Daredevil*, which during Miller's run became associated for the first time with Japanese martial arts mythology. Since his first appearance in 1964, Matt Murdock had been depicted as a boxer and gymnast: It was Miller who reimagined him as a martial artist, gave him ninja allies (the Chaste) and a ninja love interest (Elektra), and pitted him against a clan of evil ninja warriors (the Hand). *Teenage Mutant Ninja Turtles* (1984–2014) began as a black-and-white comic-book parody of Miller's *Daredevil*, complete with an evil ninja clan called "the Foot" (a parody of Miller's Hand), but swiftly became extremely successful in its own right, contributing powerfully to the popularity of ninjas in American popular culture and triggering a brief boom in black-and-white comics which almost destroyed the North American comics industry (Nicholson 129; Gabilliet 94–95, 147; Costello and Cremins 10). So overwhelming did the ninja glut become that by 1987 Eternity Comics had to promise its readers that there would be "no more ninjas here at Eternity, other than those that we already have" (*Blade of Shuriken* no. 3).

This ninja craze stoked preexisting American interest in East Asian martial arts cinema, within which action heroines had become relatively commonplace by the mid-1980s. Given this, and the precedent set by Miller's Elektra, it is unsurprising that this era saw the appearance of numerous martial arts heroines in

American superhero comics, including *Whisper* (1983), Katana (1983, in *The Brave and the Bold*), Gennin Kimura (1984, in *Samurai*), *Shuriken* (1985), *Ninja* (1986), *Samuree* (1987), Ichi-kun (1987, in *Ninja High School*), and *Scimidar* (1988). Perhaps the clearest sign of the growing popularity of female ninja characters in comics was the 1989 *X-Men* storyline in which the relatively obscure white superheroine Psylocke was captured by Elektra's old enemies the Hand, who physically and mentally transformed her into a hypersexualized East Asian ninja assassin. This transformation was not undone at the end of the story, and massively boosted Psylocke's popularity over the years that followed, making her second only to Elektra as a model for subsequent "bad girl" superheroines (Madrid 92–93).

Many of these martial arts superheroines imitated the East-meets-West backstory of Miller's Elektra. Whisper was an American woman trained in martial arts by her Japanese stepfather, though to his disappointment she refused to "be Japanese" (*Whisper* vol. 1, no. 1). Shuriken was a half-American, half-Japanese woman, trained in martial arts by her father in Japan before moving to America. Ninja was a mixed-race woman taught martial arts by her Asian grandfather, Samuree was a white American girl raised by a community of martial artists on a fictional East Asian island, and Psylocke was literally a white woman transformed into an Asian martial artist by evil magic. Storylines about characters grappling with their mixed heritage were common, often taking the form of showdowns with yakuza gangsters or ninja clans whose efforts to drag these Westernized heroines back into the world of traditional Japanese culture had to be violently resisted. While these stories clearly echo contemporaneous anxieties about the threat that Japanese corporate power (generally imagined at the time as collectivist, anti-individualist, and neofeudal in character) might pose to American capitalism, they also express aspirations toward female empowerment, made easier to articulate by projecting the figure of the oppressive patriarch onto some imagined Asian "other" such as a Japanese *oyabun*, *daimyo*, or ninja lord. Again, *Whisper* is emblematic, here. In its first issue, a traditionalist yakuza boss calls for a woman to attend him in his bathhouse, patronizingly declaring: "What an easy life you lead, woman. You care for and are cared for. . . . You know perfect joy through service, and you want for nothing" (*Whisper* vol. 1, no. 1). But Whisper has taken the woman's place, and instead of offering the "care" and "service" expected of a woman like her she instead forces the man's head underwater until he gives her the information she requires, demonstrating that she actually wants a great many things—knowledge, power, agency—that men like him are highly unwilling to give her.

The most significant of this crop of martial arts heroines was featured in *Shuriken* (1985–1991). *Shuriken* began as the self-published project of the Black American comic artist Reggie Byers, who also worked as a penciller on *Robotech: The New Generation* (1985–1986), a manga-style comics adaptation of the then-popular *Robotech* anime series (Cremins 105–107). Steeped in manga culture,

Byers drew *Shuriken* in a black-and-white manga style that was still uncommon in America at the time: As he wrote in his first editorial, "My work is very influenced by that wonderful JAPANESE ANIMATION style art," a phrase which suggests that Byers assumed his readers would not recognize the word "manga" (*Shuriken* vol. 1, no. 1). *Shuriken* told the story of a female ninja named Kyoko and her struggles to disentangle herself from "the Organization," an order of ninjas for hire. Despite its bloody subject matter, however, Byers kept the tone of the original series light and playful, with Kyoko depicted as a principled and heroic character whose morals put her increasingly at odds with her employers.

Each issue of *Shuriken* featured a backup story by another writer, frequently with female protagonists. ("Don't ask me why, but I love female lead characters!" Byers wrote in the issue 1 editorial—a trait that may have been instrumental in drawing him toward manga, where female protagonists were more common than in American comics.) In issue 4, Byers announced that the next issue would feature a backup story by R. A. Jones called *Scimidar*, but he changed his mind between issues, printing a full-page explainer in issue 5. He had rejected the *Scimidar* strip, he explained, for "basically moral" reasons: He estimated that its content would offend 30 percent of his readers, and maintained that even if they *weren't* offended they shouldn't be exposed to such material (*Shuriken* vol. 1, no. 5). Reading between the lines (and extrapolating from Jones's own subsequent statements, discussed below), it is clear that what troubled Byers about *Scimidar* was its overt sexual content, and that the 30 percent of readers he wished to protect from it was his estimate of the proportion of underage readers his comic had. *Scimidar* then languished for two years before being published as a standalone title in 1988.

The gap between *Shuriken* and *Scimidar* was strongly symbolic of the way that American superhero comics in general were moving in their depiction of action heroines. By the standards of 1980s superheroines, Kyoko was not a particularly sexualized character, and the comic seemed keen not to alienate female readers. Byers dedicated the first issue to his mother, and the reader Kathy Li, who wrote in to issue 2 warning Byers not to lean too far into the current "overglut of ninja stories," swiftly became involved with the comic, even appearing as the (entirely nonsexualized) cover model for issue 5, the very issue for which Byers rejected *Scimidar* (Cremins 112–113). Its storylines were sympathetic to Kyoko's difficulties as a woman in a male-dominated industry, and engaged with issues of workplace sexism, albeit in the fantastical context of an association of ninja assassins: Kyoko's male co-workers resent equal status being given to a woman, one of her clients objects to being assigned a female bodyguard, and her employer even has an anxiety dream about being murdered by one of the other ninjas, who is furious at him for "making me feel inferior to your little Shuriken" (*Shuriken* vol. 1, no. 1, 5, 9). The original series has a strong emphasis on female friendship and on the importance of women standing up for one another in the face of indifference from male authority figures. In issue 2, Kyoko saves her friend Joan from

FIGURE 4 Kyoko is unimpressed by police protection, in *Shuriken* vol. 1, issue 2 (1985), written and drawn by Reggie Byers. Note the patch on Doug's trembling shoulder, which reads "THE LAW."

an assassin while the male police officer Doug stands by uselessly, and in issue 9, Kyoko's own problems with the police are only defused when a policewoman intervenes in a show of female solidarity (*Shuriken* vol. 1, no. 2, 9).

Scimidar also aimed to appeal to female readers, but Jones had very different ideas about how to achieve this. As he wrote in his first editorial:

> I want you to love [Scimidar] as well—especially if you also are female. That's why I hope all you girls and women out there will write and tell me what you think of Scimidar. I want you to tell me what you like, and—just as important—what you don't like about my portrayal of her. And if you're a man, I hope you'll pass along a copy to your sister or lover, wife or mother. Comments are sincerely requested—from both genders. (*Scimidar* vol. 1, no. 1)

In the next issue, Jones explained *why* he wanted to reach a female audience. Noting that very few comics "feature a solo female as the lead character," and that most of these were merely "exercises in T&A," he lamented that women had become almost entirely alienated from American comics:

> It is an inescapable fact that comics have lost a great portion of the female audience they once held. To me, it is just as undeniable that we have to get them back.
>
> One of the best ways to do this is to create female characters that women can enjoy. Characters who are strong without being bitches. Characters whose sensuality is a natural outgrowth of their personality and not merely a sop to adolescent male fantasies. Characters who can stand alone, but who thrive on

> their relationships with the men and women around them. Characters with at least two dimensions, rather than one. (*Scimidar* vol. 1, no. 2)

Jones clearly viewed *Scimidar* as a more serious attempt to create "female characters that women can enjoy" than *Shuriken*, which he backhandedly praised as an "entertaining comic" whose readership "was largely composed of adolescents (with protective parents)," and which had thus been unable to accommodate the "raw" and "uncensored" comic that he had written for it (*Scimidar* vol. 1, no. 1). Scimidar herself was in many respects similar to Shuriken and the other comic book martial arts heroines of the period: She wore a formfitting costume and fought with bladed hand weapons reminiscent of Elektra's sais. In other ways, however, she was more unusual, with a heavy emphasis placed on her sensuality, her sexuality, her spirituality, and her status as "poet, dreamer, [and] lover" (*Scimidar* vol. 1, no. 1). Her superpower was the classically feminine gift of empathy, which allowed her both to sympathize with her friends and to reflect back the homicidal mania of her enemies. From issue 3 onward she also started to be drawn in a much more overtly sexualized fashion, frequently depicted topless, or naked, or in sexual situations. Soon the comic was trading almost entirely on its inclusion of explicit sex and sexualized violence, and Jones's regular remarks about issues selling out suggest that this strategy brought it considerable commercial success.

It might initially seem perplexing that a writer whose stated purpose was to break away from mere "exercises in T&A" ended up producing a comic that was, essentially, superheroine pornography. However, Jones's editorials make clear that this was very much in keeping with his vision of "authentic" femininity, and with his objective of giving the comic what he called "a deep psycho-sexual slant" (*Scimidar* vol. 1, no. 2). Jones's interpretation of what it meant for women to be "strong without being bitches" meant, in practice, leaning into a deeply mystificatory view of femininity, which is represented in *Scimidar* as being intuitive, empathic, amoral, irrational, and, above all, hypersexual. Scimidar's psychic abilities are depicted as deeply bound up with her sexuality, and on multiple occasions she appears to orgasm while carrying out psychometric readings (*Scimidar* vol. 1, nos. 2–3). She is a devotee of free love who rejects monogamy and has implicit or explicit sexual relationships with almost every other recurring character, including her own brother and an evil lesbian villain whom she later kills (*Scimidar* vol. 1, nos. 1–4; vol. 3, no. 1). The fact that no women ever *did* write in to tell Jones what they thought of his comics (or, if they did, he never printed their letters) did not prevent him from pronouncing confidently on what he took to be "true" femininity, and the natural attraction that supposedly existed between it and "true" masculinity, which in the series is embodied by the almost comically macho biker hero Gitano. When Gitano visits a club in which male strippers perform for a female audience, the narrator asserts: "Conventional wisdom of 40 years past stated that women were not aroused by such open displays of raw male sexuality. The purveyors of such wisdom most often did *not* wear skirts" (*Scimidar* vol. 2, no. 4).

Given its essentializing gender politics and its identification of "true" femininity with mystical irrationality and sexual availability, it is unsurprising that *Scimidar* was deeply hostile to feminism, despite its notional commitment to female empowerment. (The claim that it was non-skirt-wearers who questioned the appeal of "raw male sexuality" could easily refer to gender nonconforming women as well as men.) Complaining that "comics have almost universally portrayed producers of adult sexually-oriented material as being sleazy, exploitative flesh-peddlers," Jones devoted the fifth issue of *Scimidar* to a story in which its heroine defends the Playboy Mansion from an assault by violent antipornography feminists, modeled on the real-world feminist group Women Against Pornography, who are led by a butch caricature named Cher Trype (i.e., "sheer tripe"). Cher's attempts to argue against "a system which reduces women to the status of mere sexual objects" are depicted by the comic as both absurd and hypocritical, as she encourages her own followers to expose their breasts to gain media attention. When they attack the Playboy Mansion (while topless, naturally), Scimidar and Gitano gleefully murder the almost-naked women in large numbers to defend Hugh Hefner from their feminist rage (*Scimidar* vol. 2, no. 1). The same issue even included a *Playboy*-style centerfold pinup, featuring a nude image of Scimidar. Amid this overt pandering to his porn-reading male audience, Jones continued to position himself as a conscientious opponent of censorship and sexual repression, insisting in his editorials that his use of sex and violence was not "gratuitous," and that *Scimidar* was a serious "psycho-sexual drama" that constituted "a sincere effort to explore what it is in the human animal that leads it to mix savagery and sensuality" (*Scimidar* vol. 2, no. 1).

By the time Jones wrote this issue, Byers was no longer writing and drawing *Shuriken*. Following the crash of the black-and-white comics market it had been sold to Eternity Comics, which meant it shared a publisher with *Scimidar* (Cremins 108–110). In the hands of its new author S. A. Bennett, however, *Shuriken* remained sympathetic to its heroine's struggles against objectification. In *Hellbender*—a story which sees Kyoko's musician friend Joan targeted by a misogynistic serial killer—Joan delivers a critique of media sexism which clearly applies as much to comic books as to the music industry: "I don't *like* it, but a certain amount of objectification goes with the territory. The music business is all about fulfilling people's dreams . . . and feeding them fantasies. *That* guy's fantasy was a world where ugly guys with dirty blonde hair can have sex on demand with bimbos" (*Shuriken: Hellbender*).

Shuriken thus drew the connection between media objectification and misogynistic violence that *Scimidar* resolutely refused to make. As Joan says, "If you're a woman, it's hard *not* to feel like a target, just walking down the street." The result is a plague of men like the titular Hellbender who are unable or unwilling to disentangle their sexual desire for women from their longing to hurt

FIGURE 5 *Scimidar* vol. 2, issue 1 (1989), which traded on antifeminist messaging and female nudity. Written by R. A. Jones, pencils by Rob Davis, inks by James Baldwin.

them: As Kyoko tells him, "There must be a great big equal sign between sex and violence in your head." In this context, Kyoko's determination to defend Joan from Hellbender becomes a gesture of female solidarity in the face of omnipresent male violence, one that hints at forms of queer intimacy very different from Scimidar's pornographic pansexuality. "You know something? I *really* love you," Joan tells Kyoko. "Don't make fun! It's important you know just how much you mean to me" (*Shuriken: Hellbender*).

Shuriken and *Scimidar* coexisted uneasily at Eternity in 1990–1991, offering two very different models of what an independent "solo female" comic might look like. That tensions persisted between the two titles is obvious from a 1991 *Shuriken* storyline in which Kyoko battles a psychotic female assassin called Serrate, who is obviously (and explicitly) modeled on Scimidar: The narcissistic Serrate wanders around boasting about how she is "very sensitive" and "almost empathic," even while her actions demonstrate psychopathic disregard for human life (*Shuriken* vol. 2, no. 4). In the letters pages the authors of *Shuriken* defended

FIGURE 6 Kyoko encounters Serrate, a parody of Scimidar, in *Shuriken* vol. 2, issue 4 (1991). Note that Serrate's costume and dialogue are much more sexualized than Kyoko's. Written by S. A. Bennett, drawn by Wes Abbott.

their decision to continue depicting Kyoko as a basically heroic character despite the growing fashion for violent antiheroines, arguing that her reluctance to kill helped to distinguish her from "the current rash of 'psycho' heroes," a rash which presumably included the casually murderous Scimidar (*Shuriken: Cold Steel* no. 4). Even so, Kyoko's character hardened noticeably once she was no longer being written by Byers, coming closer to the ninja assassin heroine norm that had been established by characters like Elektra, Ninja, and Whisper. By 1989 the once-heroic Kyoko muses: "I'm really not a very nice person. I was more worried about the stains on my sofa than the dead boy in the hallway" (*Shuriken: Cold Steel* no. 4).

Neither *Scimidar* nor *Shuriken* was exactly a "bad girl" title: *Scimidar* comes close, but its visual aesthetics are still those of 1980s comics, and its heroine's dreamy amorality is fundamentally incompatible with true "bad girl" rage. *Shuriken*, despite its ninja-heavy plot, was still ultimately a "good girl" comic: One reader even wrote to the Eternity series to say "I hope that we will still get the good girl art that the book was full of" (*Shuriken: Cold Steel* no. 4). But they, along with the thong-wearing martial arts heroine Samuree from Continuity Comics, were very much signs of things to come, and the steady drift of all three titles toward greater violence and more sexualized costume designs clearly prefigured the rise of the "bad girl" trend, the visual style of which drew heavily upon both manga (as with *Shuriken*) and pornography (as with *Scimidar*). In particular, the move from *Shuriken* to *Scimidar* can be seen as marking with some precision the pivot toward "bad girl" comics, that is, away from an attempt to market female protagonists to female readers and toward a focus on the existing male comic-buying audience, who wanted as much sex, violence, and nudity as possible. Sadly, the lesson Eternity seems to have drawn from their respective sales figures was that the safest option was to lean into soft-core pornography, and that "creat[ing] female characters that women can enjoy" would have to wait for another day.

"Hot-Looking Bad Girl Comics": The Takeoff

The closest thing the "bad girl" trend has to a birthplace was the 1991 San Diego Comic Convention, at which Everette Hartsoe arrived with three hundred hand-numbered preview copies of his first comic book, *Razor: Souls of Darkness.* As Hartsoe later recalled, the story was an instant hit, paving the way for the rapid expansion of his newly founded company London Night Studios (Boom). This story of a violent female vigilante who murders criminals with blades attached to her arms had obvious debts to the then-popular comics *Elektra*, *Wolverine*, and *The Punisher*, and a Goth-infused visual style derived from the indie revenge comic *The Crow* (1989), which had become a surprise success (Voger 51). But while the constituent parts of *Razor* came from elsewhere, the manner in which it remixed them made it an important model for the works that followed.

Like *The Crow*, *Razor* tells a story of violent revenge set in a crime-filled urban hellscape. Both comics grew out of personal tragedy: James O'Barr wrote *The Crow* after his fiancée was killed by a drunk driver, while Hartsoe's *Razor* drew on his desires for revenge after the murder of his younger sister, Roberta (Boom). In *The Crow*, however, women only ever appear as victims, preyed upon by violent men: When criminals murder the protagonist Eric and his fiancée Shelly, it is *he* who refuses death in order to avenge *her*, not the other way around. Eric's heroic status is established by the way he acts as a protector and avenger of women—Shelly, a little girl named Sherri and her drug-addicted mother Sandy, even a female cat named Gabriel—all of whom are depicted as being unable to protect or avenge themselves. Despite his Goth stylings and sadistic violence, Eric's gender politics are staunchly traditional, even sentimental. Sending Sandy back to her daughter, he quotes Thackeray, telling her, "Mother is the name for God in the lips and hearts of all children," while to Sherri, who appears to be about nine years old, he says: "I'm sorry for everything that has happened to you . . . and for everything that is going to happen to you" (*The Crow*). He clearly takes for granted that his is a world in which growing up female leads inevitably to suffering: a world in which rather than making things happen, like Eric, girls like Sherri and Shelly can only try to endure the things that happen *to* them.

Razor takes *The Crow*'s black-and-white world of nihilistic urban violence and inverts its gender roles. If *The Crow* expressed O'Barr's fantasy of being able to avenge his fiancée, then *Razor* was Hartsoe's fantasy of being able to avenge his sister—but rather than telling the story of an avenging elder brother, which is what Hartsoe wanted to be in real life, the agent of vengeance is here reimagined as an avenging elder *sister*. Whereas *The Crow* depicted women as white-on-white angels, whose white skin, hair, and clothes are menaced on all sides by masculine darkness, in *Razor* it is the woman rather than the man who takes on the black hair, black clothes, and black bloodstains of the avenger. Like Elektra before her, Razor is highly sexualized and armed with phallic stabbing weapons, with which she murders every man foolish enough to cross her path. But whereas Miller's *Elektra: Assassin* depicted its heroine as a hallucinatory, mythic figure, seen primarily from the dazed perspectives of the men who stare at her through veils of lust and fear, Hartsoe treats Razor as an action protagonist much like any other. Its success thus marks the point at which the violent, aggressive, hypersexualized, castrating woman became commercially viable in comics, not as a villain or a dreamlike mythic archetype but as a viewpoint character.

Razor emerged from a preexisting world of black-and-white indie horror comics such as Tim Vigil's *Faust* (1988–2012), Joseph Linsner and Joseph Monks's *Cry for Dawn* (1989–1993), and O'Barr's *The Crow* (1989). Looking back on this era, Linsner recalled how "there was a HUGE valley between us and the mainstream guys" (Sewer Mutant). The figure of the "bad girl" action heroine turned out to be the missing ingredient that allowed Hartsoe to escape from this ghettoized world into commercial success. *Razor* began regular publication in 1992, and a year later it was reliably selling ten thousand copies per issue (*Razor Annual* no. 1). Its success was noticed by other creators and publishers, and after this the takeoff was rapid. Billy Tucci, who had been thinking of writing a comic about a male martial artist, changed his mind and decided to write about a female one, instead: The resulting character, Shi, appeared first in an issue of *Razor* before appearing in her own series in 1994 (*Shi: Art of War 1998 Tourbook*). DC's *Huntress*, which had been canceled in 1990, was relaunched in 1994, with its heroine reimagined as a more disturbed and violent Razor-style vigilante. Nira X, who first appeared in the black-and-white indie comic *Zen: Intergalactic Ninja*, began starring in her own comic book in the same year. Lady Death, who originally appeared in Brian Pulido's *Evil Ernie* as a hallucination of the protagonist, was rewritten as a real character with her own comic book in 1994, which became so successful that it was soon selling sixty thousand issues per month (Inness 145). Warrior Nun Areala, who debuted as a supporting character in Ben Dunn's manga series *Ninja High School*, got her own series in 1994. Shotgun Mary, who had initially been one of *her* supporting characters, followed suit in 1995.

Events accelerated in 1995–1996. Dawn, who had previously appeared only on the covers of Monks and Linsner's horror anthology *Cry for Dawn*, became an actual character in Linsner's *Dawn* (1995–1996). Kabuki and Witchblade first appeared in *Shi* crossovers before starring in their own series, which began in 1995 and 1996, respectively. Vampirella, who had been relaunched in 1991, was steadily rewritten to be more of a "bad girl" character, especially in *Vampirella Strikes* (1995–1996), while the inspiration for all the rest, *Elektra*, was relaunched in "bad girl" style in 1995. Other important examples from the 1992–1996 period include *Widow* (1992–1997), *Catwoman* (1992, 1993–2001), *Mantra* (1993–1996), *Ghost* (1993–2000), *Barb Wire* (1993–1995), *Angela* (1994–1995), *Vamps* (1994–1999), *Vamperotica* (1994–1999), *Zealot* (1995), *Cybernary* (1995–1996), *Double Impact* (1995–1996), *Lady Rawhide* (1995–1997), *Lady Justice* (1995–1997), *Hari Kari* (1995–1998), *Purgatori* (1996–2002), *Darkchylde* (1996–1997), *Avengelyne* (1996–1997), *Allegra* (1996), and *Vampfire* (1996–1997).

Like most new genres, "bad girl" comics became increasingly codified as time went on. In 1994 they were all still very different from one another: Aside from the fact that they both had violent and highly sexualized female protagonists, little connected a martial arts comic like *Shi* with an erotic horror comic like *Vamperotica*. By 1996 the formula was becoming much more set: Their heroines wore lingerie or fetish gear, fought with edged weapons, killed without remorse, and spent a lot of time naked. Readers were swift to notice just how quickly these titles became almost interchangeable. "I hope you have a story to tell," wrote one reader of the short-lived vampire comic *Flesh & Blood* (1995–1996), "or your Book will be just another Bad girl Book" (*Flesh and Blood* no. 2).

This process of homogenization can be seen very clearly in *Widow*, which was one of the earliest examples of the trend. The original *Widow* storyline, *Flesh and Blood* (1992–1993), tells the story of a crazed scientist who experiments on his adopted daughter, Emma, causing her to transform into a spider monster during sex and eat her lovers. The scientist uses drugs and hypnosis to keep Emma ignorant of her true nature, while carrying out further experiments to turn her curse into a "sexually transmitted mutagen" that will mutate any man who has sex with her and survives. This storyline, which is clearly shot through with anxieties over patriarchal control, female sexuality, and sexually transmitted disease, positions Emma as simultaneously an object of abject horror and erotic fascination, but hardly as a protagonist: Instead, she is merely the passive victim of her father's madness and her own uncontrollable desires, and she appears to perish at the end of the story. Over the following years, however, Emma was steadily rewritten as an increasingly active and heroic character, until by 1996 she was effectively just an unusually violent superheroine with spider-based superpowers. In 1992 her character design—a beautiful young woman with fangs, claws, and spiked spider legs emerging from her naked body, ready to impale any man who approached her—clearly marked her as a horror monster, a symbolic embodiment of male anxieties over the castrating phallic woman and the infectious, destructive power of female sexuality. By 1996 these same characteristics just made her another "bad girl" heroine, suitable for crossover soft-porn adventures in which she had lesbian trysts with the vampiress Luxura from *Vamperotica* (*Widow/Luxura: Blood Lust* no. 1).

Collectively, despite their objectifying art styles, these early "bad girl" stories were much more concerned with female agency than most of those that came later. The most coherent feminist messages were advanced by *Mantra*, which explored the difficulties experienced by its male hero after being reincarnated into a female body; *Ghost*, which depicted its heroine's battle to bring down the exploitative patriarchal institutions that destroyed her life; and the original series of *Vamps*, which told the story of a group of female vampires struggling to free themselves from male control. *Cybernary*, which told the story of two women whose intermingled minds are trapped within the body of an escaped sex robot, can be read as a parable about a woman's struggle to develop a coherent independent identity in a world that insists on objectifying and commodifying her in purely sexual terms: This theme was strongest in the earliest *Cybernary* stories, published in *Deathblow*, which were sadly cut off by the death of their twenty-three-year-old creator Nick Manabat in 1995. *Allegra*, in which a female super soldier gradually learns that her entire world is an illusion created by her male commander to keep her under control, is essentially a study in gaslighting: Her liberation comes when she learns to trust her own memories, and to stop ignoring the parts of his story that don't quite make sense. *Dawn* and *Witchblade* are both about the search for feminine spiritual resources that can be marshaled against oppressive patriarchal institutions, while *Widow*, *Kabuki*, and *Lady Death* all depict women fighting to reclaim their autonomy from their controlling, abusive fathers. Even *Vampfire* and *Purgatori* tell the stories of vampire lesbians striking back at the misogynistic and homophobic world that scorns them, although in *Purgatori*'s case this battle mostly took the form of fetishistic catfights between women in bikinis.

The phrase "bad girls" took slightly longer to attach itself to the genre, not entering common usage until 1994. Each month, *Wizard* published a "top 10" list of the comics that had sold particularly well during the previous month: In July 1994 this list included the first issues of *Shi*, *Lady Death*, and *Vengeance of Vampirella*, all of which had sold out the month before and which the article collectively referred to as "bad girl books." (Its author may have been thinking of a 1991 *Captain America* storyline in which three semi-reformed female supervillains, Black Mamba, Asp, and Diamondback, combine the initials of their code names and start collectively referring to themselves as the "B.A.D. girls" [*Captain America* vol. 1, no. 385].) Commenting on the success of these titles, the article noted: "We appear to be witnessing 'The Dawn of the Hot-Looking Bad Girl Comics.' It seems that this once-underground segment of the collecting community has come aboveground, giving some of the latest bad girl books large secondary market presence" (*Wizard* no. 35, 139).

As this passage indicates, what happened in 1994 was not the birth of the trend but the moment that trend went mainstream, no longer the domain only of "underground" black-and-white indie comics such as *Widow*, *Serpentyne* (1992), or *Vampyre's Kiss* (1990–1992). Previously, "Hot-Looking Bad Girl Comics" had been aligned with niche horror and pornography, transgressive and hard to find: From 1994, they became part of the mainstream business of comics retail. The article notes that these titles traded openly on the sex appeal of their heroines, and that their fans were "mostly guys, we imagine": Shi has "the requisite killer bod," Lady Death is "an extremely healthy female embodiment of death walking around in tiny underwear," and Vampirella "is proof that in comics, hot babes are indeed hot!" It also praised their writing—"it's actually not a bad story"—but was clearly under no illusions that this was their primary selling point.

In October 1994, *Wizard* devoted an entire article to the trend titled "Bad Girls," which marked the point at which the name attached itself indelibly to the genre. Its author, Rogers Cadenhead, opened by declaring: "For years, the conventional wisdom in comics has been that female characters can't succeed in their own books. After spirited efforts with protagonists like Wonder Woman and She-Hulk, companies resigned themselves to the fact that their largely male audience largely wants to read about large males" (*Wizard* no. 38, 42). However, Cadenhead noted that this situation had changed rapidly: "Suddenly, the battle for reader dollars has become a battle of the sexes." The sudden shift in the market took retailers by surprise, leading them to underorder copies of *Vampirella* and *Lady Death* due to their established expectation that comics with female protagonists had "an extremely underground (read: minimal) following" (*Wizard* no. 38, 44). The article noted that women mostly had negative reactions to the trend, quoting Colleen Doran as saying that "most women readers find this stuff repulsive, causing them to turn right around and walk out of the store in disgust," but that their (male) creators defended them as "a tribute to women," even though "most women observed that the images were 'sexist' and 'exploitative'" (*Wizard* no. 38, 44, 47). (One woman's description of them as "strong independent bimbos" deftly sums up their combination of heroic agency and objectified disempowerment.) A survey carried out by Hank Bordowitz concluded that the trend was essentially sustained by simple sexism: "Another fanboy summed up this survey with what appears to be the general consensus of the male readers (who make up the majority of comic readers) polled: '[These portrayals are] exploitative of the female body; however, I don't find this objectionable.' That attitude will keep 'bad girls' around for some time to come" (*Wizard* no. 38, 47).

However, as the creator of *Mantra*, Mike Barr, pointed out, this alone was not sufficient to explain why female protagonists had suddenly gone from being a commercial disadvantage to a commercial asset: "As the idea that female characters don't sell books" fades from currency, a new perception is forming: that the books are selling because attractive female characters sell books.

> "Of course, if you put a beautiful woman in a bikini, it's going to sell," writer Barr recalls being told after *Mantra* began to garner attention. "I'm hearing both sides now."
>
> Barr says that if that was the case, it would've been done a long time ago. "If that's all it took, everyone would have done it." (*Wizard* no. 38, 46)

Barr was correct: Beautiful women in bikinis had been commonplace in American superhero comics for decades, but it was only in the 1990s that they became capable of sustaining their own titles. Partly, as I shall discuss, this was due to the changing nature of the American comics market, which relied ever more heavily on a core audience of white middle-class men with substantial disposable incomes: In this sense, going all in on commodified female sexuality can be seen simply as a response to shifting audience demographics. But it also reflected a broader cultural shift, one that was hinted at in Cadenhead's byline: "*Rogers Cadenhead is a freelance writer based in Texas who swears he saw Thelma, Louise, and Selina pass him on the highway*" (Wizard no. 38, 46). *Thelma and Louise* (1991) had come out just three years before and was widely seen as a cultural milestone, insofar as it represented the moment when a feminist revenge film with lesbian subtexts could be released as a mainstream film, albeit a hugely controversial and divisive one (Henry 17; Dole 86; Owen, Stein, and Vande Berg 198). By gesturing to it here, Cadenhead suggests that the "bad girl" comics might be interpreted as part of the same cultural trend.

Once the "bad girl" name had been attached to the genre by *Wizard*, it swiftly started to be used by the publishers themselves. A 1995 advertisement for a crossover between the indie superheroines Cynder and Nira X described it as "a bad girl brawl-fest!" (*Nira X* vol. 3, no. 1). Blackout Press published *Bad Girls of Blackout* (1995), which brought together their "bad girl" characters Violet, Ice, Ms. Cyanide, Lady Vampre, and Hari Kari. Academy Comics published *Amazon Gazonga: Bad Girls of the Jungle* (1995), in which a bikini-wearing Amazon warrior learns to reject the misandric ways of her people. CFD publishing—originally formed to publish *Cry for Dawn*—brought out the art book *CFD's Pin-Up Bad Girls* (1996), and the parodic "Lady Bad Girl" appeared in *Lethargic Lad* (1996). By 1999 even DC Comics featured a knife-wielding supervillain called "Bad Grrl," clearly intended as a send-up of the trend, while London Night studios, who had done so much to start the craze in the first place, published a book called *Beyond Bad Girls* (1999), hinting at a desire to diversify (*Action Comics* vol. 1, no. 756). Shortly afterward, London Night ceased publication. For them, as for many other 1990s indie comics publishers, it turned out that what lay "beyond bad girls" was nothing whatsoever.

Bad Girl Backlash: Women Write Back

In 1995, one year after *Wizard* observed the "bad girl" trend going mainstream, AC Comics (who at the time were the leading publisher of retro "good girl" titles such as *Femforce*) published a comic entitled *Bad Girl Backlash*. Written and drawn by women, it provided a range of female perspectives on the unfolding "bad girl" genre.

In her introduction to the comic, Rebekah Black wrote:

> I can offer some areas in which those women I have had contact with seem to agree. One is that the majority of "bad girl" titles that are on the market today are clones of the first few such books and they *all* depend primarily on a focus on sex and violence for sales and the use of revenge and anti-heroism as the primary motivations for action. While many women are pleased to see strong female lead characters dominating the interest of readers, most would like to see some variety in the types of female leads that are given validity by virtue of "good sales."
>
> If you name several of the first contemporary titles considered "bad girl" books, many women will say these achieved popularity through an interesting story idea as well as sex, violence and antiheroic motivations. As for those first few titles, many women agree there is definitely a place in the market for these books. As for the multitude of clones that are not well written and have jumped on the proverbial bandwagon, enough is enough. Women can do more than look good and behave violently. (*Bad Girl Backlash* no. 1)

Black didn't specify which works she has in mind when she refers to "those first few titles," but from context she probably meant comics such as *Razor*, *Shi*, and *Vampirella*, which initially placed a heavy emphasis on storytelling as well as sexualized imagery. The objection of her informants was not to these but to the commercialized mass production of their imitators, which threatened to drive all other forms of female representation out of comics, resulting in a comics industry where female characters can *only* "look good and behave violently." Objections were also made to the near-uniform appearance of these characters, all of whom were tall, slender, big breasted, and scantily clad, and to the way they were posed, especially the "*boobs out, rear out poses*" that had already become a stylistic signature of "bad girl" comics. Much of the comic was devoted to mapping out what superheroines might look like if they were given more practical clothing and more realistic body types, and one strip even poked fun at oversexualized female costumes by demonstrating what male characters would look like if they were dressed in the same way—a concept that would be redeployed in 2012 by the Tumblr page "The Hawkeye Initiative" as a way of demonstrating the persistent sexism of American comic book art.

Bad Girl Backlash also expressed concerns at just how violent and vengeful the "bad girl" heroines were depicted as being, arguing that "their creative teams depend too much on the appeal of *revenge, big breasts, lots* and *lots* of hair, and *really* skimpy outfits." As a character in one strip explained:

> Comic book racks are filled with titles that have been classified as *bad girl*. We decided to do the *bad girl backlash* because many women object to the imbalance. There are more *bad* female characters than there are *good* or *heroic* ones. There are *too many* characters marketed by focusing on sex, violence, and skimpy costumes. Some women also object to the fact that the bodies of most superheroines are drawn to look like six foot tall models and their costumes are impractical . . . others say *that's* OK as long as women aren't depicted as whiny, whimpy, or brainless. What *I* hate most is the lack of humor, heroic motivations and lack of moral values. (*Bad Girl Backlash* no. 1)

The book offered qualified praise for *Shi*, though its authors were wary of its revenge-driven plot and the skimpiness of the lower half of her outfit. It noted the turn *Vampirella* had taken toward much bloodier storylines, comparing her 1990s incarnation to previous versions of the character—"I guess mine was a *good girl* vampire and this one is a *bad girl!*"—and arguing that earlier eras of comics had managed to produce "a *few* strong female characters" without having "each breast as large as their head" and "costumes as skimpy as can be found on *some* of today's female characters." An opinion piece by Scott Siencin clearly laid out the underlying logic of the genre:

> Question: Why can't female comic book characters kick butt like their male counterparts?
>
> Answer: For the most part, they can . . . so long as at least ninety percent of their flesh is exposed, they're written like male adolescent wish fulfillment fantasies, and they're drawn to look like they've just been peeled off the cover of Penthouse. (For heaven's sake, we don't want readers to start thinking of women as people, now do we? That would threaten the status quo?). (*Bad Girl Backlash* no. 1)

As Siencin points out, female agency and female sexualization were permitted in these comics on an essentially one-for-one ratio. The more female characters were allowed to "kick butt," the more they were also drawn and written like "male adolescent wish fulfillment fantasies," to ensure the resulting narrative did not ultimately "threaten the status quo." He acknowledges that not all "bad girl" titles are alike, praising *Whisper* and *Kabuki*, and expresses the hope that "at the heart of the whole 'bad girls' comics movement is the spark of something that one day could lead to more comic-book titles like Kabuki," stating: "Women want strong female characters. Audiences in general deserve them."

At the same time, however, Siencin acknowledges that the current situation was ultimately the result of economic forces. The reason so much interchangeable "bad girl" material was being published was simply because "readers keep buying the stuff!" The question, then, must be: Where did this demand come from? What was it about the mid-1990s American comics market that made this material so appealing to its target audience, when that same audience had displayed so little interest in it just a few years before? It is this question which the next chapter aims to address, by placing the "bad girl" genre within the context of larger trends of the American comic book industry.

2

Killer Bodies

"Bad Girls" and the American Comics Industry

Looking Like Progress: "Bad Girls" Comics in Context

The "bad girl" trend did not arise in a vacuum. Subsequent chapters will discuss its fraught relationship with feminism, but it was also shaped by other factors: distribution networks, changing art styles and production methods, shifting trends in the fashion and beauty industries, and the growing influence of manga and comics "for mature readers." All of these must be understood to make sense of the genre's rapid rise and even more rapid decline.

Given how dated they now appear, it is important to emphasize that to many readers in 1994, "bad girl" comics *looked like the future*. The overblown valuations published by *Wizard* seemed credible precisely because many collectors believed they were witnessing the beginning of something genuinely important. Compared to most Marvel and DC titles, these comics appeared more "modern" due to their incorporation of manga aesthetics, their inclusion of sex, violence, nudity, and homosexuality, and their focus on powerful women at a moment when "female empowerment" was a key element of the cultural zeitgeist. Just as "dark and gritty" characters like Venom and Wolverine had come to define the comics of the early 1990s, with consequent rewards for those fans who owned the now-scarce issues in which these once-obscure characters first appeared, in 1994–1996 it was briefly possible to believe that characters like Shi and Razor would go on to define the genre's future, in which comics would not only be dark and gritty but dark, gritty, and *female led* (Wright 280).

However, the speed with which demand for such comics collapsed following the industry-wide crash of 1996–1997 demonstrates the extent to which it was the product of a very specific moment in cultural history. The rise of the "Image style" in American comics, coupled with the shift to digital coloring, facilitated the development of art-led genres defined by their highly stylized visuals, of which "bad girl" comics became a prime example. The influx of Japanese popular culture, the influence of third-wave feminism, and the mainstreaming of pornography collectively primed the American comic-reading public to want to read about powerful, highly sexualized heroines in an environment in which actual anime, manga, and adult media were still relatively difficult to get hold of, leading them to seek approximations of their desired objects in comic books instead. The "bad girl" trend also developed in parallel with the growing prestige of comics for mature readers, such as those printed by DC's Vertigo imprint—a form with which the "bad girl" genre initially had considerable crossover. Indeed, the genre can perhaps best be understood as resulting from a moment during which the traditions of manga, pornography, and Vertigo-style mature graphic novels briefly overlapped within the context of a comics market that was temporarily rich in high-spending collectors eager to seize upon the next big thing. As soon as these conditions no longer pertained, the genre shriveled rapidly.

In this chapter I shall discuss these cultural crosscurrents: the development of the "bad girl" art style, the influence of manga, and the overlap with "mature readers" comics and pornography. I shall then discuss the commercial contexts within which "bad girl" comics were marketed, distributed, and sold to draw out the specific characteristics of the mid-1990s comic book market within which the genre's brief efflorescence took place.

"Unspeakable Fantasies!": The Rise of "Bad Girl" Art

The "bad girl" trend was heavily art driven. Image Comics, which did so much to foster it, was well named: Founded by a group of seven comics artists, its focus was always on visual rather than verbal storytelling (Voger 57–58; Gabilliet 149). Describing the foundation of Image, Todd McFarlane was dismissive of the importance of comics writers when compared to artists, asserting that "maybe the artwork is more important":

MCFARLANE Well, mostly it was artists, so I just told them, for the most part, just ditch your writer, you know? Grab control of the reins . . .

[. . .]

GARY GROTH *Did it ever occur to you that a lot of these artists might not know how to write?*

> MCFARLANE [LONG PAUSE] You know, uh, that really didn't occur to me because that never occurred to *me*, you know what I'm saying? I mean, fuck, I didn't let some little thing like not being able to write stop *me*, so I didn't really see where that should actually be that much of a problem. (Groth, "Todd McFarlane Interview" 62, 46)

"Bad girl" comics took this "art first" tendency to an extreme. The chief selling point of each comic was that it provided a sequence of pinup images depicting violent women in skimpy outfits, and for those images to add up to an actual story often seems to have been viewed as an optional extra. As one unusually honest reader explained, "I love the art work and that's what really pulled me in. . . . If a girl isn't good looking enough to me on the outside, why the hell would I want to get to know her on the inside?" (*The Tenth* vol 2, no. 12).

As a result, there is a degree to which discussing the genre in terms of story content represents a category error: While their plots certainly had similarities, "bad girl" comics were defined first and foremost by their art style. This style coalesced in 1993–1994, in the work of artists such as Jim Balent, Mike Deodato, Ben Dunn, Everette Hartsoe, Steven Hughes, Joseph Linsner, Bill Maus, Louis Small Jr., and Billy Tucci. As Mike Madrid and Carolyn Cocca note, aside from the pinup art that had always influenced comic-book depictions of women, its chief influences were supermodel fashion, manga, and pornography: All forms that were very much on the rise in the early 1990s (Cocca, *Superwomen* 11; Madrid 94).

As I have discussed, Hartsoe and Linsner came to the genre from the world of alternative, porn-adjacent, black-and-white indie horror comics. They brought their fetish aesthetics with them: Their "bad girl" heroines often resembled dominatrices, and wore fetish-inspired styles featuring straps and corsets. Tucci came from fashion design—he later collaborated with the famous fashion designer Anna Sui on his comic *Ju-Nen* (2004–2005)—and he drew his heroines in fashion magazine style, with extremely long legs and slender, tapering figures. Dunn's background was in manga, which he played an important role in introducing to the American market, and his "bad girls" were derived from the female protagonists of 1980s Japanese shonen and *hentai* media (Brienza 160). Hughes began his career drawing for Aircel Comics, which, like Dunn's Antarctic Press, published a mixture of manga-style adventure comics and pornography for the late 1980s black-and-white "T&A" comics market (Nicholson 130). Balent began drawing action heroines in the sci-fi comic *Evangeline* (1987–1989)—an early example of the "warrior nun" archetype that Dunn subsequently reimagined in "bad girl" form in *Warrior Nun Areala*—but he, like Louis Small Jr., developed his signature "bad girl" style during his work on *Vampirella*. It was in *Vampirella* that Balent first started drawing his heroines with exaggerated, artificial-looking breasts—a look which, at the time, had been newly popularized in American pornography, with female porn stars increasingly undergoing plastic surgery to obtain the cartoonish bosoms their audience had started to expect (Negra 120). Maus, meanwhile, began his career drawing semi-pornographic parodies of then-popular superhero comics, with titles like *X-Farce*, *Blandman*, and *Cyberfarce*—send-ups of *X-Force*, *Sandman*, and *Cyberforce*, respectively. His shift in 1994 to drawing and writing the "bad girl" comic *Nira X* may be taken to mark the point at which "porn parody" and "mainstream superhero comic" became effectively interchangeable.

The context within which these artists worked was heavily influenced by the rise of Image Comics, whose founders were noted for their bombastic, manga-influenced art styles: what Anna Peppard called "the stylistic excess that would soon define the Image brand," and which Matthew Pustz described more bluntly as Image's "often cluttered, highly exaggerated, usually sexist style of art" (Peppard, "Is That a Monster" 92; Beaty and Woo 79; Pustz 89). The Image style abandoned the relative realism and grid-based layouts of mainstream 1980s superhero comics, shifting to low-panel-count pages filled with stylized figures that were often depicted twisting, leaping, kicking, and screaming. Two founding Image artists—Jim Lee and Marc Silvestri—also became famous for their hypersexualized female characters and exaggerated gender dimorphism during their respective runs on Marvel's *X-Men*. The super-teams they created for Image in 1992, *WildCATS* and *Cyberforce*, exhibited this tendency even more clearly, with readers admitting to buying them partly for their bikini scenes (*Cyberforce* vol. 2, no. 6). Their female members—the swordswomen Cyblade and Zealot, the female gunslinger Ballistic, and the stripper-turned-superheroine Voodoo—provided important templates for subsequent "bad girl" character designs: Zealot was even described in her first appearance as "sex and violence, all rolled together with a bad attitude" (*WildCATS* no. 1). The Image style was widely imitated, and this, coupled with the growing influence of manga, paved the way for "bad girl" characters to make the jump from alternative to mainstream comics in 1993–1994 (Voger 65). It was this that allowed artists like Hartsoe, Linsner, and Hughes to escape the ghettoized world of black-and-white porn-horror comics, achieving commercial success with *Razor*, *Dawn*, and *Lady Death*, respectively.

The distinctive elements of the "bad girl" comics style may be swiftly described. The regular grid used by older superhero comics is gone: Instead, each page is divided into a small number of irregularly shaped panels, usually no more than six, sometimes only one. Splash pages are common, and if there are more than three panels, one is usually much larger than the others, visually subordinating the rest. Gutters between panels are usually either black or absent: The broad white gutters used in older comics are rare. The page is brightly colored, with lakes of black and garish bursts of red—an effect enabled by the shift to digital coloring and away from newsprint paper, which allowed 1990s comic books artists to use much smoother and brighter colors than the murky inks of the past.

The resulting layout is dominated by one or more idealized female figures moving under enormous torsion, their spines arched or twisted, hips and breasts jutting out at sharp angles. They exemplify Scott Bukatman's description of the comic book superheroine as embodying a parodically exaggerated version of femininity:

> The fetishism of breasts, thighs, and hair [is] so complete, that the comics seem to dare you to say anything about them that isn't just redundant. Of course the female form has absurdly exaggerated sexual characteristics; of course the costumes are skimpier than one could (or should) imagine; of course there's no visible way that these costumes could stay in place; of course these women represent simple adolescent masturbatory fantasies (with a healthy taste of the dominatrix). (112)

Whereas older comics tended to draw characters in long shot, situated within their drawn environments and confined to their individual panels, these heroines loom into massive close-up, filling the page, transcending their environments (which are often not drawn, replaced with abstract colors or speed lines), and smashing through whatever remains of the panel grid. Compared to superheroines in earlier comics they are much more likely to be posed with legs wide apart, their arms flung out in dramatic poses: Subordinate panels are often devoted to close-ups of their faces, with huge eyes framed by waterfalls of hair. Often these figures are naked, or nearly so: If they are clothed, their costumes cling like a second skin. Around them pinwheel other, lesser figures, usually men, tumbling limp as ragdolls, mown down by the heroines' swords, or guns, or martial arts. Often the cause of the men's defeat is very unclear, as though they have died simply from coming near the heroine. These secondary figures are often poorly defined, their clothes baggy, their bodies blocky, their faces sketched in. The women, by contrast, are drawn in great detail, with every line of their figures visible, even when this would seem improbable in context. (Clothes that mysteriously cling to every side of the breast as though painted onto the bosom rather than draped over it, and nipples that remain clearly visible through multiple layers of clothing, are staples of "bad girl" art.) Impossibly long legs kick out toward the page's corners. Long hair swings theatrically around the main figure like a cape. All sight lines converge on the heroine's bosom.

Cocca succinctly describes the archetypal "bad girl" superheroine body as being "large-breasted and small-waisted, long-haired and long-legged," and Jeffrey Brown offered a similar checklist: "huge, gravity-defying breasts, mile-long legs, perpetually pouty lips, and perfectly coifed big hair" (Cocca, *Superwomen* 12; Brown, *Dangerous Curves* ch. 2). That these heroines all had very similar body types reflected the ever-narrowing beauty ideals of the period: As Diane Negra noted at the time, "A growing frankness about sexuality and the body have accompanied an ever more specific sense of what ideal femininity should look like" (119). Insofar as they had a real-world model it was Pamela Anderson, who played the "bad girl" superheroine Barb Wire in the 1996 film of the same name. However, while their bodies reflected the norms of American pornography, their

FIGURES 7A, 7B, AND 7C Three classic "bad girl" page compositions. Top left from *Lady Death: Between Heaven and Hell* issue 2 (1995), written by Brian Pulido, art by Steven Hughes, colors by Jason Jensen, lettering by Dave Lanphear, letters by Comicraft. Top right from *Warrior Nun Areala vs Razor* (1996), written by Joseph Wolfe, art by Ben Dunn, coloring by Pat Duke and Joseph Weltjens. Bottom from *Shi: The Way of the Warrior* (1996), written and drawn by William Tucci, inked by Nelson Asencio, lettering by Mada Design.

page layouts owed more to 1990s supermodel fashion photography, which—like "bad girl" comic art—frequently revolved around one or more goddess-like female figures, dynamically posed with legs outstretched.

In 1990s fashion photography, a combination of high waists, high heels, and camera angles were often used to give the impression that the model's legs made up two-thirds of their actual height. In "bad girl" comics, these became the actual proportions of the female characters—just as the extreme thinness of 1990s supermodels, which in reality was the result of extreme diet and exercise regimes, was depicted in "bad girl" comics as the natural default shape of women's bodies. The combination of supermodel thinness with porn-star bustiness led to some "bad girl" heroines being drawn with truly bizarre figures, giving rise to the improbable "two balloons on a broomstick" bodies that swiftly came to be associated with the lower-status end of the genre. In 1999 the comics author Lea Hernandez expressed her frustration at "the Victoria's Secret model with a backache-sized tit job being presented as a heroine for me [in comics], her goodness as a role model directly related to her breast size."

The same narrowness apparent in the permitted range of "bad girl" body types can be seen in their depictions of race. Given the huge number of East Asian "bad girl" characters, and the importance of Black, Latino, and Asian artists in the style's development, it would not be quite accurate to call it a "white" aesthetic—but it was certainly a very *pale* aesthetic, which made heavy use of the paleness of Northern European and East Asian skin tones to achieve exaggerated visual contrast effects. Tucci often mentioned the influence of the *Playboy* artist Patrick Nagel on his style: Nagel famously drew women with snow-white skin, a look Tucci paid homage to in his series *Year of the Dragon* (2000). (In Tucci's *Shi,* the heroine's white war paint is explicitly inspired by a Nagel poster hanging on her wall.) White-skinned heroines emerging from black shadows, surrounded by red bloodstains, swiftly became a "bad girl" cliché. Crusade Comics even published one series, *Shi: Black, White, and Red* (1998), in which these were the only three colors used.

Given that the success of *Vampirella* and *Lady Death* made Louis Small Jr. and Steven Hughes two of the highest-profile Black comics artists in America overnight, it is tempting to read an element of parody into their drawings of the whiter-than-white undead women who made them famous (Voger 76). The hint is especially strong with Lady Death, who can easily be read as a caricature of white beauty ideals: With her snow-white skin, hair, and eyes, which lack even pupils for contrast, she is literally so white that she's dead. If it was, however, then it was a parody whose readers clearly took it at face value. Darker skin tones among "bad girl" heroines were extremely rare: According to their respective texts, Elektra was Greek and Catwoman was Latina, but they were drawn with the same skin colors as any other white characters. The vampire queen Purgatori was Egyptian, but in her very first appearance her demonic transformation turned her skin bright red. When she eventually regained her North African skin tones in 2001, her title was canceled a year later.

The revealing styles promoted by 1990s women's fashion also fed into "bad girl" character designs. When a reader wrote in to the Image series *The Tenth* (1997–2000) to complain about its scantily dressed and frequently naked female leads, asking "are they both supposed to be super-sluts[?]," the artist responded that he was only imitating current supermodels and youth fashion trends: "In the summer time, girls wear mini skirts and tank tops and big high heeled shoes (especially in the last two years)—does this mean most of America's youth are dressing like sluts? Of course not. . . . For Zorina, she's an aspiring supermodel/actress and Espy—well, she can't help it if her clothes rip off when she over-uses her telekinesis!" (*The Tenth* vol. 2, no. 6). One form of fashion culture that proved particularly influential on the "bad girl" aesthetic was Victoria's Secret lingerie catalogues, which were ubiquitous in 1990s America: As Jane Juffer points out, in the years before the rise of internet pornography, it was an open secret that such catalogues were often used as masturbation material (148). Silvestri admitted to using Victoria's Secret catalogues as references for the female characters in *Cyberforce*, and as the decade progressed the swimsuit special issues were increasingly joined by Victoria's Secret–style "lingerie specials" like *Lady Death in Lingerie* (1995), *Vamperotica Lingerie Special* (1995), and *Bethany Vampfire: Lingerie Secrets* (1998) (*Cyberforce* vol. 2, no. 9). When Alias Enterprises entitled their 2005 "bad girl" comic *Victoria's Secret Service*, they were only acknowledging what had long been known: That many "bad girl" character designs originated as copies or tracings of lingerie models.

The perspective of these comics mirrors that of the normative heterosexual male gaze, in which all attention always leaps toward the body of the most conventionally attractive woman present. She gets the splash page and the main panel: Everyone and everything else is merely set dressing. As I have discussed, the question of whether the ability of women to attract and hold such a gaze constituted a state of empowerment or degradation was much debated by American feminists at the time. In *Backlash*, Susan Faludi built on earlier critiques by second-wave feminists to argue that the fashion industry in general, and the lingerie industry in particular, acted to degrade and disempower women (203–236). This argument was opposed by Camille Paglia, whose books *Sexual Personae* (1990), *Sex, Art, and American Culture* (1993), and *Vamps and Tramps* (1994) celebrated fashion photography and pornography as expressions of female power: As she put it, "Sex *is* power, and all power is inherently aggressive" (*Sexual Personae* 23). This debate was so familiar within early 1990s popular culture that it actually plays out in the experimental Image Comics series *The Maxx*, where Julie (a "pro-sex" third-wave feminist) has an argument with an older woman, a second-wave feminist who is visually coded as a hippie:

> They had the same old argument.
> Steinem!
> Paglia!

> PAGLIA??!
> STEINEM?!?
> MISOGYNY disguised as liberalism!
> HUMOURLESS TOTALITARIANISM!
> You're buying into the same old MACHO posturing that's holding us back!
> YOU'RE buying into the culture of VICTIMIZATION and staying HELPLESS! (*The Maxx* no. 4)

This conversation is framed by a page-filling image of Julie wearing a cutout top. In her imagination, Julie is "the Leopard Queen," a "bad girl" warrior who is "beautiful and feral as the great beasts she runs with"—a clear allusion to Clarissa Pinkola Estés's *Women Who Run with the Wolves*, which had been published the year before (*The Maxx* no. 1). Here Julie dominates the page like the "bad girl" heroine she likes to imagine herself as being, but she isn't drawn or posed like one: Instead, she looks down, diffident, as though doubting the strength of her "pro-sex" position. But *The Maxx*, whose primary subject was the long-term psychological consequences of sexual abuse, was unusual in presenting both sides of the argument. The "bad girl" comics that followed mostly wanted Paglia without Steinem, insisting that their works were meant to celebrate the strength and beauty of their heroines, and dismissing the idea that their art might constitute "MISOGYNY disguised as liberalism."

It is notable that while several "bad girl" comics were written by women—most notably Mary Jo Duffy (*Catwoman*) and Christina Z (*Witchblade*)—far fewer were *drawn* by them. There were some exceptions: *Witch Hunter* (1996) and *Wynonna Earp* (1996–1997) were drawn by Joyce Chin, who went on to make a career drawing "bad girl" comic covers, while *Vampfire* was written and drawn by Holly Golightly, who had a background in porn comics and later married the *Catwoman* artist Jim Balent. Probably the best-known female artist to work in the genre was Amanda Conner, who began her career as an assistant to Bill Sienkiewicz and served as his model for Elektra in *Elektra: Assassin* (Ray). Conner drew for *Vampirella*, *Tomoe*, and *Painkiller Jane*, offering a slightly less pornographic interpretation of the "bad girl" aesthetic. As one *Vampirella* reader wrote approvingly, "Conner has lowered the cup sizes without sacrificing a hint of Vampi's unearthly beauty" (*Vampirella: Death and Destruction* no. 1).

For the most part, however, the style was practiced by men. This was noticed at the time, as the foreword to Sandra Chang's *Akemi* (1997) makes clear:

> Another cliché comes tumbling down: A story drawn with the talent of a maestro, filled with stunning, sexy, and provocative girls can only be the work of an exacerbated [*sic*] macho male driven by unspeakable fantasies! Well, think again. Sandy [Chang] is a ravishing young woman whose temperament is rather calm and reserved. She loves beauty and femininity. She stands fearless

before the unbridled violence of her imagination and her art comes as a master's stroke." (*Akemi* no. 1)

The language here shows that, as a woman drawing "bad girl" art, Chang was recognized as being highly unusual, and that the vast majority of such works were indeed produced by "macho male[s] driven by unspeakable fantasies," whose reasons for drawing "stunning, sexy, and provocative girls" required little explanation. In any case, describing *Akemi* in this way was either an overstatement or a marketing tactic, as the comic was firmly at the milder end of the "bad girl" spectrum. It also lasted only one issue before being brought down by the collapse of its publisher, Brainstorm Comics, thus ending the genre's only chance to see what an Asian "bad girl" action heroine written and drawn by an actual Asian woman might have looked like.

The fact that this foreword stressed that Chang was not just female but "a ravishing young woman" further emphasizes the extent to which all female power and value in "bad girl" comics was understood to be contingent upon sex appeal, even in fields like comic book penciling which could not possibly be affected by the physical appearance of the artist. Given the rampant fetishization of East Asian women in the genre, the description of Chang as "calm," "reserved," and loving "beauty and femininity" may well have been intended to reassure readers that she also conformed to the relevant stereotypes of Asian femininity. Nor was this the only example in which the sexualization of fictional women in "bad girl" comics was extended to the real women who worked on them. The Homage Studios *Swimsuit Special* (1993) included a drawing by Silvestri of their editor, Cynthia Sullivan, posing in a bikini in "bad girl" style: One can only hope the page was published with her approval. (The same issue referred to the superheroines it featured as "super-models," emphasizing the crossover between fashion and comic-book imagery.) *Witchblade* included photos of its female writer and editor, and printed letters from male readers offering to date the former and praising the beauty of the latter (*Witchblade* no. 13, 56). When Conner started drawing *Vampirella*, readers wrote in asking if she was single (*Vampirella: Death and Destruction* no. 2).

As I have discussed, the year "bad girl" art really took off was 1994: the same year as the now-famous "Hello Boys" Wonderbra advertising campaign starring Eva Herzigová. Like the comics already discussed, this campaign was premised on the assumption that the truly desirable bosom would be an *exaggerated* bosom: Thus the need for the push-up Wonderbra to enhance the wearer's cleavage. The ad's accompanying text made clear that the resulting look was designed for the male gaze, the "Boys" whom Herzigová was supposedly greeting. Its implicit promise was that this look, correctly performed, would grant the wearer power over men, a power apparently evidenced by widely reported claims that male drivers found the billboards so distracting that they crashed their cars (Alexander). The poses Herzigová struck for the campaign would not have looked out of place on a "bad girl" comic splash page: Indeed, one of them, in which she leans forward while half turning her torso toward the viewer, rapidly became a stock "bad girl" pose. The accompanying ad text was, "Or are you just pleased to see me?"

Plastered across billboards, Herzigová's larger-than-life image loomed over real-world streets in the same way that "bad girl" heroines loom over their page layouts: Mythic figures of idealized female sexual power, like the pagan goddesses celebrated by Paglia, whose strength was at the same time completely contingent on their willingness and ability to follow male sexual scripts (Paglia, *Sexual Personae* 8, 26). Within their stories their power may be real but it is also sharply circumscribed, available only to those whose bodies, behaviors, ethnicities, and sexualities were compatible with the genre's extremely restrictive norms. Given its overwhelming emphasis on a model of female empowerment created by men, for men, and premised entirely on performing for the male gaze, "Hello Boys" could easily have acted as a slogan for the entire "bad girl" art style.

"The Spirit of the *Buyuden*": Amerimanga

The "bad girl" genre cannot be understood without reference to its relationship with anime and manga, which crept gradually into mainstream American culture over the course of the 1990s (Brienza 43). In Japan manga is written in all genres, from realistic queer love stories to violent fantasy epics, but in the United States it was initially marketed primarily to the existing American comics-buying audience, which at the time was overwhelmingly young and male. The material translated into English was thus disproportionately shonen manga and anime, that is, works aimed primarily at teenage boys. Most American comics readers only gradually became aware of the *seinen*, *shoujo*, and *josei* manga categories, which were aimed at men, girls, and women, respectively.

Consequently, if manga meant anything at all for most mid-1990s American readers, it meant shonen manga: giant robots, female nudity, and martial arts. The first such works to find American audiences—*Akira* (manga 1982–1990, film 1988), *Dirty Pair* (anime 1985–1988, comics 1988–1995), *Bubblegum Crisis* (anime 1987–1991), *Dragonball* (manga 1984–1996, anime 1986–1997), *Gunbuster* (anime 1988–1989), *Ghost in the Shell* (manga 1989–1990, film 1995), *Battle Angel Alita* (manga 1990–1995, anime 1993), *Gunsmith Cats* (manga 1991–1997, anime 1996–1997), and *Ninja Scroll* (anime 1993)—were mostly shonen, and their appeal was strongly linked to their inclusion of more violence and nudity than was common in American comics and animation at the time. Six of these nine franchises also had female leads, and when *Wizard* interviewed American comics artists about their favorite manga, they mostly cited female-led action titles such as *Gunsmith Cats*, *Battle Angel Alita*, and *Ghost in the Shell* (*Wizard* no. 62, 36–40). The American release of pornographic *hentai* anime such as *Legend of the Overfiend* (1987–1996) and *La Blue Girl* (1989–1992) strengthened the association between anime, manga, and extreme scenes of sex and violence: As one character in a 1997 *Gen13* comic explains, the reason he watches anime is because it's full of "sex and blood and giant robots and lesbo schoolgirls" (*Gen13 Bootleg* no. 8). The founders of Image were heavily influenced by manga, and Dark Horse published English editions of several manga series in comic book format (Gabilliet 168; Lopes 154). The fact that both companies began publishing much more violent, sexualized, non-code-approved superhero comics in 1992–1993, kick-starting the "bad girl" craze in the process, must be understood partly as an attempt to produce American comics capable of competing with their Japanese rivals among the young male audiences crucial to their success.

The genre's attitudes to Japanese culture were highly conflicted. Its debts to manga, in terms of both form and content, were obvious: As well as frequently using manga-inspired art, complete with large eyes and speed lines, these comics were awash with ninja, samurai, yakuza, robot battle suits, and similar borrowings from Japanese popular culture. The figure of the Japanese female martial artist was clearly an object of erotic fascination for their target audience, and hypersexualized East Asian action heroines appeared in many "bad girl" series, including *Warrior Nun*, *Shi*, *Tomoe*, *Purgatori*, *Jade Warriors*, *Jade*, *Kabuki*, *Immortal II*, *Hari Kari*, *Mortal Kombat*, and *Bloodpool*. *Silver Sable*, which appeared at the start of the trend in 1992, included an Asian lesbian assassin named Amy Chen as a supporting character: Its writers remarked that readers were always requesting more of her, and if the series had been published a few years later she would probably have been the main protagonist (*Silver Sable* no. 32). Even "bad girl" characters who *weren't* Asian often *looked* Asian. Readers of *Cyberforce* wrote to the comic asking hopefully about Cyblade's ethnicity, having concluded from her hair and skin tone that she was probably Asian, and were disappointed to learn that she was actually meant to be French (*Cyberforce* vol. 2, nos. 4–5).

With the exception of the deeply researched *Kabuki*, Asian heroines in "bad girl" comics were usually depicted through a haze of Orientalist stereotypes, constantly talking about their honor and their ancestors, quoting Sun Tzu and Musashi, and waving katanas. Asian organizations, meanwhile, appeared in many of these comics as antagonists, often depicted in classic "yellow peril" terms as cruel, perverse, anti-individualist, and indifferent to the value of human life. In *Witchblade*, for example, the invading yakuza are shown to be much worse than the Italian American mafia, while in *Jade Warriors* the yakuza turn out to be a front for a dragon-worshipping doomsday cult, and the Japanese villains in *Silver Sable* are willing to kill and die for Japan's economic supremacy. Several series, including *Shi*, *Jade Warriors*, and *Kabuki*, told stories about Japanese heroines rejecting, and sometimes destroying, the Japanese institutions which raised and trained them. The late "bad girl" series *Kumori* (2004–2005) even features a Japanese samurai heroine who only starts to wonder whether killing people on her clan's orders might be wrong after being lectured by a male

American superhero who is literally called "the Great White." "You can't just take somebody's *word* for it, you have to see it for yourself and make your own decision," he explains to her—an insight that had apparently never occurred to Kumori during her years in Japan, which here as elsewhere is depicted as conformist, collectivist, and conservative, desperately in need of American individualism to liberate its people in general and its women in particular (*Kumori* no. 2).

This sense of simultaneous attraction to and repulsion from Japanese culture is most obvious in *Shi*—one of the highest-profile titles in the "bad girl" wave of 1994–1996, even though its author strongly rejected the label. *Shi* was unusually serious in its engagement with Asian culture, filling its pages with visual quotations from ukiyo-e prints and devoting a spin-off series, *Senryaku* (1995), to illustrating *The Thirty-Six Stratagems* of Wang Jingze. The Japanese American cartoonist Stan Sakai praised the series as superior to its competitors in the field of "bad girl" Orientalism:

> I've seen samurai walruses, penguins, squirrels, robots, assassins, and women . . . lots of women. . . . Most of them had no respect for the source material and the creators never bothered to do much research beyond what they had read in another comic book. I was always glad when they were canceled. And then I read William Tucci's *Shi*. . . . He captures the *spirit* of the buyuden—tales of valor popular in medieval Japanese literature. He conveys the ideals of bushido (duty, honor and loyalty) and contemporizes them for today's world. (*Shi: The Way of the Warrior* no. 2, Fan Appreciation Edition)

Shi tells the story of a woman torn between the warrior traditions of her father (a Japanese martial artist) and the religious teachings of her mother (an American Catholic missionary). Over the course of the series these come to stand for a split between the East—depicted in Orientalist terms as honorable and spiritual but also hierarchical, implacable, and in thrall to ancient tradition—and the West, which is modern and chaotic but also individualistic, empathic, and capable of forgiveness and change. Despite Tucci's obvious fascination with Japanese art and history, the Japanese organizations in the series were all ultimately depicted extremely negatively and condemned for their violence and ruthlessness, with repeated references to the cruelty of the historical Japanese persecutions of Christianity. The heroine, Ana, is able to escape the cycle of violence that threatens to consume her precisely because her Japanese warrior identity is counterbalanced by her Western Christian morality, while her Japanese friend Tomoe, who has no such counterbalance, spirals away into murderous insanity. Not coincidentally, Ana ends the series with a white American boyfriend, whereas Tomoe's implied homoerotic crush on Ana—a relationship that would pull her back toward her Japanese heritage—goes unconsummated.

In 1996 Tucci took the then-unusual step of publishing a spin-off *Shi* series drawn in manga style: He even released a "Rising Sun edition" in which the cover was in Japanese and the interior art was in black and white, just as it would be in a Japanese manga magazine. But the editorial made clear that this engagement with manga had strict limits: "After this initial three-issue story arc concludes, we'll be revisiting Yukio, Sabre, Hondo, and the rest in new adventures, each exploring a different manga genre. Weird monsters, giant robots, invaders from space . . . you name it, we'll do it (although, we'll skip emulating some of the racier stuff, like *LA BLUE GIRL* or *DEMON BEAST INVASION*. Sorry, but Shi just isn't that kind of gal)" (*Manga Shi* no. 1).

Just as *Shi* emphasized the need for Ana to keep her engagement with Japanese traditions within the limits prescribed by Western religious morality, so *Manga Shi* enacts a similar engagement with Japanese manga culture, drawing on its more socially acceptable elements while simultaneously maintaining some distance from its reputation for extreme "tentacle rape" pornography—a reputation that was enhanced in 1997 when the controversial bad-girl-adjacent horror pornography comic, *Verotika*, began publishing its own *hentai* manga spin-off, *Verotika East*. The prelude issue, *Manga Shi* ½, depicted Ana sealing a tentacled demon behind a magical portal, implicitly locking it out of her series and reassuring her readers that while this might be manga, it won't be *that* kind of manga. To emphasize the point still further, the first issue of *Manga Shi* included a sneak preview of *Shi: Heaven and Earth*, in which Ana has to save her Catholic mother from a Japanese sect that seeks to martyr her. It is a story that confirms once again that she (and *Shi*) are ultimately on the side of American Christian morality against a Japanese culture that is figured as limitlessly violent and perverse, no matter how good it also happened to be at drawing comics.

After *Shi* blazed the way, several "bad girl" series published manga spin-offs, including *Nira X Anime* (1997), *Warrior Nun Manga* (2000), *Jade: Redemption* (2001–2002), *Manga Darkchylde* (2004–2005), and *Witchblade Manga* (2007–2008)—*Witchblade* and *Warrior Nun* were even published in *tankōbon* form. Vampirella's manga spin-off, *Vampi* (2000–2005), featured genuinely disturbing levels of sadistic violence that sometimes verged on snuff pornography, presumably on the assumption that such material would be more acceptable if drawn in manga style. Bill Maus, the creator of *Nira X*, explained that "my art was inspired by the creativity of manga," and welcomed *Nira X Anime* as a chance to "[push] a bit more manga style which was the original idea for the book when first conceived" (*Cynder Nira X* no. 1; *Nira X: Soul Skurge* no. 2). Tucci even expressed hope that works such as *Manga Shi* might open new Japanese markets for American comics:

> What I discovered was that a lot of women read comics in Japan and that it's exciting to read about a Japanese woman living on her own in New York.

> So we feel that this is going to work both ways. This is opening up the Japanese market for US books and it's also giving American mainstream readers a good introduction to manga. . . . This is basically our way of saying to the Japanese: 'Hey! Here we go! We can do it like this too!'" (*Wizard* no. 59, 34)

In retrospect, what is most striking about this idea is its naivete: Having just discovered the existence of *josei* manga, Tucci already imagined competing with it on its own ground. While Tucci's attempts to write seriously about women made him genuinely unusual by the standards of mid-1990s American superhero comics, his comics were shallow compared to the novelistic complexity of contemporaneous *shoujo* or *josei* manga, and the idea that a Japanese female audience would flock to a series like *Manga Shi* seems far-fetched when they already had works like *Neighborhood Story* (1995–1997) written by, for, and about Japanese women. What actually happened was the opposite: Once translated manga began appearing in the United States, it rapidly obtained a large readership among American women, who had been alienated from mainstream American comics culture by its persistent sexism (Williams and Lyons 12; Nicholson 158; Lopes 154–155). Particularly important here was the *shoujo* series *Sailor Moon*, which achieved growing popularity in America in 1997–1998, especially among female audiences (Brienza 51). Writing in 1999, Hernandez argued that the hypersexualized heroines of American comics, which she described as "chromium multivariant oops-my-tittie-fell-out 1-to-4 short-packed speculator specials" compared poorly to "Sailor Moon (who really does kick ass)" (Hernandez).

As already mentioned, initial efforts to sell manga in America aimed primarily at the existing comics-buying audience. When Viz started publishing translated *shoujo* manga they even offered a false definition of the genre, clearly anxious that if it was perceived as being "for girls" (which it was), then it might alienate their existing audience, which was mostly male: "Shô.jo (sho'jo) n. 1. Manga appealing to both female and male readers. 2. Exciting stories with true-to-life characters and the thrill of exotic locales. 3. Connecting the heart and mind through real human relationships" (*X/1999* vol. 1, inside cover).

Some manga series were heavily adapted to meet the assumed tastes of their target market (Brienza 120). Keith Giffen's adaptations of *Battle Royale* (2000–2005, English edition 2003–2006) and *Ikki Tousen* (2000–2015, English edition 2004–2010), which remain infamous in American manga fandom, are a case in point: Both were extensively rewritten, and the latter even had its title changed to *Battle Vixens* to make it sound more like a "bad girl" title. By the early 2000s, however, it was becoming clear that manga had a much larger potential audience outside the traditional comic-shop demographics, with manga sales increasing 300 percent between 2000 and 2002 (Gabilliet 101; Brienza 58; Beaty and Woo 118; Lopes 155). Interviewing female manga readers in 2005, Sarah Glazer concluded that "girls long ago abandoned American superhero comics, a market increasingly dominated by adult male collectors" (Glazer). American comic shops were slow to recognize the importance of manga, which consequently ended up being distributed through mainstream bookshops, cutting comic shops out of the fastest-growing section of the American comic book market and contributing to their decline (Gearino 76; Brienza 51; Nicholson 158).

What is perhaps most dismaying about this episode is that Tucci was not wrong to see the arrival of manga as an opportunity. The 1994–1996 moment could have been a turning point for the American comics industry: a chance to learn from the growing popularity of both manga and DC's Vertigo imprint and pivot toward comics more engaged with female readers and female perspectives. Indeed, many "bad girl" comics creators, including Tucci (who said of *Shi* that "I'd like a lot more women to read it"), David Mack (creator of *Kabuki*), and Linsner (creator of *Dawn*), clearly understood themselves to be doing exactly this (*Wizard* no. 42, 44). To understand why the genre ultimately had the opposite effect, alienating female readers from American comics so completely that they flocked to manga instead, it is important to consider its vexed relationship with more "literary" comics—and especially with those that, at the time, were starting to be referred to as "graphic novels."

"Bad Girls Make the Most Interesting Characters": Bad Girls and Comics "for Mature Readers"

In 1994, *Wizard* magazine began to hype a comic named *Drama*. *Drama* was a plotless experimental art comic drawn by Linsner, featuring a series of dreamlike allegorical sequences shot through with sexual fantasy imagery and intimations of queer desire, and ending with five continuous pages of illustrated quotations from Hindu, Jewish, Islamic, Christian, and Buddhist sacred texts. Willfully obscure and gleefully esoteric, it seems like the last thing that would be picked up on by a mainstream commercial publication like *Wizard*—and so it surely would have been, were it not for the fact that the magazine had pegged Linsner's Dawn as a "bad girl," and hence identified *Drama* as a "bad girl" book.

The late 1980s and early 1990s saw some crucial developments in the more artistically ambitious side of American comics. The success of titles such as *Watchmen* (1986–1987), *V for Vendetta* (1982–1985, 1988–1989), *Sandman* (1988–1996), and above all *Maus* (1980–1991) demonstrated that an Anglophone audience existed for comics of novelistic depth, and that the medium could be used for stories more sophisticated than the monthly action-adventure superheroics with which it had become associated (Gabilliet 92). A year after *Maus* made comic book history by winning a Pulitzer Prize in 1992, DC established a new imprint, Vertigo, to publish comics "for mature readers": Both *Sandman* and *V for Vendetta* were retroactively reclassified as Vertigo titles (Beaty and Woo 18; Williams and Lyons 26). While they continued to be sold monthly in comic-book form, Vertigo's titles were also collected into trade paperbacks that were sold at regular bookshops, allowing its graphic novels to reach audiences outside those who frequented comic shops (Gabilliet 208; Licari-Guillaume, *Vertigo* 61). Vertigo comics such as *Sandman* were marketed to an older demographic than most other DC comics, and it was swiftly observed that they also proved more popular with female readers (Williams and Lyons 23; Wright 290; Gearino 75–76; Groth, "Vertigo" 54–55; Pustz 13, 84; Licari-Guillaume, *Vertigo* 42).

The first title published by Vertigo was *Death: The High Cost of Living* (1993), a *Sandman* spin-off featuring a personification of death who manifested as a beautiful woman with snow-white skin (Pustz 86). The fact that only a year separated Vertigo's *Death* from Chaos! Comics's *Lady Death*—another white-skinned comic-book death goddess who sometimes appeared alongside her Vertigo counterpart on *Wizard* magazine's monthly "Top 10 Heroes and Villains" lists—is a reminder of just how much the two trends initially overlapped. Vertigo's graphic novels, and other "mature readers" comics of the same period, made extensive use of the graphic sex, nudity, and violence that had been denied for so long by the Comics Code: As Isabelle Licari-Guillaume writes, they were "united by a common 'adult' tone, allowing for profanity and explicit sexual situations" (*Vertigo* 81). Many of the authors most associated with "mature readers" comics, including Neil Gaiman, Grant Morrison, and Alan Moore, wrote "bad girl" comics during the 1990s: Gaiman wrote *Angela* (1994–1995), Morrison wrote *Vampirella* (1997–1998), and Moore wrote *Voodoo* (1997). Comics like *Dawn*, *Shi*, *Kabuki*, and *Ghost* all subsequently came to be seen as "bad girl" series, but when they first appeared in 1993–1994 they were presented as entries into the then-new genre of Vertigo-style adult comics, marked out as such by their more explicit content and their focus on female perspectives.

The overlap between Vertigo's "mature readers" comics and the nascent "bad girl" genre is clearest in the feminist vampire series *Vamps*, which was published by Vertigo from 1994 to 1999. As its author, Elaine Lee, wrote in her first editorial: "I am so bored. Bored with all this 'what-a-female-character-has-to-be' stuff. Can't have an evil thought or a skimpy costume or a selfish motive or big breasts. Can't be submissive (that's sexist) and can't fight back (that's reverse sexism). Can't have any kind of fault or personal failing that might serve to make her interesting, because she has to serve as a role model. . . . Everybody knows that bad girls make the most interesting characters" (*Vamps* vol. 1, no. 1). As Lee makes clear, in 1994, writing a series about "bad girls" with "evil thought[s]," "skimpy costume[s]," "selfish motive[s]," and "big breasts" could still be associated with comics that aimed to be mature rather than juvenile—and indeed, despite its lurid subject matter, *Vamps* was a genuinely mature series in a way that most subsequent "bad girl" comics were not, offering a serious and unsparing look at sexism and abuse. This was the context that authors like Mack, Eric Luke, and Linsner *thought* they were writing for as they began their respective series. With its extreme violence, dark supernaturalism, and film noir stylings, Luke's *Ghost* invited comparisons with Miller's *Sin City* (1991–2000) and Vertigo's *Hellblazer* (1988–2013), while the occult mysticism and metaphorical metanarratives of Linsner's *Dawn* connect it to contemporaneous works such as *Sandman*, *Death*, *From Hell* (1989–1996), *The Maxx* (1993–1998), and *The Invisibles* (1994–2000). Similarly, works like Ann Nocenti's *Typhoid* (1995–1996), a feminist thriller written as a critique of misogynistic violence, in which fragments of the heroine's splintered mind fight over whether she should be a "good girl" or a "bad girl," or Peter Milligan's *Extremist* (1993), in which a woman becomes a leather-clad enforcer for a secret society of sadomasochists in order to investigate her husband's murder, clearly ask to be understood as both "mature readers" comics and "bad girl" comics simultaneously.

It can hardly be overstated just how preoccupied the "mature readers" comics of this era were with the relationship between sex and violence, and especially with the relationship between political and sexual repression. *Watchmen* explored how the violent authoritarianism of the superhero might be understood as an expression of damaged and abusive sexualities. *V for Vendetta* and *Luther Arkwright* (1987–1989) both examined how sexual sadism could thrive within repressive and puritanical political regimes: *The Invisibles* took this even further, with its community of queer sexual radicals rebelling against an oppressive occult order founded on sexual exploitation. *The Maxx* was about the consequences of sexual violence (including the use of "superheroic" fantasy identities as psychological defense mechanisms), while *From Hell* used its occult interpretation of the Ripper murders to argue that sexual violence against women constituted the symbolic foundation of Western civilization. In many of these series, queer sex-positive libertine heroes were pitted against vast systems of oppression that sought either to eliminate sexuality or to reduce it to just another form of sadistic abuse. Even comics that were overtly pornographic in character, such as *Verotika*, returned frequently to the sexual hypocrisy of the political and religious right. Indeed, it was one story on this theme—a ghastly horror narrative in which the rape and murder of a suburban girl turns out to have been orchestrated by her seemingly upstanding father for his own erotic gratification—that led to the police seizure of *Verotika* issue 4 during the controversial Planet Comics case of 1995 (CBLDF Case Files). (Verotik subsequently started publishing their own "bad girl" series, *Satanika*, which ran from 1996 to 1999.)

The earliest "bad girl" comics emerged from this milieu, and clearly understood themselves as progressive in depicting liberated, sex-positive heroines taking a stand against their oppressors. The influence of these works can also be seen on a formal level: *Shi: The Way of the Warrior* (1994–1997), *Kabuki: Circle of Blood* (1995), and *Dawn: Lucifer's Halo* (1995–1996) are examples of early "bad girl" comics that were written as Vertigo-style graphic novels, with sustained storytelling over several issues building toward an overarching conclusion. Not coincidentally, all three wore their literary and intellectual ambitions on their sleeves, engaging frequently with topics such as art, history, philosophy, and religion. However, in an era of notorious instability in the comic book market, it was a huge risk for a small indie company to commit to a long-form novelistic narrative. Given the delays that plagued the industry, such works often took years to complete, shedding readers with every issue: It proved much safer to produce a succession of short, accessible storylines, with attention-catching, sales-boosting "issue 1" comics every few issues, and to rely on "bad girl" art and variant covers to sell the resulting books. As indie publishers crowded into the "bad girl" market, few attempted to emulate the model of *The Way of the Warrior*, whose much-delayed sixteen-issue storyline took three whole years to finish. Instead they mostly opted to follow the highly profitable example of *Lady Death*, whose first miniseries featured just three issues, straightforward plotting, rudimentary characterization, and chromium covers.

As a result, the commercial consolidation of the "bad girl" genre in 1995–1996 entailed not only an ideological shift toward postfeminism but also a *formal* shift: away from the Vertigo-style graphic novel, with its intellectual and novelistic ambitions, and toward the three- or four-issue miniseries, built primarily around fight scenes and pinup art. Chaos! Comics became particularly proficient in this form, with works like *Lady Death: The Odyssey* (1996), *Purgatori: The Vampire's Myth* (1996), and *Chastity: Theatre of Pain* (1997) telling basic but effective action-horror adventure stories in just three or four issues, while also providing numerous opportunities for hypersexualized battles between their growing stable of "bad girl" characters.

Further evidence of the market's preferences for such series can be seen in *Warrior Nun*: Its first two miniseries (*Warrior Nun*, 1994–1995; *Rituals*, 1995–1996) traded successfully on campy action and sex appeal, but when it shifted to more serious stories about Vatican corruption (*Scorpio Rose*, 1996–1997) and the Holocaust (*Warrior Nun*, 1997–1998), readers punished it with falling sales. Finally the series creator, Ben Dunn, offered an apology: "Based on the initial sales of the first and second series, I knew I was on the right track. But I let things slide and I made mistakes with *Warrior Nun*, choices that I now wish, given another chance, I could do differently. Well, here is that chance. I believe that this new series will explore the WARRIOR NUN universe as I intended" (*Warrior Nun: Resurrection* no. 1). The new series in question was the three-issue miniseries *Warrior Nun: Resurrection* (1998–1999), which took the franchise back to its apolitical, high-camp roots. It may or may not have been what Dunn "intended," but it was clearly what his readers seemed to prefer. Similarly, when Vampirella shifted toward mythic metanarrative in *Vampirella: Death and Destruction* (1996), one reader complained that the resulting comic looked as though it were "assembled by stitching together cut-up Vertigo comics." Praising Vampirella as "the first and the best of the scantily-clad blood babes, the archetype for the current flood," he objected to "the implication that somehow Vampirella is not good enough to read on her own, but must be 'validated' with high-flown intellectual concepts such as lost myths and stories of power" (*Vampirella: Death and Destruction* no. 2).

A comparison between the 1995 graphic novel *Kabuki: Circle of Blood* and the 1996 miniseries *Purgatori: The Vampire's Myth* casts this contrast between "high-flown intellectual concepts" and "scantily-clad blood babes" into sharp relief. Both are "bad girl" narratives concerned with themes of female rebellion, and both feature abundant nudity and violence, but their tones could hardly be more different. *Circle of Blood* tells a complex story of intergenerational trauma over the course of six issues: It is self-consciously literary, drawn in austere black and white, and demonstrates deep engagement with Japanese history and culture. *The Vampire's Myth* tells a straightforward three-issue story about a lesbian vampire killing everyone she meets: It is gleefully pulpy, drawn in lurid colors (mostly red), and shows a total disregard for historical or cultural accuracy. (At one point, a samurai warrior visits Egypt in 2000 B.C.; at another, men in 1990s Shanghai are drawn wearing conical bamboo hats.) *Circle of Blood* is deeply interested in the tormented psychology of its characters, which it explores in novelistic depth, whereas *The Vampire's Myth* depicts a world driven entirely by rage, lust, and fear. *Circle of Blood* explores intersectional systems of racial and sexual oppression, devoting much of its story to a critique of Japanese patriarchy and the oppression of the Indigenous Ainu people. *The Vampire's Myth* is unburdened by any such sensitivities, depicts all women as huge-breasted sex objects, and makes heavy use of racist stereotypes—especially in relation to the African vampire, Kabala, who is depicted as an animalistic jungle-dwelling savage in a fur bikini. *Circle of Blood* had only a niche audience, languishing near the bottom of the monthly sales ranks. *The Vampire's Myth* was the top-selling graphic novel in the month that it came out (Comichron).

The Vampire's Myth is not without a level of demented creativity—in one memorably bizarre scene, the heroine is attacked by a flock of bat-winged vampire tigers—and it too drew upon Japanese sources, with its author citing Go Nagi's *Devilman* (1972–1973) as a key influence (*Purgatori: The Vampire's Myth* no. 0). But if works like *Circle of Blood* demonstrate why the creators of the "bad girl" genre briefly hoped that it might widen the appeal of American comics beyond their core white male audience, the speed with which they were supplanted by works like *The Vampire's Myth* shows why this did not actually come to pass. Having initially overlapped heavily with the Vertigo-style graphic novel, the genre quickly came to define itself *against* it, trading on its ability to offer stories that were action-packed, unpretentious, accessible, and short. From their earlier graphic novel influences they retained only the gore, and the nudity, and the conviction that by telling stories full of "bad girls" with "skimpy costume[s]," "selfish motive[s]," and "big breasts" they were somehow helping to move the American comics industry in the right direction.

Boom and Bust: "Bad Girl" Comics and the Business of Comic Retail

The "bad girl" fad grew out of larger cultural trends, but it also resulted from a very specific moment in the history of American comic book retail. In the 1980s, the American comic market shifted from its older "newsstand" model, in which distributors could return unsold stock to the publisher as they did with newspapers, to a "direct distribution" model in which comics were sold to retailers at a greater discount, but with no opportunity for return. As a result, comics came to be sold primarily by dedicated comic shops, which sprang up in large numbers during this period (Rogers 147–148; Gabilliet 151–152). This shift had major secondary consequences: Because comics now had to be sought out deliberately in specialist spaces, the stream of new readers began to dry up, and their overall business model shifted to focus on extracting more money from existing older readers rather than widening and diversifying the target audience (Gearino 7; Beaty and Woo 57; Rogers 149). Because their income relied on attracting smaller numbers of high spenders rather than larger numbers of casual readers, it was extremely risky for comics retailers to do anything that might alienate their regular customers, even if they might bring in new readers in the process. As Cocca notes, "The growth of the direct market intersected with the broader conservative backlash against the gains of the Second Wave of feminism," and the result was a market propped up by a relatively small audience of affluent, high-spending comic book fans who cultivated an insular and often exclusionary comic-shop culture that was frequently hostile to anyone other than white heterosexual men with high disposable income (Cocca, *Superwomen* 11–12; Robbins 7, 105–107; Gabilliet 208; Gearino 73–75; Kashtan 323; Pustz xii, 5, 8).

It is not a coincidence that 1992, the year that the "bad girl" trend began in earnest, was the same year in which Image Comics was founded, offering a serious threat to the DC/Marvel duopoly for the first time in decades (Gabilliet 149; Voger 57, 78; Rogers 153). As Hope Nicholson noted, the content produced by Image was even more heavily skewed toward straight male audiences than that of Marvel or DC:

> Some call this a revolution in the comics industry. I call it a group of men who made enough cash to form their own company and saw that it was to their advantage to do so. The content of the books was usually high action, with throbbing muscles, painted-on suits, and proportionally distorted women. Even if the company was presenting an exciting new model that let creators own their creations, Image wasn't exactly friendly to female creators or fans." (157)

One of the ways in which Image outflanked its better-established competitors was by abandoning the Comics Code, allowing them to publish darker and more violent comics such as *Spawn*—a move that Bradford Wright describes as "turning up the testosterone level" (Wright 290–291; Beaty and Woo 57). In so doing it helped to usher in the so-called Dark Age of comics, during which, as Mark Voger writes, "Mania, fervor, and obsession seemed to have replaced 'truth, justice, and the American way'" (4–6). Its comics also included more overtly sexualized content than those of Marvel and DC, taking advantage of the mainstreaming of such material in American popular culture more generally. As Madrid points out, the launch of Image took place in the same year as two other pop culture milestones: the debut of Pamela Anderson on *Baywatch*, and the publication of Madonna's *Sex* (95). (One might also note that 1992 was the year in which Madonna released her single "Bad Girl," as part of her album *Erotica*.) As Anderson and Madonna demonstrated, the media ecology of the early 1990s was one in which the boundaries between female celebrity culture and pornography were eroding fast. Image simply applied the same logic to its superheroines.

These lessons were not lost on other indie comics publishers. Many "bad girl" comics were the result of publishers racing to outdo one another in their inclusion of sex and violence, creating a widespread rush away from traditional superheroes and toward horror pornography. But American comics publishing in the 1990s was brutally competitive: The direct distribution model meant that each issue lived or died by the number of comic shops willing to order copies of it in advance, and if retailers lost confidence in the sales potential of a series then its numbers could plummet almost overnight. Plaintive editorials complaining of falling order numbers and begging readers to ask their local comic shops to stock the publisher's titles are commonplace in the indie comics of the period. (For one example among many, see the first and only issue of *Claire Voyant* (1996), which implored its readers to "tell your retailer you want future issues of Claire.") Large numbers of new comics publishers sprang up during these years, and many of them closed after publishing just a few issues (Gabilliet 151).

As a result, reading "bad girl" indie comics means getting used to broken promises. One heroine after another springs up, beset by mysterious situations and monstrous enemies. Grand storylines and terrible revelations are hinted at. Side characters are introduced, clearly with the intention of giving them spin-off titles further down the line. Editorials assure the reader that this is just the beginning of their epic plans for the character. Then, after two or three issues, the whole series is canceled, its storylines either rushed to a forced conclusion or left forever unresolved. Even major titles like *Shi* and *Warrior Nun Areala* sometimes broke off in mid-storyline (e.g., after *Shi: The Series* no. 13 or *Warrior Nun Areala* vol. 3, no. 12) when commercial realities made their continuance unsustainable.

These were economically volatile years for the American comics industry, as demonstrated by the rapid shifts in the number of American comic shops, which fell from 9,400 in 1993 to just 2,300 in 2002 (Gabilliet 151–152; Rogers 154). The speculator-driven boom of the early 1990s gave way to a crash in 1994–1995, and then a second, larger crash in 1996–1997, giving retailers the impression that "the comic market is always this series of disasters" (Gabilliet 98, 151–152; Gearino 57, 70). With desktop publishing and digital coloring still in their infancy, founding a new comic meant overcoming a whole range of practical obstacles relating to layout, lettering, color separation, and paper supply. Many new publishers clearly underestimated what they were getting themselves into, with the result that their comics regularly appeared months later than advertised, often emerging long after the excitement over them had faded, or into market conditions very different to those that had pertained when they were first commissioned (Gabilliet 150–151). Under these circumstances, a bankable "bad girl" character was an immense asset to an indie publisher, capable of attracting a devoted fan base willing to buy any number of collectibles and special editions: As Jean-Paul Gabilliet notes, aside from "very personal productions" such as *Shi*, "bad girl" comics were "a commercial solicitation pure and simple" (103). Several indie publishers, such as London Night, Crusade, and Chaos! Comics, were sustained almost entirely by the popularity of their respective "bad girl" heroines, and consequently slid into inactivity or bankruptcy once the trend started to wane.

When indie "bad girl" heroines proved commercially successful, their creators often attempted to spin their success out into a larger franchise, usually populated by yet more "bad girl" heroines. When London Night found success with *Razor*, they swiftly brought out multiple "bad girl" spin-off titles including *Poizon*, *Demonique*, *Stryke*, *Sade*, *Sisters of Mercy*, and *Tommi Gun*, most of which lasted for only a few issues. Similarly, after the success of *Shi*, Crusade Comics brought out the short-lived titles *Tomoe*, *Atomik Angels*, *Angel Fire*, and *Victoria Cross*. Antarctic Press traded on the success of *Warrior Nun Areala* to bring out a range of spin-off series, including *Warrior Nun Brigantia*, *Lillith*, and *Shotgun Mary*. David Mack's *Kabuki* had the spin-offs *Masks of the Noh* and *Scarab*, and Top Cow's *Witchblade* had *Magdalena* and *Aphrodite IX*. In each case the publisher's stated intention was to use a successful "bad girl" title as the foundation of a whole new shared comics universe, and in each case these ambitions ultimately enjoyed very limited success. Probably the most successful attempt to create a whole interlinked universe of "bad girl" characters was that of Chaos! Comics, who used the popularity of *Lady Death* to launch the titles *Purgatori*, *Chastity*, *Jade*, *Bad Kitty*, *Vandala*, and *Lady Demon*. None came close to the popularity of *Lady Death*, but Purgatori, Chastity, Jade, and Bad Kitty each accrued a respectable number of issues before Chaos! went bankrupt in 2002, which is more than their counterparts at other companies managed to achieve.

The chief means by which these publishers appealed to their core audience was through collectibility (Wright 278–279; Beaty and Woo 74–75; Roger 153). As the market for sports trading cards collapsed, large numbers of shops which had previously specialized in trading cards moved into comic book retail in the late 1980s and early 1990s. They brought with them a mindset that comics, like trading cards, could be viewed as essentially arbitrary tokens of speculative investment, their value based not on their actual art and story but on the possibility that they might one day command a high price from other collectors, at least if maintained in mint condition (Gearino 131; Gabilliet 149; Voger 7; Beaty 167). Some comics began to be published with enclosed trading cards, and one comic, *Plasm* (1993), was even published as a set of trading cards which formed a comic book when assembled in order, thus requiring buyers to collect the entire set in order to read the whole issue (Voger 101). As Wright notes, by the 1990s, comics had become the third largest collectible market in the United States, after coins and stamps—a development that stoked tensions between fans who saw comics as primarily for reading and collectors who prized them for their monetary value (Wright 279; Beaty 154–157). At first this approach merely took the form of encouraging fans to buy two copies of each comic, one to read and one to keep in mint condition for future sale, but over time publishers found more ways of selling the same comics to the same purchasers: As well as buying a single comic, one might also be able to buy preview or ashcan versions of that same comic, one or more variant cover editions (often with added extras such as foil lettering), special editions with added content, and so on (Gearino 114; Gabilliet 150; Voger 55, 97, 128–130; Beaty 170; Roger 153–154). The incentive behind owning these was the idea that, because they were produced in smaller numbers, these various special editions would one day be more valuable to serious collectors than the regular comic.

This mindset was encouraged by the rise of *Wizard* magazine (1991–2011), which included monthly price guides offering optimistic assessments of the value of comic book back issues, leading many fans to buy comics not on the basis of whether they enjoyed their content but on whether their value was likely to rise in the months or years ahead (Gearino 133; Gabilliet 149; Beaty 167–168). As comic shop owners noted at the time, such fans were usually woefully disappointed when they attempted to "cash in" their collections, and discovered that the actual market rates for their books were far below what *Wizard* had promised them (Pustz 67; *Immortal II* no. 4). *Wizard* was an important booster of the "bad girl" trend: As Bart Beaty and Benjamin Woo note, its editorial voice very much assumed that its readers were white, straight, and male, and that their comic-collecting habits would reflect this (75). Because some back issues genuinely had become extremely valuable, such as those featuring the first appearances of characters such as Wolverine or Venom who went on to become fan favorites, collectors were especially eager to buy multiple copies of comics that they thought might eventually attain such value—an eagerness that publishers capitalized on by deliberately publishing "event" comics such as "The Death of Superman" (1992), of which some fans reportedly bought up to one hundred copies, convinced that its value would skyrocket in the future (Wright 280–282; Gearino 135–136; Voger 7, 89; Beaty 172). The ultimate emblem of this trend was Jim Lee's *X-Men #1* (1991), which sold a staggering 7.5 million copies, more than any other superhero comic in history, its sales boosted by its four alternate covers (Voger 55; Beaty 170). As Gabilliet points out, the combination of the

Image-led rush away from the Comics Code with a comic-buying culture driven by speculative investment gave rise to a 1990s comics industry built around collecting, speculation, and stories of violence, all of which were traditionally male pursuits (Gabilliet 208–209). It was the confluence of all these factors that produced the "bad girl" trend, and it is not a coincidence that the comic artists most associated with the "Image revolution"—Rob Liefeld, Todd McFarlane, Jim Lee, and Marc Silvestri—all became prolific creators of "bad girl" superheroines over the years that followed.

You Have to Have Her: The Erotics of Collecting

As I have discussed, "bad girl" comics were specifically designed to appeal to the key comic shop audience of white heterosexual men, and to alienate just about everyone else. As female readers complained, the simple act of stocking such works served to mark comic shops out as hostile to anyone other than their core demographics (Paul Williams 135; Cocca, *Superwomen* 12). Highly commodified, they made little pretense of appealing to anything other than commercial realities: Their implicit message to their target audience was simply "people like you are going to want to collect books like this, so if *you* collect them first then you can sell them on for an inflated price later." As a result, it soon became commonplace for every "bad girl" title to come complete with a range of special and deluxe editions, just in case it subsequently became a valuable collector's item. It made some sense for DC Comics to bring out a special collector's edition of "The Death of Superman": In 1992, Superman was an iconic figure with over fifty years of continuous history, and the story marked a milestone in his fictional history. But "bad girl" titles like *Pandora* (1996–1999) and *Demonslayer* (1999–2000) were published with a range of special editions from their first issues onward, long before there was any evidence that they would have a lasting audience or indeed any audience at all, as though their status as highly collectible future classics was already assured.

An important part of the context from which "bad girl" comics emerged was the trading card market, which in the 1990s overlapped heavily with the market for comic books. As mentioned, many of the new comic shops that opened during the early 1990s boom years started as trading card shops, and only subsequently diversified into comics. The trading card market initially focused on sports, but as it became entangled with comic book culture a growing number of new trading card sets appeared reproducing art from comic books, or from the lurid covers of paperback science fiction, fantasy, and horror novels (Gabilliet 156–157). This art was often highly sexualized: The 1992 trading card set reproducing the art of the then-popular fantasy artist Ken Kelly is a good example of the trend, with one card after another featuring the same trinity of a hulking barbarian hero, a deformed and leering villain, and a prone or chained nearly-naked woman for the other two to fight over. Further examples of fantasy trading cards bearing sexualized images of women can be seen in the 1994 "Amazons and Angels" set, which featured images by the fantasy artist Chris Achilleos.

The early 1990s comic and trading card shop was thus one in which collecting and trading stylized images of ultrasexualized women were already commonplace, even before the rise of the "bad girl" trend. "Bad girl" comics, with their endless rare special editions and alternate covers, invited their readers to collect them like trading cards: Indeed, some of their marketing gimmicks, such as rare holographic or chromium editions, were used in the trading card market first (Beaty 168). Unsurprisingly, many "bad girl" titles (including *Shi*, *Ghost*, *Luxura*, *Avengelyne*, *Dawn*, *Warrior Nun*, *Razor*, *Widow*, *Vampirella*, and *Witchblade*) also had associated sets of trading cards reproducing their art: These sets inevitably including the most sexualized images of their respective protagonists, thus reducing the eroticized bodies of their heroines to commodified tokens of exchange. Sometimes the comics seemed to exist primarily for the sake of their associated collectibles, rather than the other way around. The original *Snowman* series (1995–1996) ran for only three issues, but still had a full range of collectible figurines and trading cards showing off its improbably proportioned female characters. An even more extreme example was *Sinthia* (1997–1998), whose two published issues were outnumbered two to one by the four tie-in action figures depicting its swiftly forgotten heroine.

The "bad girl" comics took full advantage of the erotics of collecting. Matt Hills writes that collectibles gain value through "the durability of fans' attachments," and Beaty concurs: "The deep personal relationship that the fan develops with his or her obsession almost inevitably seems to manifest itself in the form of a collection" (Matt Hills 35; Beaty 155). Beaty describes the act of collecting as transforming "an affective (Freudian) fetish into an economic (Marxian) one," and argues that the affective logic of collecting is primarily driven by nostalgia—but in the case of "bad girl" comics and their associated collectibles the economic fetish value of the collected object was inescapably intertwined with its sexual fetish value, and the primary affective response evoked was not nostalgia but lust (Beaty 154, 157). When a comic like *Pandora* was emblazoned with the name and the (hypersexualized) image of the fetishized heroine, it offered its purchaser the fantasy that to own it was in some sense to own *her*, too, and the economic desirability of the comic book was thus ineluctably bound up with the sexual desirability of the heroine whose name and image it bears. The vast proliferation of "premium editions" produced for these comics, with limited print runs, alternate art, chromium covers, leather bindings, and so on, speaks directly to this urge. Pustz describes how collectors seek the "sense of closure," achieved "by completing a set," but in the case of these comics this "sense of closure" was deliberately conflated with the illusion of erotic mastery (81). The more complete the collection, the more total the collector's symbolic ownership of the heroine becomes.

The trend for embossed covers, such as those of *Catwoman #1* (1993) or the embossed red foil edition of *Purgatori: The Vampire's Myth* (1996), added a tactile element to the eroticized act of collecting. With a regular cover the buyer could only *look* at the heroine, but by purchasing a special embossed edition he could *feel* her, too, making it possible to experience her exaggerated curves through the fingertips as well as the eyes. Collectible figurines and posable action figures, which proliferated during these years, placed the same heroines literally into the hands of their collector, available to be posed and positioned at will. In extreme cases the craze for variant editions led to comics such as the 2006 *Lady Death / Shi* crossover: Technically the entire story consisted of only two issues, but the *true* fan would want to own not just every version of issue 1 (thirteen variant covers, including one printed on red leather) and issue 2 (eight variant covers, including one which appears to show the two heroines being assaulted by an octopus) but also issue 0 (twenty variant covers, including one printed on canvas) and the special preview issue (twenty variant covers, including one that seems to depict the two heroines comparing bust sizes). The casual consumer who bought just two comics could read the story, but only the hardcore collector who bought all sixty-one could feel that they truly *owned* it, and hence owned the heroines whose names it bore. That even the creators of these comics may have become weary of such devices by this point is suggested by one of the variant covers for issue 2, which depicted the two heroines locked in battle while apparently endless numbers of *Shi* and *Lady Death* variant comic books rain from the sky behind them.

This dynamic of eroticized ownership, which had always been implicit in the collection of sexualized comic-book art, was rendered much more explicit in the 1990s when indie publishers began producing special editions of their comics with higher prices and alternate covers that depicted their heroines wearing more revealing costumes than in the regular edition. This process reached its logical conclusion in 1996 when both London Night Studios and Lightning Press began printing "nude editions" of their comics, a practice swiftly imitated by competitors such as Avatar Press. As Lightning's vice president Steven Zyskowski explained, "I figured, since the comics industry is dominated by the male consumer, they'd do just about anything to get their hands on a *Hellina* nude variant comic" (*Wizard* no. 44, 19). Sold at higher price points, and kept in opaque sealed bags to keep them from the eyes of anyone other than their purchasers, these nude editions offered an elevated level of symbolic intimacy to the customer willing to pay a higher fee, with the removal of the comic from its bag constituting a form of striptease. Everyone else in the comic shop might have seen their imagined object of desire, but only the purchaser of the nude edition could claim to have seen her *naked*.

These sexualized special editions proliferated through the "bad girl" era. They went hand in hand with the multiplication of "swimsuit specials": plotless art books filled with pinup drawings of female (and occasionally male) comic book characters in revealing swimwear (Madrid 97; Peppard, "Is That a Monster" 91–92). These had started with Marvel Comics in 1991, but were swiftly imitated by virtually every "bad girl" title (e.g., *Vamperotica Swimsuit Special* [1994)], *Lady Death Swimsuit Special* [1994], *Razor Swimsuit Special* [1995], *Avengelyne Swimsuit* [1995], *Gamorra Swimsuit Special* [1996], *Darkchylde Swimsuit Illustrated* [1998]), and were soon joined by books of borderline-pornographic "bad girl" pinup art such as *Lady Death in Lingerie* (1995) and *Top Cow Secrets* (1996). The nadir came with the publication of the "bad girl" anthology comic *Threshold* (1998–2006) by Avatar Press, in which each issue was printed with a variety of covers, each depicting a different heroine in a different form of undress and engaged in a different form of sexual activity. The customer selected from the catalogue which heroines he wished to see and what he wanted to see them doing (posing naked, in bondage, having sex with each other, etc.), and the publisher supplied the relevant materials and billed the customer accordingly. By this point the veneer of "empowerment" had worn extremely thin, and the relationship among heroine, consumer, and publisher had become very clearly analogous to that of sex worker, client, and pimp.

The boundary line between "bad girl" comics and pornography was always tenuous, and when *Wizard* referred to the trend as originating with "underground" comics, the word "underground" functioned at least partly as a euphemism for "pornographic" (*Wizard* no. 35, 139). The mainstreaming of "bad girl" comics was very much of a piece with the mainstreaming of pornography in 1990s media culture more generally, and within the American comics industry in particular: As Gary Groth noted in 1991, "A year ago, there may have been seven X-rated comics being published; today there are 70" (Groth, "Confessions" 5). Several important "bad girl" titles emerged from publishers such as Antarctic Press which had backgrounds in publishing pornographic comics, and some artists, such as Fauve/Holly Golightly and Sandra Chang, moved back and forth between drawing "bad girl" titles and pornography. The reliance of *Scimidar* on sex and nudity to drive sales has already been mentioned, while London Night Studios, who did more than anyone to start the trend, swiftly diversified into producing pornographic media, using their comics to advertise for models for their erotic videos (*Sheena* no. 3). The early "bad girl" title *Nira X* advertised its painted centerfolds of its barely dressed heroine as a key selling point: These were printed with ads on their obverse pages, allowing the centerfold to be removed from the comic and used as an erotic poster without damaging the (extremely tokenistic) surrounding narrative (*Nira X* vol. 2, no. 2). The indie horror anthology *Cry for Dawn*, which ultimately evolved into the "bad girl" comic *Dawn*, traded openly on its erotic content. The cover of issue 5 depicted Dawn bending over in a stock pornographic pose, accompanied by the words "DOES SEX SELL? SO FAR, SO GOOD."

It is thus unsurprising that when the pornographic magazine *Penthouse* brought out its own line of Penthouse comics from 1995 to 1998, chronicling the sexual misadventures of pornographic superheroines such as Doctor Dare and Bethlehem Steele, their plots and character designs were often not very different from those of contemporaneous "bad girl" comics. Unlike most "bad girl" titles, *Penthouse Comix* was openly and explicitly sexist: Its first issue opened with a strip in which a woman berates a man for reading "adolescent" comics and encourages him to instead read "DC Vertigo" titles (noted at the time for their large female readership) to put him "in touch with your *feminine* side," a situation that he resolves by reading "Penthouse Men's Adventure Comix," which make him into a "real man" capable of forcing the woman into sexual submission (*Penthouse Comix* no. 1). It also featured overtly antifeminist content, such as the adventures of Backlash (named after Faludi's feminist bestseller *Backlash: The Undeclared War Against Women*), who fights for men's rights in a dystopian future ruled by an evil cabal of "radical, man-hating, lesbian gender feminists" (*Penthouse Comix* nos. 4–7). In other respects, however, the main difference between these pornographic comics and the "bad girl" comics that appeared during the same years was their comedic tone, as most "bad girl" titles tended to take themselves extremely seriously.

Penthouse Comix was one of several titles to mock the popularity of the "bad girl" trend, by including pornographic stories about a bisexual supervillain called "Bad Girl" who dressed in black leather (like many actual "bad girl" heroines) and used her powers to seduce men into evil and convert women into lesbians (*Penthouse Comix* nos. 2–4). But precisely because of its overtly pornographic nature, *Penthouse Comix* was also able to depict overtly the sexual dynamics that other "bad girl" titles were only able to suggest implicitly. Scenes such as the one in which the superheroine Hericane uses her superpowered vaginal muscles to crush a supervillain's penis, not releasing him until he gives her the information she requires, merely literalized the metaphors of eroticized sexual domination that ran through many contemporaneous "bad girl" comics (*Penthouse Comix* no. 2).

As one reader noted: "What first struck me as so original was the honesty of your magazine. I find that the blatant sexuality of mainstream comics (particularly many Image and Marvel titles) today are very disturbing because while they are obviously selling sex and violence, they must do so deviously (under the cover of the skimpiest costumes)" ("Jake," in *Penthouse Comix* no. 7). As "Jake" clearly recognized, beneath the fig leaf of their female empowerment rhetoric many "bad girl" titles already effectively functioned as pornography, and the boundary between the two was blurred still further by a series of collaborations between comics publishers and adult models. Some nude editions simply featured drawings of the relevant heroines naked (e.g., *Razor: Uncut* no. 40), but others had photographs of actual nude women on their covers, styled to resemble the relevant heroines (e.g., *Razor: Uncut* no. 51). Some superheroines became closely associated with the models hired to represent them in photo shoots and conventions: Thus *Avengelyne* (1995) was jointly created by Liefeld and the former *Vampirella* model Cathy Christian, who was always credited as Avengelyne's cocreator and appeared in revealing costumes on several covers for the series. When Image released a lingerie issue of *Glory*, its primary selling point was the fact that it included photos of the "new Glory model" in her underwear (ad in *Vogue* no. 2).

At least two "bad girl" comics were the direct result of partnerships between cartoonists and adult models. *La Femme Vampirique* (1997) was a collaboration between Brainstorm Comics and the porn actor "Angel Eyes": She appeared on its cover and served as the model for its lesbian vampire protagonist, and the comic itself included nude photos of her and ads for her pornographic videos. Stranger still was *Alley Cat* (1999–2000), a collaboration between Silverhawk Productions and the *Playboy* glamor model Alley Baggett. Baggett was not only the cover model for every issue of this series but also its heroine, who was literally named "Alley Baggett" and was written as an alternate-universe version of Baggett herself, who had become a superheroine instead of a model. Tellingly, hypersexualized action figures of Alley Baggett/Alley Cat were made available right from the first issue, highlighting her status as a commodified sexual fetish object available for purchase for the right price. If readers wished to see even more of her they were directed to Baggett's website, where nude images of Alley Baggett/Alley Cat were available to anyone willing to pay a subscription fee (*Alley Cat* prelude).

Interestingly, Alley Cat's archenemy was none other than the spirit of the Marquis de Sade, whom the comic depicted as a monstrous embodiment of deviant sexuality. *Alley Cat* thus staged a symbolic battle between two forms of pornography: Alley embodies "good" porn ("vanilla" soft-core pornography such as Baggett's *Playboy* shoots), which is represented as empowering for women and compatible with normative heroic morality, whereas de Sade stands for "bad" porn ("kinky" hardcore pornography involving BDSM), which is depicted as murderous, misogynistic, and literally demonic. By insisting that Baggett and de Sade's styles of pornography are opposites rather than equivalents, *Alley Cat* thus implicitly reassured its readers that their own taste for soft-core porn was not something that they needed to be ashamed of, as it is only *other* forms of pornography which harm women and encourage sexual violence. The series included an interview with Baggett, in which she declared that she loved *Playboy*'s "vision" of women as "very strong, intelligent, beautiful, and powerful," and that she was happy to recruit other women to pose for them, effectively acting as an evangelist for the kind of commodified female sexuality that *Alley Cat* promoted and endorsed (*Alley Cat* prelude). As the arc of their publication history demonstrates, "bad girl" comics were partly born from pornography, and once their popularity receded, it was to pornography they swiftly returned. The chief difference was how much more mainstream pornography had become in the intervening years.

As I have discussed, however, it would be an oversimplification to conclude that the message of the "bad girl" craze was simply that "sex sells." Comics publishers had been using sex appeal to sell comics since the 1930s, and yet it was only in the 1990s that female-led titles reliably became commercially viable. Nor should the vengeful anger and violence of these "bad girl" heroines be dismissed as merely window dressing, as *Bad Girl Backlash* made clear that this was recognized at the time as being at least as much of a break from prior superheroine tradition as their more overt sexualization. Not *all* of their rhetoric of female empowerment was spurious, and the genre's subsequent decline should not be allowed to obscure the fact that the earliest examples of the trend were closely engaged with the same issues around sexual violence and double standards articulated by third-wave feminist bestsellers such as *Backlash* (1991) and *The Beauty Myth* (1990), and expressed on a more popular level by Riot Grrrl albums like *Revolution Girl Style Now!* (1991), as well as by feminist comic books such as the rebooted anthology *Twisted Sisters* (1991, 1994), the first volume of which was even subtitled *A Collection of Bad Girl Art*. This phase of explicit ideological engagement was brief, but it *did* happen, and it left lasting marks on the "bad girl" genre as a whole. My next chapter will thus explore the way that early "bad girl" comics such as *Ghost*, *Mantra*, and *Catwoman* were used as a vehicle for overtly feminist storytelling during the early 1990s, and their interconnections with other strands of feminist popular culture during the same period.

3

Revolution Girl Style

"Bad Girl" Comics and Third-Wave Feminism

"A Woman Gone 'BAD'": Roberta Gregory and the Feminist Context

1991, the year Everette Hartsoe took the first issue of *Razor* to the San Diego Comic Convention, was also the year in which the feminist cartoonist Roberta Gregory began publishing her own regular comic book, *Naughty Bits*. Gregory had been writing feminist and lesbian comics since the 1970s, contributing to anthology series such as *Wimmin's Comix* and *Gay Comics*, but creating her own ongoing series had previously eluded her (Galvan ch. 2). *Naughty Bits* was finally made commercially viable by the same wave of black-and-white indie comics that gave rise to early "bad girl" titles like *Razor*, and for a few years in the early 1990s it was briefly possible to think of titles like Gregory's *Naughty Bits* (1991–2004), Terry Moore's *Strangers in Paradise* (1993–2007), Julie Doucet's *Dirty Plotte* (1991–1998), and Kurt Busiek's *Vampirella: Morning in America* (1991–1992) as all forming part of the same movement, united by their distance from mainstream superheroics, their black-and-white art, and their fascination with angry, violent, queer, socially transgressive women.

These years constituted a critical moment in the history of American feminism. The Republican Party had been in power since 1980, and made no secret of its hostility to the feminist movement. The Moral Majority had disbanded in

1989, but President Bush still relied heavily on the support of the religious right, and there were widespread worries that he would restrict abortion rights if he was reelected in 1992. Bush's appointment of Clarence Thomas to the Supreme Court in October 1991, despite the allegations of sexual harassment made against him by Anita Hill, acted as a lightning rod for feminist anger at what was widely seen as Republican contempt for women's issues, prompting widespread political mobilization (Henry 16, 21; Marcus 113; Zeisler 151; Wolf, *Fire* 3–4). In the 1992 election, 45 percent of female voters voted for Bill Clinton, compared to 38 percent for Bush, making them crucial to his electoral success. Alongside Clinton, an unprecedented number of women were elected to the U.S. Senate, prompting the *Washington Post* to describe 1992 as "the Year of the Woman" (Zeisler 173). So many gains were made in such quick succession that, in 1993, Naomi Wolf announced grandly, "From the autumn of 1991 to the present, a new era has begun—the era of the 'genderquake,' in which the meaning of being a woman is changed for ever," because "women have become the political ruling class" (Wolf, *Fire* xiv).

The movement that emerged from the political mobilization of 1991–1992 had some crucial differences from the women's liberation movement of the previous generation. As Andi Zeisler notes, its key buzzword was "empowerment," a word which gained rapidly in popularity from 1992 onward (172). What its proponents desired was not just to be liberated but to be *powerful*, like the "wild women" celebrated in *Women Who Run with the Wolves* (1992), which swiftly became a bestseller and remained so until 1995. Wolf, who became one of the movement's leading spokeswomen, asserted the need for a new "power feminism" to replace the "victim feminism" of the past (Henry 28; Snyder 179). As she explained: "Victim feminism is obsolete because female psychology and the conditions of women's lives have both been transformed enough so that it is no longer possible to pretend that the impulses to dominate, aggress, or sexually exploit others are 'male' urges alone. . . . Our new opportunities will be wasted unless we develop a vision of femininity in which it is appropriate and sexy for women to use power" (*Fire* xviii).

As Elizabeth Wilson and Gillian Rodgerson wrote, "Feminists wanted a much wider recognition of women as capable, strong, and independent, and wanted women to be portrayed as such" (32). Whereas second-wave feminists had often looked askance at forms of female power which resembled the patriarchal norms they were fighting, their third-wave successors embraced a much wider vision of what female "empowerment" might look like, including manifestations such as sex work, sadomasochistic sexualities, and fantasies of physical violence (Snyder 189; Wolf, *Fire* 42–43, 237–239). Helen Zahavi's controversial bestseller *Dirty Weekend* (1991), about a woman who murders seven abusive men, was praised by several leading feminist writers, including Susie Orbach and Wolf (Zahavi). Sara Marcus notes that early 1990s Riot Grrrl activists sometimes worked as strippers, argued that sex work could potentially be empowering rather than demeaning, and that they enjoyed writing fantasies of vengeful feminist violence, elevating Lorena Bobbitt to the status of an unofficial Riot Grrrl icon (282–283, 300, 304–305).

In this context, being an "empowered" woman often meant being a very bad girl. In 1985, Sara Diamond lamented, "Where boys learn that sex makes them powerful, we learn that it makes us powerful and bad"—but by 1990, a new generation of feminist activists saw being "powerful and bad" as a badge of honor (50). Wolf called on women to reconnect with "that wild child—the inner *bad* girl," and used her writings to map out what she described as "The Bad Girl's Route to Equality" (*Fire* xviii, 242–243, 334). Marcus describes how Kathleen Hanna of Bikini Kill made a deliberate claim for "bad girl" status, while Emma Healey describes the publication of the BDSM-friendly lesbian sex magazine *Quim* (1989–1995) as "confirm[ing] the arrival of a new brand of lesbian—the lesbian 'bad girl'" (Healey 142). As Healey notes, "*Quim* deliberately placed itself in opposition to the lesbian feminist ideology that had gone before it," acting as "an angry response to what the editors saw as the prescriptive lesbian feminism of the 1980s" and "a direct challenge to the sort of lesbian feminism that had led women to attack the lesbian SM club Chain Reaction with crowbars" (142–143). The lesbian S&M zine *Brat Attack*, which was published from 1991 to 1994, was subtitled *The Zine for Leatherdykes and Other Bad Girlz*. "Bad girl" figures such as violent female vigilantes and dominatrices consequently found themselves much more at home in third-wave feminist media than they had in that of the previous decade, a shift very much in keeping with the overall third-wave tendency to push back against essentializing interpretations of what women could or should be. Judith Butler's influential *Gender Trouble* (1990) was emblematic of this wider movement within third-wave feminism toward more capacious and flexible conceptions of gender and sexual identity.

This ethos was clearly visible in the feminist comics drawn by Gregory during these years. Gregory made no secret of her political sympathies, or her views on how much was at stake in the 1992 election: As she wrote, "If Mr Bush had been re-elected, we'd be DANGEROUSLY close to reversing Roe v. Wade" (*Naughty Bits* no. 7). After his defeat, she expressed her relief: "As we begin the year 1993 on a buoyant cloud of OPTIMISM, I'm happy to be right UP there with everyone ELSE . . . at LEAST until we see how many CAMPAIGN PROMISES Bill's gonna go back on! Well, I sure hope we're gonna manage to keep our REPRODUCTIVE FREEDOM intact . . . such as it IS!" (*Naughty Bits* no. 8).

For Gregory, "freedom" was the key tenet of feminism, and she had little time for versions of feminist ideology that she saw as overly restrictive. In 1991 she wrote angrily about having had her contribution to a comic "for 'self-defined' dykes" rejected on the grounds that she was bisexual: She went on to attack such gatekeeping in her *Bitchy Butch* cartoons, which she began publishing the same year (*Naughty Bits* no. 4). In *Bitchy Butch*, the eponymous heroine is constantly wrong-footed by the way that her radical lesbian feminist ideology leaves her ill prepared to cope with the more fluid queer politics of the 1990s, leading her to rage against bisexuals (or "little coulda-been dykes," as she calls them) and to humiliate herself by becoming infatuated with someone whom she believes to be a butch lesbian woman but is actually an effeminate gay man (*Bitchy Butch*). As Gregory wrote: "I think EVERY woman who wants to call herself a 'DYKE' (and who wants to catch all the FLAK that's gonna come of it) ought to have the RIGHT to SELF-DEFINITION . . . whether you're a struggling comic book artista, or whether you make a living taking your CLOTHES off in front of STRAIGHT MEN" (*Naughty Bits* no. 4).

Gregory argued that this right to self-definition was tightly bound up with the right to self-expression: thus her decision to open the first issue of *Naughty Bits* with a deliberately confrontational comic in which a group of women physically and sexually assault a man, ultimately amputating his penis, to show male readers how women felt about the misogynistic violence of Robert Crumb's comics, which were being republished by Fantagraphics at the time. Responding to the controversy generated by this strip, in issue 3 Gregory drew caricatures of herself as a violent, castration-happy "COMIX BITCH" who described herself as "a woman gone 'BAD,'" boasting: "Bet her PEN is bigger than YOURS, too!" (*Naughty Bits* no. 3). In her defenses of sex work, bisexuality, gender fluidity, and fantasies of violent revenge, Gregory was thus very much in line with early 1990s Riot Grrrl feminism, and it was entirely fitting that her perpetually enraged character Bitchy Bitch appeared on cover art for Cockpit's 1993 Riot Grrrl album *Sick and Tired*, much to Gregory's delight (*Naughty Bits* no. 9).

It is within this context of sex work–positive Riot Grrrl activism, lesbian sadomasochism, Lorena Bobbitt, *Thelma and Louise*, *Dirty Weekend*, and the phallic, penis-severing feminist avenger "COMIX BITCH" that the earliest "bad girl" comics need to be understood. Gregory's "COMIX BITCH" was a joke, but it was a joke with a serious message, one that many of the first "bad girl" comics shared. As Gregory wrote, "A Bitchy Bitch . . . is a 'Good Girl' who's gotten TIRED of being treated like a DOG!"—a description that could apply equally well to most of the early "bad girl" heroines, as they shed their restrictive "Good Girl" identities to embark on rampages of sex, violence, and revenge (*Naughty Bits* no. 10). In 1989–1993, to write a comic about an angry, queer, socially alienated woman with a job as a sex worker and a sideline in vigilante violence was not yet the cliché that it would soon become: It was still a relatively radical act, one that meant positioning oneself closer to feminist cartoonists like Gregory or Doucet than to mainstream superhero comics. When Hartsoe's prototypical "bad girl" avenger Razor returned to the asylum where she was abused as a child to mutilate the orderly who once raped her, she was following a trail blazed years before by feminist comics like *Naughty Bits* and *Dirty Plotte*, both of which explored fantasies of castration and revenge (*Razor: Cry No More; Dirty Plotte* no. 3). As Bitchy Bitch herself declared in *Naughty Bits*, "It looks like screaming, yelling, and threatening VIOLENCE are STILL the only ways to get things DONE" (*Naughty Bits* no. 6).

Gregory wrote frequently and bitterly about the way that comic books objectified women. She explained that at Fantagraphics she'd been stuck working on pornographic comics for their Eros Comix imprint, and had created Bitchy Bitch as a response, as "something to make MEN feel as queasy as all this sexist GARBAGE makes WOMEN feel": The accompanying image shows Gregory opening a comic book and being poked in the eye by a huge pair of breasts springing out of its pages (*Naughty Bits* no. 1; Robbins 123). In the following issue she expressed her dismay at the proliferation of what she called "Mammary Envy" comics—"Little if any STORY . . . —but . . . BREASTS! TITS! KNOCKERS!"—and when *Naughty Bits* was canceled in 2004 its final cover depicted Bitchy Bitch drowning in a sea of huge, spherical breasts (*Naughty Bits* no. 2, 40). "Bad girl" comics quickly became synonymous with this kind of pornographic breast fetishism, but it is important to recall that before the appearance of Lady Death and her ilk, the earliest "bad girl" titles were often relatively sympathetic to the feminist movement of the period. They critiqued restrictive gender norms, destructive beauty ideals, sexual double standards, and the pervasive threat of male violence, and—like third-wave feminism in general—their preferred solution was not to valorize the feminine over the masculine but to break down gender binaries entirely. It is these works, in which the genre came closest to realizing its feminist potential, which form the subject of this chapter.

"Don't Let the Cat Out": *Her Sister's Keeper*

In 1984, DC Comics revived its defunct *Showcase* anthology series under the title *New Talent Showcase*, inviting submissions from previously unpublished writers and artists. Among those selected for publication was Mindy Newell: As her contributor biography explained, "Mindy sent her synopsis in to the new talent program, and some four days after its arrival, Sal Amedola passed it on to Karen Berger, who, some two weeks later, called Mindy to come in for an interview" (*New Talent Showcase* no. 5). It is easy to see why: Newell's contribution, a tragic dystopian narrative entitled "Moon River," was much more hard-hitting and tightly written than most of the other *Showcase* stories. Several more of her stories were featured in *New Talent Showcase*, and she swiftly progressed to writing for *Green Lantern Corps* and *Legion of Super-Heroes* (*New Talent Showcase* no. 10). Through her subsequent work on *Catwoman*, she would go on to play an important role in the development of "bad girl" comics during the genre's most socially conscious phase.

Newell seems to have been pigeonholed by DC as a writer for female characters. Her longest contribution to *Showcase* was a series about a superheroine called Jenesis, and over the following years she also wrote for *Wonder Woman* (1985, the first time the series had been written by a woman), *Lois Lane* (1986), and *Amethyst, Princess of Gemworld* (1986–1988). Her writing was strong, but its tone tended to be bleak, even despairing, and the serious social problems that she

FIGURES 8A AND 8B Two panels from *Lois Lane* issue 2 (1986) in which Lois struggles to get a proper hearing. Written by Mindy Newell, drawn by Gray Morrow, colored by Joe Orlando, lettering by Augustin Mas.

clearly wanted to write about matched awkwardly with the colorful comic-book characters to whom she was assigned. In August 1986, for example, Doug Moench's issue of *Batman* ended with a standard comic-book teaser: "In the next issue of Detective Comics: *The Love Killing!*" (*Batman* vol. 1, no. 398). Newell's issue of *Lois Lane*, published by DC in the same month, ended in a rather different register: "NEXT ISSUE: Some surprising revelations for Lois while she finds that the phenomenon of missing children is widespread, regardless of race, color, creed, or socioeconomic background" (*Lois Lane* no. 1).

Newell's stories for *Lois Lane* and *Amethyst* tended toward the horrific, eschewing the straightforward power fantasies and redemptive endings common in the genre. Years later, in an interview with Gail Simone, she described how she acquired "[a] reputation as a 'difficult bitch'" at the DC office because of her resistance to editorial mandates (Simone, "Questions"). Her depiction of Lois Lane as a highly driven woman who is dismissed as "raving" or "crazy" by the people around her, while her resentful male editors bury her stories in the back pages of their newspaper, may well have had a strong autobiographical element.

Newell's stories repeatedly engaged with issues of gender, and she told Simone that the work she was most proud of was a "tale of female unity" she wrote for *The Legion of Super-Heroes* (Simone, "Questions"). She was clearly skeptical of the traditional models of masculine heroism which comprised DC's stock in trade, and questioned whether extending them to women constituted a step forward rather than backward. In her author's note to *Lois Lane*, she wrote:

> The hard fact of life is that it's full of loss. Get that into your head, and you've got it made in the shade, Jack. Then nothing's gonna hurt you, and nothing's gonna touch you. But, hey, that's the American way, right? Be a man. Take a key and lock up your heart. Then throw the key away. You're not gonna need it any more.
>
> And don't think that none of this applies to you, girls. Uh-uh. You wanted equality. So take it. Be a woman. But don't cry when you discover something's gone from your life. (*Lois Lane* no. 1)

Newell's reference to "the American way" makes clear that she had Superman in mind here. Famously the guardian of "truth, justice, and the American way," Superman offered a model of how to "be a man" that was premised on invulnerability: The key to heroic masculinity was becoming so tough that "nothing's gonna hurt you," just as bullets bounce harmlessly from Superman's chest. In Newell's *Lois Lane*, Superman's stoical masculinity turns out to be useless, leading Lois to reflect ruefully on how poisonous their relationship had become:

> He used to do this all the time. Show up and rescue her.
>
> She grew to appreciate it. Even to use it to her advantage. But that was okay. They were both reporters. It was part of their job, using people. So he knew what she was doing.
>
> And he went along with it. Until one day, it didn't seem to be working anymore. (*Lois Lane* no. 2)

In her characteristically bleak reading of Lois and Superman's relationship, Newell interprets it not as a happy romance characterized by mutual love and support, or even a chauvinistic fantasy of male power and female helplessness, but as a mutually manipulative arrangement in which each is reduced to a prop in the other's narrative. There is a strong implication that by always taking on the role of invincible superheroic rescuer, Superman hasn't just stunted Lois as a person, he has also stunted *himself*. "But, hey, that's the American way, right? Be a man. Take a key and lock up your heart."

The same skepticism regarding the value of stoical heroism marked Newell's subsequent work on *Catwoman*, which appeared in the wake of Frank Miller's influential *Batman: Year One* (1988). In Miller's hands, Batman, like Daredevil before him, went from a campy costumed swashbuckler to a grim and violent vigilante locked in battle with entrenched forces of corruption. *Year One* also gave Catwoman a new origin story, as a sex worker inspired by her encounters with Batman to adopt her own costumed identity, as well as a new sidekick, the underage prostitute Holly Robinson. As befitted her status as DC's go-to writer for female characters, Newell was the first writer assigned to write about Miller's reimagined Catwoman: She wrote a four-part story in *Action Comics Weekly* (1988) telling the story of Holly's death, and strongly implying a homoerotic bond between her and Catwoman. Newell's characteristic cynicism fit well with Miller's gritty reimagining of the Batman universe, and in 1989 she was assigned to write a four-issue *Catwoman* series, the first time in the character's fifty-year history that she had been given a comic book of her own.

As I have discussed, Newell's *Catwoman: Her Sister's Keeper* appeared as part of a wave of female-led titles in the late 1980s and early 1990s, which saw characters such as Elektra, Black Canary, and Silver Sable shift from being supporting characters in male-led titles to starring in their own series. What set Catwoman apart was her long-standing status as an iconic comic-book villain: Whereas DC's *Black Canary* (1991–1992) was a straightforward celebration of female heroism, *Catwoman* invited its readers to sympathize with a "bad" woman who devoted herself to committing crimes rather than preventing them. The fact that it was released without Comics Code approval and advertised as being "suggested for mature readers" demonstrated how far the series stood outside the mainstream of 1980s superhero storytelling.

Newell's *Catwoman* covered many of the same events as *Batman: Year One*, retold from Catwoman's perspective. Audaciously, Newell even reused specific frames from Miller's comic, placing them in new contexts which radically shifted their meaning. In *Year One*, Miller gave Catwoman little in the way of inner life: She was just a karate-kicking dominatrix who decided, apparently on a whim, to exchange prostitution for cat burglary after meeting Batman. In Newell's retelling, by contrast, *Catwoman* became the story of a woman alienated from society by her experiences of gendered violence. Its protagonist, Selina Kyle, is physically and sexually abused by her pimp, and her work as a dominatrix is forced on her rather than something she freely chooses to do. Episodes in *Year One* which had seemingly depicted Selina's genuinely dominant personality and sexuality were thus recontextualized into queasy scenes in which she is finally able to express her scorn and disgust of the men who abuse her, but only because her (male) client benefits from it erotically, and her (male) pimp profits from it financially.

Newell also rewrote Selina's motives for becoming Catwoman. No longer is her alter ego adopted simply for her own amusement: Instead, following a particularly severe beating from her pimp, she cuts her hair short, takes up boxing, modifies her leather fetish outfit into a costume, and learns to use her theatrical dominatrix whip as a weapon of self-defense. In another frame repurposed from Miller, Holly describes Selina's resulting persona as "pretty queer"—a line that gains new significance from the lesbian overtones which Newell placed on Holly and Selina's relationship. Holly is quite right: In Newell's retelling, Selina's performance clearly represents a kind of drag. It marks her deliberate attempt

FIGURES 9A AND 9B Left: Selina dominates a client, in *Batman: Year One* issue 1 (1988). Written by Frank Miller, art by David Mazzucchelli, colored by Richmond Lewis, lettered by Todd Klein. Right: Selina tells her masochistic client what he wants to hear, in *Catwoman* 1, no. 1 (1989). Written by Mindy Newell, art by J. J. Birch, inked by Michael Bair. Note the exaggerated lettering given to Skunk in Newell's version, suggesting his heightened state of arousal.

to replace her old identity as "Selina" (soft, femme, vulnerable, submissive, straight) with a new identity as "Catwoman" (butch, androgynous, violent, dominant, queer) (*Catwoman* vol. 1, no. 2).

As usual, however, Newell rejected easy solutions. Far from representing Selina's transformation as straightforwardly empowering, as Miller had done, Newell was intensely alert to the way that it is always already imbricated with exploitative male fantasies. In her retelling, Selina's leather costume is chosen by her pimp, not herself, and is designed to fulfill other people's desires, not her own: When he first gives it to her, she tells him that "it's disgusting" and begs him not to make her wear it. Even her leather cat mask is originally bought to serve the double purpose of obliterating her identity—as her pimp tells her, her client "ain' interested in your *face*"—and hiding the disfiguring bruises his beatings have left on her (*Catwoman* vol. 1, no. 1). Her transformation into a merciless, black-leather-wearing avenger—exactly the kind of person that her masochistic clients must have fantasized about her being—is thus a defeat as well as a victory, one that requires the sacrifice of an earlier, more fully human version of herself. Encountering her abusive pimp as Catwoman, she attempts to seduce him, telling him: "I'm *here*, Stan—*all* of me—just for *you*." But he knows her too well to believe that her new femme fatale performance has anything to do with her authentic sexuality. "You *lyin!*" he replies. "You don' *like* bein' touched. I *knows* you don'!" (*Catwoman* vol. 1, no. 3).

As with Newell's critique of Superman, her biggest objection to Selina's Catwoman identity is precisely the trait that, by the standards of subsequent "bad girl" comics, would be the most positive thing about it. Becoming Catwoman renders Selina invulnerable. As Selina puts it: "*I* can't take it. But *she* can. The *Catwoman*—she can stand it all." Rather than seeing this imperviousness as a state of empowerment, however, Newell reads it as a terrible lack: a sign that Selina has shut herself down emotionally, like the male followers of "the American way" she critiqued in *Lois Lane*. Her adoption of her superheroic persona thus constitutes a kind of spiritual death. "*Nothing* hurts her," Selina explains. "It's like she's *dead*—oh, Maggie, it's so much *easier* being dead!" (*Catwoman* vol. 1, no. 4).

For Newell, then, Selina's Catwoman persona embodies the kind of false liberation that she had critiqued in 1986, in which "equality" turns out to just mean giving women an equal opportunity to emotionally maim themselves in the same way as the men who have been harming women since history began. When Selina discovers that Holly has been brutalized by the police, her first instinct is to respond by lapsing back into her emotionally invulnerable (and emotionally dead) Catwoman persona. But her sister, Magdalena, begs her not to, insisting that feeling pain is better than feeling nothing. "*Don't* let the cat out," she says to Selina. "*Let* it hurt" (*Catwoman* vol. 1, no. 4).

What finally drives Selina to collapse decisively into her Catwoman identity is her realization that the authorities will never care about people like her and Holly: That to the police, even relatively sympathetic police like her friend George Flannery, the bottom line will always be "she's a *whore*" (*Catwoman* vol. 1, no. 4). Terrorized by bad cops and ignored by good ones, Selina concludes that she must take matters into her own hands, regardless of the cost. When Batman tries to dissuade her from taking vengeance against the policeman who beat Holly, telling her that "he deserves a jury of his peers," she is incredulous at his naivete, replying, "There isn't a cop in this *town* who'll believe a whore over one of their own." While Batman insists that the difference between Catwoman and himself is that between crime and justice, Selina argues that the true distinction is between men, who make and enforce the laws, and women, who only suffer under them. She refuses to allow him to apprehend her "like a *good* little girl," and when he says, "So it's to be a *war* between us," she replies: "It's *always* a war between the sexes." First kissing him, and then striking him down, she snarls:

> You're just another *cop*, aren't you—smarter, cooler, more seductive—but a *cop* just the same . . .
>
> And I don't do cops. (*Catwoman* vol. 1, no. 4)

Over the decade that followed, similar stories played out in innumerable "bad girl" comics, as one violent, hypersexualized heroine after another embraced the path of vengeance to secure justice that the patriarchal authorities couldn't or

FIGURE 10 Selina's confession, from *Catwoman* 1, no. 4 (1989). Written by Mindy Newell, art by J. J. Birch, inked by Michael Bair.

wouldn't provide. What sets Newell's *Catwoman* apart from these is her clear recognition that this story is a *tragedy*, and that for a woman like Selina to be driven to adopt a violent, invulnerable alter ego as armor against men's cruelty is more to be mourned than celebrated. Like the heroine of the 1981 rape revenge film *Ms .45*, whose last and only word is "sister," Selina becomes a feminist avenger, "her sister's keeper," striking back at men who abuse women—but only at terrible personal cost, shifting into a parodic version of herself that has more in common with the dominatrix persona her clients paid her to fake than with the traumatized girl she actually is. If this is empowerment, then it is empowerment of a particularly bitter kind, and Newell makes clear that in a better, fairer world, Selina would never have had to "let the cat out" in the first place.

Take Back the Night: *Vampirella*

As mentioned in chapter 1, *Vampirella* was in many ways a "bad girl" title avant la lettre. First published by Warren in 1969, *Vampirella* ran for over a hundred issues, ending only when Warren went bankrupt in 1983. It then slid into dormancy until 1991, when Harris Comics—presumably encouraged by the appearance of female-led titles such as *Catwoman* and *Huntress*—published a four-issue miniseries entitled *Vampirella: Morning in America*. It was written by the then-little-known Kurt Busiek, who subsequently described it as "the point I became a writer." In Busiek's hands, *Vampirella* became more overtly political than it had ever previously been: Its subtitle alluded to Reagan's famous 1984 "Morning in America" campaign, but its politics were anything but Reaganite. Instead, it portrayed America under Reagan and Bush as an empire of fear and false promises, with Vampirella as a countercultural "bad girl" heroine given the task of ending this long era of national night.

At the start of *Morning in America*, Vampirella has been missing for ten years (i.e., since the beginning of Reagan's presidency), having vanished fighting a "cult of chaos" on Wall Street. America has changed for the worse since her disappearance:

> America underwent a *sea-change*. She wanted things: nice *clothes*, fast *cars*, a quick *high*. Time to *play*, and the *toys* to play with.
>
> And she didn't care what it *cost*, so long as it didn't have to be paid for until *later*. America wanted it *easy*. America wanted it *now*.
>
> And the creatures of the dark *laughed*, because they wanted things *too*. And *bargains* could be made. And it was *good*.
>
> And *this* time, the creatures swore, they would *not* be defeated. They learned to work *together*. And learned to make the human power structure an *extension* of their own. (*Vampirella: Morning in America* no. 1)

In Vampirella's absence these "creatures of the dark" have formed themselves into an "unseelie congress," which gathers by night in the Senate chamber and secretly rules over America. Combined with the title, the metaphor is not subtle: Reagan's government made deals with the devil, especially those Wall Street chaos cultists (i.e., the acolytes of unregulated capitalism), and let the monsters in. They no longer need to operate in the shadows: As Vampirella's ally, Adam Van Helsing, explains, "The cult of chaos is looking to make *converts*—and what better way to do it than through the *mass market*?" Vampirella discovers to her horror that their grimoires are now bestsellers: "The *Crimson Chronicles*. The *Bible of Blood*. The most evil occult volume in the *world*. Once there were only a few copies in existence. Now it's available in *supermarkets*! *What has this world become?*" (*Vampirella: Morning in America* no. 2). The result is an America where everyone still pretends that things are normal, but where the underlying social fabric has disintegrated almost completely: where "people don't travel so much these days" and "you don't stay outside at night—for *any* reason" (*Vampirella: Morning in America* no. 1).

Vampirella's allies fear that she has been killed or captured, but the truth is sadder: She just got old. Like many 1970s counterculture activists, she has declined into drug addiction:

> She does not know *how long* she has been taking the drug. She does not remember a time when she *didn't* take it.
>
> All she can think about, as the smell fills the air, is the *rich, acrid* taste of it—and the way it dulls the *pain* inside her. (*Vampirella: Morning in America* no. 1)

But the drug doesn't just take away her pain: "It also took away her *memory*, her *identity*, her *youth*. When she woke up, she was a teacher in a *girl's school*—an *old, bitter* woman" (*Vampirella: Morning in America* no. 2).

The back cover for issue 1 eloquently summarizes its scenario. Three girls from Vampirella's school walk past a tattered poster for her comic book, advertising "issue #113 on sale Sept '81," marking the exact moment of her disappearance. (In reality the Warren series ended with issue 112 in March 1983, so the never-released issue 113 would have been due in May 1983: The dates have been reshuffled to match the political timeline.) Over it has been posted a fashion ad for "LUXURY TIME!," symptomatic of the 1980s consumerism which the comic linked so insistently with the nation's social unraveling. Below this, half obscured, is a third, newer poster, displaying a raised fist and the words: "PROTEST! TAKE BACK THE NIGHT!" The lurking figure of Shroud, the comic's life-draining villain, creeping after the girls in the shadow of the U.S. Capitol demonstrates exactly why, and from whom, it is so imperative for them to "TAKE BACK THE NIGHT." "Take back the night" marches were a staple of 1980s feminist activism: While the earliest marches dated back to 1975, the slogan was popularized by the publication of Laura Lederer's *Take Back the Night: Women on Pornography* (1980). When Vampirella reawakens, she begins to take back the night in a very literal sense, slaughtering the predators who have flourished in the darkness during the nation's long Reaganite decline.

One of Busiek's shrewdest moves comes with his handling of Vampirella's infamously revealing costume. When it first appears it is sent by Shroud as a gift to his chosen victim, the schoolgirl Chelsea Cantrell: In this context, the garments are clearly aligned with predatory male sexuality, constituting an attempt to force premature and inappropriate sexualization onto a vulnerable teenage girl. Seeing Chelsea wearing it, the "*old, bitter*" Vampirella responds with slut-shaming, victim-blaming rhetoric, telling her: "Young ladies should be *careful* what they wear—so much in this world depends on *first impressions*" (*Vampirella: Morning in America* no. 1). However, when Vampirella regains her identity she also reclaims her costume, wearing it into battle as she begins to "take back the night." In this context the same garments take on a very different meaning, aligning her with the real-world 1980s "take back the night" slogan: "However we dress—wherever we go—yes means yes and no means no!" ("International History of TBTN"). The comic thus recognizes that the significance of such costumes can change radically depending on context. Worn by Chelsea, it is a degrading marker of her forced participation in Shroud's misogynistic fantasy, but when worn by Vampirella, the same garments become assertions of a woman's right to walk the streets unmolested, regardless of how she happens to be dressed.

Vampirella's notional enemies are monsters, but her *real* enemy is Reaganite consumerist individualism. "*What is this 'Justice,' this 'Liberty,' but a means to an end? A way to make it easier for you to attain that which you truly want?*" asks the demon Nuberus. (Vampirella impales him on the Washington Monument.) She is almost defeated by the undead Southern "big oil" senator Bane, a kind of demonic George H. W. Bush, who mesmerizes his followers with promises of "two cars in every *garage*" and "*more* for your dollar": "Somewhere within them, they know the promise is a *lie*. But they don't care. They have learned to *live* with lies. And the promise is *so beautiful*" (*Vampirella: Morning in America* no. 4, 2). Fighting him is "like fighting a *freight train*," and to defeat him Vampirella has to abandon her old standards of feminine self-restraint: "She was always fighting *two* fights[.] The one on the *outside* and the one on the *inside*—Always *holding back* her—*her*—*her own freight train*—" (*Vampirella: Morning in America* no. 2). Vampirella's previous "good girl" femininity is thus depicted as a state of continuous and exhausting self-repression, one that she must renounce in order to unlock her true power. Faced with enemies like Bane, she discards her old codes against killing and drinking blood, committing herself to life-or-death struggle. As she explains, "The world has gone *bad* in the last ten years. It's crawling with *evil things*—*evil people*—surely I can find *someone* who deserves to die!" (*Vampirella: Morning in America* no. 2).

Morning in America thus makes many of the same rhetorical moves as subsequent "bad girl" comics, pitting a violent, barely dressed female vigilante against forces of entrenched corruption and criminality within a context of social decay, and endorsing her decision to employ lethal force against her enemies. What sets it apart from its later imitators is the specificity of its political reference points.

It offers a much more coherent critique of the sociopolitical problems Vampirella faces, showing how what starts with an innocent-sounding promise of "*more* for your dollar" can end with near-total social breakdown in which everyone knows that "you don't stay outside at night." Within the context of "take back the night" activism, it becomes possible to view Vampirella's costume as a confrontational gesture of defiance against those who blame women for their own victimization, and to read her impatience with "*holding back*" as necessitated by her struggle against a social order that relies on fear, apathy, and gender conformity to maintain the status quo. Subsequent "bad girl" comics mimicked Busiek's iconography while increasingly disregarding his politics, resulting in works that were either basically apolitical ("bad girl" vigilantes vs motiveless evil) or specifically reactionary ("bad girl" vigilantes vs the lawless urban underclass): For their heroines to dress in nearly nothing and solve their problems with lethal violence was increasingly represented not as an appropriate response to a specific set of social problems but as simply and straightforwardly good in and of itself. In 1991, however, writing about a physically and sexually empowered woman taking back the night from the powers that be still just about qualified *Vampirella* as a countercultural project.

In the third issue of *Morning in America*, Vampirella has a dream. To mark this sequence out from the rest of the comic, it was drawn by two guest artists, both with strong queer feminist credentials: Colleen Doran, whose sympathetic portrayal of gay love had won a cult following for her series *A Distant Soil*, and Trina Robbins, who since designing Vampirella's costume in 1969 had become primarily associated with feminist "wimmin's comix" (Misemer 12–15). Their involvement shows that a work like *Morning in America* still had a foot in both camps: It could be read as a crowd-pleasing action-horror title about a half-naked vampire woman killing demons, but at the same time it was a work with a serious political message which drew self-consciously on traditions of feminist activism and linked itself stylistically to the black-and-white alternative comics of the 1980s. Such collaborations help to demonstrate why, before 1994, "bad girl" comics like *Vampirella* were still regarded as being closely aligned with the world of indie comics counterculture rather than as the purely commercial products they rapidly became.

"Weighed Down by Beauty": *Defiant*

Newell left DC in 1990, and when Catwoman was next given a comic of her own it was written by the British comics writer Peter Milligan. 1992 saw the cinematic release of *Batman Returns*, which pitted Batman against Catwoman and Penguin: In line with Miller and Newell's reimaginings of the character, the film depicted Catwoman very much as a dominatrix, complete with black leather bodysuit and whip. To accompany the movie DC released stand-alone graphic novels for both characters: *Catwoman: Defiant* (1992) and *Penguin: Triumphant* (1992).

Catwoman's subtitle emphasized a theme that had been developing in portrayals of Catwoman since Newell's series: that she was not just an opportunistic criminal but a self-consciously "defiant" figure who set herself against the existing social order, especially in matters of gender. Her depiction in *Batman Returns* emphasized this: Murdered by her corrupt employer, she returns like an avenging ghost to take vengeance on a world that treats women like her as expendable. Played by an icy Michelle Pfeiffer and directed by Tim Burton in characteristically Gothic style, Catwoman became an almost vampiric figure, all pale skin and red lips and black leather, haunting the city by night. (Being an enthusiast for Gothic literature, Burton may well have recalled that Carmilla, the lesbian vampire from Sheridan Le Fanu's 1872 novel, transformed herself not into a bat but into a cat.) Wolf saw the film as exemplifying her new style of "power feminism," describing it as a work in which "Catwoman becomes the archetype of bad-girl sexuality, the sexuality of the anti-victim" (*Fire* 244). She also praised Newell's *Catwoman* comics, demonstrating that at least one leading third-wave feminist writer was paying attention to the changing trends in the American superhero comics market (244–245).

Milligan's *Defiant* sees Catwoman battling against a masked crime boss called Mister Handsome, who collects beautiful objects so that he can destroy them, a mania that his followers attribute to his grief at the death of his wife. He wants to capture Catwoman because he is fixated by her beauty, which he describes in disturbingly fetishistic terms. ("Enjoy the limbs. Long. Languid. Leather. Notice the perfect arc of her supple spine.") When he captures Catwoman, he chains her to a statue of Venus, so that she is literally "weighed down by beauty," and leaves her to be devoured by a monstrous "Beast"—but she is saved by a woman claiming to be his wife, Mary. Mary tells Catwoman that Mister Handsome faked her death and left her to die because he was disgusted by her fading beauty, which rendered her beastly in his eyes. Catwoman agrees to kill Mister Handsome for her, but in a final twist it turns out that Mister Handsome *is* Mary, who killed him and took his place before he had a chance to murder her for losing her looks. Mary has arranged events like this so that she can be killed by Catwoman, whom she regards as the perfect beauty. Catwoman leaves her to be killed by the Beast instead.

This story emblematizes two key concepts in early 1990s feminism: the idea of gender as performance, popularized by Judith Butler's *Gender Trouble* (1990), and the idea of "the beauty myth" articulated by Wolf in her 1990 book of the same name. As Wolf argued, "We are in the midst of a violent backlash against feminism that uses images of female beauty as a political weapon against women's advancement" (*Beauty Myth* 10). Mary, as a woman with the capacity to be "the best criminal mind in Gotham," poses a potential threat to the status quo, and it is thus essential for men like Mister Handsome to insist that she waste her energies in an endless and ultimately impossible battle to conceal her "beastly" physicality beneath a suitably beautiful exterior (28). As Mary explains to

Catwoman, "My husband was a lover of *beautiful things*. He loved women, but only *beautiful* women, *feminine* women. . . . [The beast lived] inside all women, as far as my husband was concerned" (*Catwoman: Defiant*). Mister Handsome's masked male enforcers, the Model Army, thus act as living embodiments of the social processes which compel women to comply with restrictive and oppressive models of beauty, by force if necessary.

As Butler emphasized, there was nothing inevitable about this linkage of female biology with traditionally feminine beauty ideals and social standards. As she wrote in *Gender Trouble*, "Gender is the repeated stylization of the body, a set of repeated acts within a highly rigid regulatory frame that congeal over time to produce the appearance of substance, of a natural sort of being" (43–44). *Catwoman: Defiant* is full of these instances of "stylization," most notably in the uniform suits and masks worn by the Model Army which reduce them to parodies of normative masculinity. As Butler argued, however, such "regulatory frame[s]" were always unstable:

> Gender ought not to be construed as a stable identity or locus of agency from which various acts follow; rather, gender is an identity tenuously constituted in time, instituted in an exterior space through a stylized repetition of acts. The effect of gender is produced through the stylization of the body and, hence, must be understood as the mundane way in which bodily gestures, movements, and styles of various kinds constitute the illusion of an abiding gendered self. (Butler 179)

"The illusion of an abiding gendered self" is exactly what Mary creates when she replaces her husband as "Mister Handsome." By talking, dressing, and acting like a man, she is able to occupy a male role in society, regardless of her female biology. (In 1993, Milligan explored similar ideas in *The Extremist*, in which a woman dons her husband's face-concealing costume and takes on his social role without anyone noticing the difference.) The Model Army act as enforcers of gendered norms, but the secret behind their suits and masks turns out to be the fact that they can be worn by *anyone*: As long as they are sufficiently macho, *anyone* can "be a man." As she lies dying, Mary confesses to Catwoman that being "Mister Handsome" came more naturally to her than being "Mary" ever had, telling her that "playing the role of that man was easier than playing the role I'd tried to play all my life, the role of the beautiful, feminine woman" (*Catwoman: Defiant*).

It would be possible to read Mary / Mister Handsome as a trans man: Certainly life as an ultramasculine crime boss seems to suit her better than life as an ultrafeminine trophy wife, allowing her to blossom into new forms of power. But her behavior—obsessively destroying beautiful, "feminine" objects, orchestrating her own execution at Catwoman's hands—hardly bespeaks a mind at peace with its new identity. Instead, Mary's tragedy appears to be her inability to reconcile her "beauty" (= feminine) and "beast" (= masculine) personae as aspects of a single identity. Within the beauty myth paradigm she is in thrall to, if she cannot be a "beauty" then she cannot be a "real woman," meaning that the only thing she can be is a "real man," which is to say a violent, beauty-destroying "beast." Mary admires Catwoman precisely because she has achieved the fusion of masculine and feminine traits that have eluded her, saying to her: "Even when you're beastly, you're still beautiful . . . Could that be because you have come to terms with it? Because your beauty and your beast are reconciled?" (*Catwoman: Defiant*). Catwoman is thus offered to the reader as a positive model of "masculine" femininity, juxtaposed with the failed model of Mary / Mister Handsome. Catwoman exists outside the (male) law, but she still has a moral core, unlike the psychotic Mister Handsome: As she says, "I might be a lot of things, but I'm not a killer." She combines "masculine" strength with "feminine" beauty: Watching her, Mister Handsome croons, "Her body will be hard, very hard. And yet . . . there will be softness, too." Unlike Mary / Mister Handsome, she is not "weighed down with beauty." *It* serves *her*, not vice versa.

These reconciliations are made possible by Catwoman's feminist politics, which allow her to define herself by her own standards rather than in relation to men. From the start, *Defiant* positions Catwoman as a self-consciously feminist character: Set upon by Mister Handsome's men, she asks, "Doesn't your *Mister Handsome* realize that when a lady says no . . . she means . . . *no!*" ("No means no" was a newly popular slogan at the time, popularized by the Canadian Federation of Students in a 1992 sexual assault awareness campaign [Canadian Federation of Students].) When Batman arrives, she tells him: "I don't ask anyone for help. Especially a *man*" (*Catwoman: Defiant*). Mary remains trapped within binaristic gender thinking in which woman is to man as weak is to strong, victim is to perpetrator, beauty is to beast, but Catwoman, having discarded such binaries, is free to define and perform her gender in whatever way she sees fit. It is these politics that allow her to escape the pernicious beauty myths that damage and destroy other women.

Compared to *Her Sister's Keeper*, *Defiant* thus offers a much more hopeful vision of the cultural work that the "bad girl" antiheroine might be able to accomplish, very much in line with the pivot from second- to third-wave feminist thought that had occurred in the intervening years. Emerging from a feminist politics which saw male aggression as harmful and female empathy as tragically undervalued, Newell understandably saw Catwoman's adoption of a violent, androgynous persona as being, at best, a mixed blessing. Yet it was just such critiques of the traditionally masculine, and valorizations of the traditionally feminine, that Butler warned against. As she wrote in the tenth anniversary edition of *Gender Trouble*: "It seemed to me, and continues to seem, that feminism ought to be careful not to idealize certain expressions of gender that, in turn, produce new forms of hierarchy and exclusion. In particular, I opposed those regimes of truth that stipulated that certain kinds of gendered expressions were found to be false or derivative, and others, true and original" (viii).

In 1989, Newell had depicted Catwoman's "bad girl" persona in tragic terms, as a state of living death, but by 1992, the popularization of Wolf and Butler's ideas had paved the way for Milligan to offer a much more optimistic interpretation of such gender-fluid self-fashioning. Later writers would use this as a kind of ideological blank check, allowing them to assert that any combination of masculine violence and feminine sex appeal was "empowering" simply because it cut across conventional gender binaries, but *Catwoman: Defiant* stands as a reminder of the brief moment when "bad girl" superhero comics still remained in close dialogue with the latest trends in feminist thought.

"Is This Damn Body All Men See?": *Mantra*

In 1982, the longtime DC comics writer Mike Barr began a series entitled *Camelot 3000*. Its premise was that when aliens invade Earth, King Arthur returns and rallies his knights to defend the planet: The twist was that the knights had all been reincarnated into new bodies, and some were now of different genders or ethnicities than they had previously been. Seeking the reborn Sir Tristan, Arthur's allies attend the wedding of a soldier, Owen McAllister, assuming that Owen must be the reincarnated knight. But in fact, Tristan's soul now inhabits the body of Owen's bride, Amber—and upon recalling his past life, he calls off the wedding, telling Owen that "I'm not the woman either of us thought I was." Cutting his hair with his sword, he rejects both his name and his gender as "Amber," asserting his identity as "Sir Tristan" even while still wearing his wedding dress (*Camelot 3000* no. 3).

What follows is clearly a trans narrative. Tristan constantly corrects people who call him "lady" instead of "sir," or "Amber" instead of "Tristan," or encourage him to wear dresses instead of suits. When he meets his lover Isolde, who has reincarnated as a woman, she is unbothered by his shift in biological sex—but he is tormented by it, feeling unable to love her as she deserves while he remains trapped in the "wrong" body. Only in the final issue, when regaining his male body proves impossible, does he reluctantly accept a new identity as a genderqueer butch woman in a lesbian relationship with Isolde instead—a conclusion which the series depicts as a happy ending.

In *Camelot 3000*, Tristan's story was only one plot thread among many. Barr, however, was clearly not finished with the idea, and in 1993 he began writing *Mantra* for Malibu Comics, which again told the story of a man reincarnated into a woman's body. Its protagonist, Lukasz, is a warrior in the service of a wizard named Archimage. He was recruited centuries before to fight Archimage's rival Boneyard, and each time he dies Archimage sends his spirit to possess another man's body and continue the fight. In the first issue, however, Archimage is defeated by Boneyard, and Lukasz's soul is displaced into the body of a woman named Eden Blake. Like Tristan in *Camelot 3000*, Lukasz spends many issues trying to find his way back to a male body, before finally accepting his/her new identity as a woman in issue 20.

Like *Catwoman: Defiant*, *Mantra* is strongly engaged with Butlerian notions of gender as performance. Simply being biologically female doesn't mean Lukasz knows anything about being feminine, and no part of his new gender comes naturally to him: "Being a woman" is something he has to learn, one step at a time, as he grudgingly learns how to apply makeup, walk in high heels, and develop suitably "feminine" interests in cooking, cleaning, childcare, hygiene, appearance, and weight (*Mantra* vol. 1, no. 1, 2, 10, 11). Other parts of his introduction to femininity are much harsher, as he swiftly learns that his new body makes him a target for his culture's pervasive sexual violence. Over the course of his adventures, Lukasz is repeatedly subjected to attempted sexual assault, and threatened by enemies with forced marriage, forced impregnation, and rape. Longing for the physical and social power that came with his previous male bodies, he concludes ruefully that "women were born hostages" (*Mantra* vol. 1, no. 1, 4, 7).

Much of *Mantra* reads like a study in gender dysphoria. "This is all *wrong*," Lukasz thinks, looking at his newly female body. "The rhythm, the movement, the center of gravity . . . and *breasts* . . . what do women *do* with them[?]" (*Mantra* vol. 1, no. 1). He rages against the way that his female biology bars him from the male homosociality he craves—"Can't I ever be friends with a man? Is this damn body all men see?"—and when a comrade praises Lukasz for bravery, telling him that "you've got more balls than most *men* I know!" his unspoken response is "I wish . . . !," yearning for a biologically male body to match his traditionally masculine behavior (*Mantra* vol. 1, no. 12, 13). Through his forced feminization, however, Lukasz gains a new understanding of male privilege. He comes to realize that Boneyard's villainy is just an extension of the pervasive violence of normalized misogyny. When Boneyard dismisses him as "just a *woman*" and looks at him "as though I was his personal *property*," Lukasz reflects: "Why should he be any different from any *other* man I've met since becoming a woman?" (*Mantra* vol. 1, no. 4). He visits a world where men and women live in single-sex communities, with heterosexual couples stigmatized as "perverts" and "deviants," pushing him to recognize how culturally contingent his norms of gender and sexuality really are (*Mantra* vol. 1, no. 13). His love affair with the spirit of Eden Blake, the woman who previously inhabited his body, symbolically represents his deepening appreciation of his own femininity: Eden encourages him to "*accept* your role as a woman," and he expresses his love for her by kissing his own female reflection in the mirror (*Mantra* vol. 1, no. 16). The eponymous "mantra" is "change, growth, power," a mantra that Lukasz ultimately fulfills by merging with Eden into a single identity, achieving personal empowerment by transcending reductive categories of masculinity and femininity. As in *Camelot 3000*, accepting a queer female identity is thus depicted as a crucial step in Lukasz's growth as a person.

Reading *Mantra* alongside *Camelot 3000*, it becomes clear how close Barr's view of gender is to that articulated by Butler. Tristan and Lukasz initially rage against being "women" because they have not yet disentangled their notions of sex from those of gender, and hence believe that being biologically female also requires them to be socially feminine (and heterosexually interested in men). Once they accept that there is no necessary connection between the two, and that "being a woman" is compatible with loving other women and behaving in traditionally masculine ways, they are able to let go of their anxieties and start identifying as (queer, gender-fluid) women rather than men. *Camelot 3000* is the simpler of the two: Tristan never stops preferring masculine self-presentation, but moves over the course of the series from identifying as a straight trans man to identifying as a butch lesbian. *Mantra* is more complex, because while Tristan never wavers from adhering to a masculine ideal, Lukasz gradually comes to see the strict masculinity of his previous incarnations as woefully inadequate, and to genuinely embrace many aspects of femininity in a way that Tristan never does. By Barr's (and Butler's) standards, this marks Lukasz as someone who has gone further than Tristan in disentangling sex and gender: not only accepting that male presentation might be compatible with female biology, but willing and able to freely combine "male" and "female" traits without any regard for whether they conform to social expectations. Lukasz is finally able to announce "I'm a woman" precisely because he/she no longer feels those words carry any kind of socially prescriptive power, or that "being a woman" is in any way incompatible with his/her identity as a warrior (*Mantra* vol. 1, no. 20).

In 1993, giving a female character their own comic—not a limited miniseries, like *Her Sister's Keeper* or *Morning in America*, but an open-ended, ongoing series—was still seen as a risky move. In August 1994, Barr wrote:

> I'm proud not only because *Mantra* is one of the top Ultraverse titles, but because it seemed as though we had so much working against us. Most everyone was nervous about the idea of a solo heroine, reciting the oft-heard dictum "women characters don't sell." Truth to tell, even some higher-ups here at Malibu were concerned. The first issue of *Mantra* also contains the first appearance of Warstrike, because it was thought that Mantra might need a male co-star to attract readers!
>
> [. . .]
>
> In fact, there are precious few women solo characters in comics at all—and of those who aren't spin-offs from other titles, hyped mini-series or female versions of male characters, *Mantra* is #1! (Okay, in a way, Mantra is a female version of a male character, but you know what I mean.) I'm not claiming Mantra is any kind of feminist statement . . . but when you consider the fact that she's a female character, holding her own in a field that's overwhelmingly male-dominated, I'm not ruling it out either! (*Mantra* vol. 1, no. 13)

There is much to unpack here. Barr was correct that many superheroines were "female versions of male characters," with individuals such as Supergirl or Batgirl deriving much of their appeal from their connections with their male originals. By observing that, "in a way," Mantra is *also* "a female version of a male character," Barr invites us to think of such characters in transgender terms, as examples of fundamentally male figures transposed into female bodies. (If Supergirl, for example, is "a female version of Superman," then to what extent is she "really" female?) But given that Mantra, at this point in the story, still very much understood himself to be a man trapped in a woman's body, in what sense can he be described as a "woman solo character" or "a female character, holding her own in a field that's overwhelmingly male-dominated"? What does it imply that this rare example of a successful comic about a "woman solo character" was actually about a man? And in what way might this be understood as "a feminist statement"?

What *Mantra* calls attention to is that female characters were able to flourish in 1990s comics precisely by *acting like men*. As I have discussed, the form of femininity celebrated by "bad girl" titles like *Razor* and *Witchblade* was primarily defined by hyperbolic machismo: Its chief virtues were courage, stoicism, aggression, and a capacity for violence. What gives *Mantra* a more credible claim to be a feminist statement than the works which followed it was its focus on the tensions between this version of "masculine" femininity and the more traditional forms of femininity that their heroines were simultaneously expected to adhere to. The struggle to simultaneously "be a man" (fight, master "masculine" tools such as weapons, demonstrate courage and toughness) and "be a woman" (care for children, master "feminine" tools such as high heels and makeup, demonstrate sensuality and sensitivity) causes Lukasz tremendous distress, and it is only once he recognizes that there are real problems with the version of masculinity he idealizes—that, in fact, the warrior masculinity he aspires to is troublingly close to the villainous masculinity he defines himself *against*—that he is able to bring the two sides of himself into happier equilibrium. By the end of the series Lukasz has realized the futility of Archimage's centuries-long conflict with Boneyard, during which he possessed one man after another simply to send them to their deaths in battle, and he embraces his new identity as a woman precisely because it offers an escape from the eternal deadlock of a masculinity defined only by heroic bloodshed. In this, *Mantra* contrasts starkly with subsequent "bad girl" titles such as *Exposure* (1999–2000) which depicted "masculine" battle prowess and "feminine" sexual self-objectification as two sides of the same coin, each accompanying and facilitating the other, with the tools of sex and violence represented as virtually interchangeable sources of personal empowerment. "You were *right*, Lisa" yells one of the barely dressed heroines of *Exposure* as she uses her stiletto heel to impale an attacking vampire. "I'll never be caught *without* high heels again!" (*Exposure* no. 1).

Mantra's engagement with gender issues attracted much praise from its female readership. The comic's (female) editor invited women to write in with their views on Mantra's "feminine masculinity," and most of the printed responses were positive: One complimented the comic because "it addresses the issues that millions of women face in life today without drowning us in soapsuds," while another saw its handling of social issues as distinctively modern, calling it "a book for the 90s" (*Mantra* vol. 1, no. 3, 5, 6). One reader asserted that women don't read comics because of their reliance on oversexualized heroines who act "like men in women's bodies," praising *Mantra* for engaging with these themes in a more sensitive fashion, though another letter lamented the comic's apparent view that it took a male soul to make a strong woman and called it to take a more explicit stand against sexism (*Mantra* vol. 1, no. 7). Other letters suggest that the comic pushed some readers to reconsider their views around gender, with readers worrying over which pronouns to use for Lukasz, questioning whether it was wrong for straight men to be attracted to a woman who was "really a man," speculating on the relationship between Lukasz's gender and sexuality, and suggesting that many men might enjoy the experience of inhabiting female bodies (*Mantra* vol. 1, no. 3, 6, 8). In 1999, Jenny North, the creator of the online Transgender Graphics and Fiction Archive, even created a "Mantraverse" fan site celebrating the character—a hint of the significance that the series had for trans comic readers back in the 1990s, at a time when trans issues were otherwise all but invisible in mainstream comic books (North).

The one thing female readers *did* object to was Mantra's costume, which even its editor freely admitted was included simply to attract male readers (*Mantra* vol. 1, no. 7). On the level of plot, *Mantra* was in many ways a more progressive work than *Camelot 3000*, but the same cannot be said for its art. In *Camelot 3000*, Tristan was almost always shown dressed like a man, in line with the androgynous beauty ideals of the 1980s: Lukasz, by contrast, is magically compelled to wear an incredibly skimpy costume which he himself describes as "painted-on," and which serves no purpose except to show off his breasts, legs, and buttocks to the reader. The comic thus engages in continuous sexual objectification of its protagonist, even as it emphasizes the ways in which women are harmed and humiliated by being reduced to objects for the male gaze.

In issue 20, when delivering his/her final, rapturous acknowledgment of his/her own femininity—"My name is Lukasz. I'm a warrior. My name is Mantra. I'm a wizard. My name is Eden. I'm a woman."—Lukasz is *still wearing* the same magical armor forced on him back in issue 1, bare thighs and cleavage now proudly displayed, apparently having accepted that such self-objectification is simply part of being female. Like many subsequent "bad girl" titles, *Mantra* thus found itself caught between its desire to gain artistic and ideological credibility by attracting female readers through its writing and the economic necessity of pandering to the lucrative, straight, male comic-buying market through its art. This tension between art and story, already apparent in earlier comics such as *Elektra*, would become even more prominent in the next early "bad girl" series, *Ghost*.

FIGURE 11 Lukasz laments his objectifying costume, in *Mantra* issue 1. Written by Mike Barr, pencils by Terry Dodson, inked by Al Vey, letters by Tim Eldred.

"Let Me Tell You About Men and Women": *Ghost*

Malibu Comics was not the only company to launch its own superhero universe in 1993. Lured by booming sales in superhero comics, Dark Horse launched its own shared universe in June 1993, hubristically entitled "Comics' Greatest World." A range of sixteen titles was initially envisaged, but market competition was brutal, and cancellations came thick and fast. By May 1996, these sixteen had dwindled to just one survivor: *Ghost*.

Like many early "bad girl" titles, including *Razor* and *Shi*, *Ghost* told the story of a woman's search for revenge in a dark, crime-filled cityscape. Unusually, however, the person she was trying to avenge was *herself*: Its protagonist, Elisa Cameron, wakes up spectral and amnesiac, and spends the rest of the series investigating the murder of the woman she used to be. In the hands of its initial writer, Eric Luke, this investigation led Elisa to position herself explicitly as a feminist avenger, using her ghostly powers to destroy men who prey on women: pornographers, misogynistic serial killers, businessmen who sexually exploit female employees, and cult leaders who gather harems of female followers. The revenge she took on them was often brutal—*Ghost* was published without the approval of the Comics Code, so Luke was free to be as violent as he liked—and multiple readers wrote in to express their discomfort with Elisa's uncompromising feminist rage (*Ghost* vol. 1, no. 2, 3, 4, 5, 7). As one (male) letter writer complained, the trouble with Elisa was that she was "an unsympathetic character. She's hard to like" (*Ghost* vol. 1, no. 3).

If *Mantra* drew on the works of Butler, and *Catwoman: Defiant* drew on Wolf, then *Ghost* drew on Andrea Dworkin. Elisa's vision of gender relations comes straight out of Dworkin's *Pornography* (1981), a work that was still being bitterly debated at the time in books such as Elizabeth Wilson and Gillian Rodgerson's *Pornography and Feminism* (1991) and Susan Cole's *Pornography and the Sex Crisis* (1989). Dworkin argued that "the major theme of pornography as a genre is male power," and that the normalization of pornography was central to the maintenance of patriarchy, because "male supremacy depends on the ability of men to view women as sexual objects" (*Pornography* 24, 113). Indoctrinated by porn to hate and despise women, men became all too eager to suppress them through violence and terror.

Dworkin argued that violent media formed part of the "legend of terror" through which men maintain power over women. As she wrote:

> But first, there is the legend of terror, and this legend is cultivated by men with sublime attention. In epics, dramas, tragedies, great books, slight books, television, films, history both documented and invented, men are giants who soak the earth in blood. Within the legend men have great chances and are the carriers of values. Within the legend, women are booty. (16)

Dworkin regarded male stories about female violence with deep skepticism: Describing a dominatrix in a pornographic novel, she argued that "she is a fantasy, as opposed to a symbol: the power attributed to her nowhere resonates in the real world" (30). In her view, genuine narratives of female resistance to male power were simply too dangerous for patriarchal culture to permit: "Physical strength in women that is not directly harnessed to 'women's work' becomes an abomination, and its use against men, that is, as power, is anathema, forbidden, horribly punished" (14). It was this taboo that she aimed to break in her subsequent novel *Mercy* (1990), which ended with its heroine devoting herself to violent resistance against male terror, declaring: "I went out; at night; to smash a man's face in; I declared war. My *nom de guerre* is Andrea One; I am reliably told that there are many more; girls named courage who are ready to kill" (*Mercy* 333).

Dworkin assumed that objectification of women and intolerance of female violence would inevitably go together, as both resulted from the same horror of female power. When she wrote *Pornography* in 1981 this was probably true, but by the 1990s the correlation had broken down with the proliferation of powerful heroines in mainstream media who were also depicted in sexually objectifying ways. The "bad girl" comics of the early 1990s were *full* of "girls named courage who are ready to kill," most of whom took special delight in "smash[ing] a man's face in." Contrary to Dworkin's predictions, male readers did not recoil from them: Instead, they devoured them, eagerly reading comics about angry women brutalizing evil men as long as the women in question were depicted in a sufficiently sexualized fashion. As I have discussed, these comics often drew on feminist ideas, at least at first, but they also drew heavily on pornography, the very genre which Dworkin saw as perpetuating women's oppression and justifying their revolutionary rage. Nowhere was this uncomfortable double allegiance more clearly visible than in *Ghost*.

In the first issue of *Ghost*, aptly titled "A Man's World," Elisa offers a rather Dworkinian account of gender relations after carrying out the first of her many massacres:

> You think that was *cold?* You think that was a little . . . *heartless*? Let me *tell* you about hearts. Let me tell you about *men* and *women*.
>
> Let me tell you about how men *treat* women. Men treat women like *meat*. Meat that gets slammed around. Hey—that *phrase*: meat that gets slammed around. Does it get you a little *excited* to think of a woman like that?
>
> *Sure* it does.
>
> Gets you *twitching* just a little, hmm? Well, you want to know the *truth*? I'm going to slam *you* around, a *lot*.
>
> It's going to *hurt*. It's going to hurt so much it won't even be a *little* exciting. And *then* I'll think about letting you live. (*Ghost Special* no. 1)

Like Dworkin, Elisa insists on the direct relationship between objectifying pornography and misogynistic violence, as when she sees a man open fire in a strip club: "He's shooting the strippers. He's skipped the show. This is the fastest way to turn a woman into an *object*" (*Ghost* vol. 1, no. 2). As she later remarks, "What a man feels when he looks at a naked woman he doesn't know, doesn't even care about . . . He thinks *that's* power" (*Ghost* vol. 1, no. 3). The result is a world in which men reflexively brutalize and humiliate women, driving Elisa, like Dworkin's Andrea One, to violent revenge on their behalf.

Elisa's ghostly power of intangibility is explicitly framed as a way for her to undermine the physical and emotional hardness through which her enemies define their masculinity. As she explains:

One thing about men: they love *walls.*
They love to *build* walls. Big, thick, towering walls. The taller the better.
Nothing like a huge wall to show the *measure* of the man.
Me . . . ?
I pass right through walls.
It's what I do. (*Ghost Special* no. 1)

As a ghost, Elisa is able to penetrate her male victims at will. She penetrates their physical walls, and she penetrates their emotional walls by showing them that they are never safe. Finally, she penetrates the walls of their own bodies—usually with messily lethal results, as when she sticks her hands into men's chests and materializes her fingers inside their hearts, thus demonstrating that she is, in a very literal sense, a heartbreaker. Her brutal executions of her enemies, and her ever-escalating body count, prefigured the hyperbolic violence of later "bad girl" heroines. However, like Newell's *Catwoman* and Barr's *Mantra*, *Ghost* acknowledged the limitations of simply answering male violence with female violence, and Elisa's reign of retributive terror was depicted by Luke as something that she ultimately learned to outgrow.

Luke's *Ghost* thus resembled a version of Newell's *Catwoman: Her Sister's Keeper*, told in reverse: Indeed, the parallels are so strong that it is hard to believe they are coincidental. Newell told the story of how a woman (Selina) is driven by institutionalized misogyny to become a violent avenger (Catwoman), abandoning her friends and sister along the way. Luke's heroine *starts* as a violent avenger (Ghost), driven purely by the desire to punish misogynistic violence, and gradually relearns how to be a woman (Elisa) by rebuilding relationships with her sister and friends. Catwoman shares her city with a male vigilante, Batman: When they meet, she first kisses him, then strikes him down, rejecting his masculine methodology as incompatible with hers. Ghost *also* shares her city with a male vigilante, X, who dresses, like Batman, in black: Initially she hates him, seeing him as just another violent man throwing his weight around, but when trapped in a dream together they first kill each other, then have sex with each other, after which they come to recognize one another as complementary allies rather than enemies (*Ghost* vol. 1, no. 21). (In a Dworkinian touch, Elisa initially rejects X because she associates his name with misogynistic X-rated porn movies.) *Catwoman* ends with Selina's final estrangement from her sister, Maggie, whereas *Ghost* ends with Elisa's final reconciliation with her sister, Margo, whom she literally carries in her arms, devoting herself to becoming exactly what Selina is not: her sister's keeper (*Ghost* vol. 1, no. 36). Selina abandons a heterosexuality which has brought her nothing but abuse for her "queer" alter ego; Elisa starts off queer, hating men so much that the only attraction she admits is toward another female vigilante, only to gradually acknowledge that she is sometimes attracted to men as well (*Ghost* vol. 1, no. 19, 21, 32). Some level of gender fluidity remains, however, and when she does finally sleep with a man, it is *she* who penetrates *him*, using her intangibility to achieve full-body interpenetration of his passive, sleeping body (*Ghost* vol. 1, no. 31).

Newell told the story of how "Selina" became lost within "Catwoman," but just as Mantra reconciles his/her warrior identity ("Lukasz") with his/her feminine identity ("Eden") in *Mantra* issue 20, so Elisa ultimately reconciles her warrior identity ("Ghost"), which hates men, with her feminine identity ("Elisa"), which is capable of loving them, in *Ghost* issue 32—a development which the comic clearly views as positive. It would be tempting to read this as a simple parable about Elisa's need to shift from militant, gender-essentialist, radical lesbian separatism to a more gender-fluid third-wave feminism, but many of the lessons she learns along the way are classic second-wave axioms about the importance of sisterhood, the need for female solidarity and female friendship, and the recognition that traditionally feminine traits like empathy have just as much value as traditionally masculine traits like violence. (As one villain tauntingly tells her, "You're so angry that you're thinking like a *man*" [*Ghost* vol. 1, no. 13].) Like *Mantra* and *Catwoman*, *Ghost* takes the view that violent revenge can only ever be part of the solution to institutional sexism, and when a dream sequence positions Elisa as a sidekick to a parodically macho superhero named Killblade, she quickly realizes just how empty a life of pure vengeance and aggression really is (*Ghost* vol. 1, no. 3). As the comic shows, Elisa's quest for vengeance has reduced her to a ghost rather than a person, and she needs to rehumanize herself before she can become a genuine force for redemption rather than simply an agent of tit-for-tat violence in an interminable war between the sexes.

On the level of plot, *Ghost* is thus engaged in a critique of pornographic culture and an exploration of possible avenues of resistance and reform. At the same time, however, the very comics that are so strident in their critiques of pornography are themselves pornographic, with Elisa's exaggerated curves and cleavage-baring, slit-to-the-waist costume ensuring that she is continuously objectified for the scopophilic pleasure of the assumed heterosexual male reader. Adam Hughes, who drew the first issues of *Ghost* and established the look of the series, was famous for his pinup art: As one reader admitted, the reason he first bought the comic was because it was "Adam Hughes, and hence, gratuitous T&A" (*Ghost* vol. 1, no. 13). (The following year, Hughes began drawing pornographic cartoons for *Penthouse Comix*.) Elisa's costume is never explained or justified in-universe: Editorial mandates were presumably involved, and the editor, Randy Stradley, ultimately admitted that he was the one who had insisted on Elisa wearing high heels after female readers objected to her habit of wearing high-heeled pumps into combat (*Ghost* vol. 1, no. 24). (His explanation was that her costume was meant "to give men pause.") As the fifteen other titles from Comics' Greatest World were canceled one after another, one letter writer grimly summed up the situation: Despite being a "well-written comic," *Ghost* had become a work that "can only survive by the grace of the lead character's cleavage" (*Ghost* vol. 1, no. 32). Debbie Byrd, who ran the letter column from issue 14 to give it what the editor called "a woman's

FIGURE 12 Elisa's cleavage-baring costume, from *Ghost* 1, no. 6 (1995). Written by Eric Luke, pencils by Scott Benefiel, inked by Jasen Rodriguez. Note the phallic imagery of the train entering the tunnel, its arch mirroring the arch of her legs.

perspective," was blunt about the reasoning behind Elisa's costume. Lamenting the trend for all superheroines to have "DD breasts" and "5-inch heels," she remarked: "But we've got to keep the men reading, huh?" (*Ghost* vol. 1, no. 14, 18).

Luke's writing sometimes strikes a rather passive-aggressive note on the subject of Elisa's costume. In the "Killblade" dream sequence, Elisa complains that she is required to wear "this suit that I'm always falling out of," even though "it makes no sense as a fighting outfit," but the sexist costume Killblade forces on her isn't much different to the outfit that she inexplicably wears every issue (*Ghost* vol. 1, no. 3). At the same time, however, Luke's plots frequently catered to the same sexist impulses that they critiqued. Elisa defeats a string of misogynistic villains, but usually not before they've had a chance to thoroughly humiliate her, allowing readers first to sadistically enjoy her degradation and then to piously applaud its punishment. In an interview with *Wizard*, Hughes expressed his mixed feelings about the scenes that Luke asked him to draw for the series:

> I just sent in the artwork on the strip club sequence and got a call from Mike [Eury] saying that some of the women at Dark Horse were a little upset by it, because it's a strip club and I show strippers there doing what strippers do, which is take their clothes off. I was bothered by that at first, but then I got to thinking—women should be upset by a strip club. If I drew a strip club that didn't bother them, then I wouldn't be doing my job. A reader, especially a woman, who feels that way is in exactly the right mood to read that story, because Ghost herself is offended by the club and what goes on there. (*Wizard* no. 45, 40)

Hughes here acknowledges the notional antipornography message of *Ghost*, according to which strip clubs are something "women should be upset by." However, there was no guarantee that the comic's male readers *would* be "bothered" or "offended" by the scene: Indeed, the reason "the women at Dark Horse" were upset by it was almost certainly because they knew that most of *Ghost*'s target audience would find it arousing rather than offensive, and would consequently view the comic as pandering to the strip-club aesthetic rather than critiquing it. (Hughes certainly does not seem to have made any effort to make the club seem unappealing in his art, despite the extremely critical captions Luke paired it with.) Elisa frequently echoes Dworkin's rhetoric, but if Dworkin herself ever saw these comics she would no doubt have concluded from such scenes that they, like dominatrix pornography, were really expressions of male dominance, despite their pretenses of female empowerment (*Pornography* 36). The comic's constant nudity and sexualized violence clearly alienated some of its female readers, who wrote in to express their discomfort, leaving Byrd with the awkward job of imploring them to "try not to be too offended" (*Ghost* vol. 1, no. 16, 19).

Ghost thus found itself in the invidious position of marketing a comic with a clear antipornography feminist message using borderline pornographic imagery as its primary selling point. In doing so, it came ever closer to the boundaries of what, over the course of its run, came to be known as "bad girl" comics. As early as 1995, readers were expressing their worries that *Ghost* would become "what my local comic shop owner calls a 'bad girl': a gorgeous, scantily-clad woman with big guns," and praising it to the extent that it managed to avoid "the temptation to let this book descend into 'bad girl' hell": "Thank God for progressive feminism. Maybe the solid female characters will overrun the 'Bad Girls'!" (*Ghost* vol. 1, no. 6, 19, 20, 26, 28). By 1997, with sales in decline, readers worried that *Ghost* had been overshadowed by the "bad girl" craze, and survived "mostly because of the 'bad girl' costume the character wears" (*Ghost* vol. 1, no. 23, 32). Byrd expressed her bewilderment at the popularity of "bad girl" comics—"There's no story behind the characters, just page after page of girls with unrealistic bodies, wearing unrealistic clothing, fighting against seemingly everyone"—and saw *Ghost* as a welcome exception to such "bimbos" (*Ghost* vol. 1, no. 26). But while *Ghost* undoubtedly had more ambitious writing than the median "bad girl" title, in other respects they were very similar. The primary reason it survived while the fifteen other titles from Comics' Greatest World were canceled was because market conditions had shifted to favor titles about "gorgeous, scantily-clad women with big guns"—an aesthetic that *Ghost* itself had helped to popularize back in 1993.

Ultimately, the market won out. Luke's run on *Ghost* ended in 1998, with the title canceled due to low sales: Rebooted five months later with a new writer, it swiftly became exactly the kind of "bad girl" title that readers had previously asked Dark Horse to promise it would never become, with Elisa rewritten as a merciless assassin whose clothes kept falling off (*Ghost* vol. 1, no. 28). In 1993, *Ghost* had been, if not entirely in keeping with the discourses of antipornography feminism, then at least in close dialogue with them. But by the time it was finally canceled in 2000, few traces remained of the self-consciously feminist work that it had once aspired to be, before its writing was decisively overpowered by its pinup art.

Real Girls: *Strangers in Paradise*

Strangers in Paradise, which was written and drawn by Terry Moore from 1993 to 2007, is not normally classed as a "bad girl" comic. With its self-consciously literary style, its slice-of-life storytelling, and its introspective focus on queer love and friendship between its female leads, Francine Peters and Katina Choovanski ("Katchoo"), it deliberately distanced itself from the hypersexualized superheroics which dominated most American comics in the 1990s. It gathered a large female audience, many of whom expressed their delight at finding a work they enjoyed amid a genre that otherwise seemed determined to alienate them—"I only read you and Neil Gaiman" was a common refrain in the letters pages (*Strangers in Paradise* vol. 2, no. 6). By 2000 its own ads declared that "*SiP* is one of the strongest female reader titles in the industry" (*Strangers in Paradise* vol. 3, no. 34).

In 1994, the Dark Horse editor Diana Schutz credited *Strangers in Paradise* with being the first work to make her fellow Dark Horse employee Debbie Byrd (already cited for her work on *Ghost*) take an interest in comics:

> Debbie is bright and funny and sexy. She's also warm and sympathetic and emotional. She likes black lace and jewelry and fancy drinks with little umbrellas. And she doesn't like comics: in fact, she's completely indifferent to them.
>
> In short, Debbie Byrd is a Real Girl.
>
> [. . .]

> Over a year later, Debbie has now not only read every issue of *Strangers in Paradise* to date, she actually *collects* them this from a woman who, despite her seven years employ at Dark Horse, once very matter-of-factly explained to me that she didn't read comics, didn't much like them, to tell the truth. This from a high school Homecoming Queen—like I said, a Real Girl. A Real Girl who now runs out to the local comics shop every other month, anxious to pick up her *reserved* copy of *Strangers in Paradise*, the *only* comic book she cares to read. (*Strangers in Paradise* vol. 2, no. 1)

The essentialist implication that only a traditionally feminine "Homecoming Queen" can be "a Real Girl" is troubling, but Schutz's message is clear: Byrd here acts as a representative example of all the women who currently don't read comics but might start if they were more like *Strangers in Paradise*. As Schutz explained, "We need Real Girls—*civilians*—as readers, and we need Real Girls—*humans*—to read about. Enter Francine Peters and Katina Choovanski" (*Strangers in Paradise* vol. 2, no. 1).

The idea expressed here by Schutz was one that was repeatedly expressed by Moore's admirers, including Byrd herself: that his heroines were "Real Girls" in a medium mostly populated by adolescent sex fantasies (*Strangers in Paradise* vol. 2, no. 1, 6; vol. 3, no. 2; Pustz 169). During a guest appearance in *Gen13*, Francine and Katina were even depicted as "real women" protecting the comics industry from the improbably proportioned "bad girls" bent on destroying it (*Gen13* vol. 2, no. 13C). Moore received much praise for the physical and psychological realism of his female characters, and he frequently expressed his dismay at the state of mainstream American comics, lamenting the industry's lack of interest in women as anything other than sex objects. His disdain for the "bad girl" genre was obvious from a 1996 issue in which a sleazy video rental employee is depicted reading a comic emblazoned with cartoonishly busty women in bikinis, entitled "Bad Girl Comix: Death Tits" (*Strangers in Paradise* vol. 2, no. 10).

However, when *Strangers in Paradise* began in 1993, the gap between it and the early "bad girl" titles was much narrower than it subsequently became. It was originally published by Antarctic Press, which was primarily associated with pornographic manga and anthropomorphic animal comics: Moore himself quipped that Antarctic Press was "a fun company heavily populated by naked animals and cute Japanese girls. Or is it the other way around?" (*Strangers in Paradise* vol. 2, no. 7). Nor was this a particularly surprising place for the title to begin. Taken in isolation, the initial three-issue run of *Strangers in Paradise* tells an anarchic story about a violent lesbian avenging herself on her best friend's unfaithful boyfriend, with black-and-white art, threats of castration, and lots of sexual content: more or less exactly the terrain of alternative indie black-and-white comics from which the earliest "bad girl" titles were then arising. Like many comic authors over the next few years, Moore quickly recognized that his angriest female character was also his strongest creative asset, writing: "When I

FIGURE 13 Video Pat consoles himself with a copy of Bad Girls Comix, in *Strangers in Paradise* 2, no. 10 (1996). Written and drawn by Terry Moore.

began writing *Strangers in Paradise*, I thought it was a story about Francine and her roommate, Katchoo. By the second or third issue I realized it was actually a story about Katchoo and her roommate, Francine. Katchoo just took over. She does that" (*Strangers in Paradise* vol. 1, no. 1, 1997 edition).

As a queer, aggressive, physically capable young woman with a history of sex work and violence and a long list of grievances against society in general and men in particular, Katchoo bears more than a passing resemblance to other early "bad girl" heroines such as Newell's Catwoman or Luke's Ghost. As I have discussed, Byrd, who tirelessly championed *Strangers in Paradise*, also acted as a spokeswoman for *Ghost*. Moore himself was moving in "bad girl"–adjacent territory at the time: He drew pinup art for the 1993 issue of Antarctic Press's *Ninja High School Swimsuit Special*, from the pages of which the influential "bad girl" series *Warrior Nun* emerged the following year, and he designed a gun-wielding, bikini-wearing heroine named Kaippe for Caliber Press (*Strangers in Paradise* vol. 1, no. 3, 1997 edition). He recommended the comics of Frank Miller and Kurt Busiek, who at the time were closely associated with the early "bad girl" heroines Elektra and Vampirella, respectively, and he praised the work of David Mack, whose series *Kabuki* (1994–2009) came to define the more artistically serious end of the "bad girl" genre (*Strangers in Paradise* vol. 3, no. 4). Mack returned the favor by drawing a picture of Kabuki standing alongside Francine and Katchoo in a police lineup, all bad girls together (*Strangers in Paradise* vol. 1, no. 1, 1997 edition).

Given the reputation that *Strangers in Paradise* developed for slow-burn, emotionally literate drama, it is somewhat startling to realize just how much "bad girl" material it actually contains. There are conspiracy thriller plots involving secret, all-female organizations of assassins; there are evil murderous East Asian lesbians with knee-length hair; there are battles between female gunslingers and female martial artists; there are scenes in which Katchoo breaks into criminal bases wearing a black bodysuit; there are many, *many* scenes in which Katchoo beats people up while yelling about how much she hates men. The themes it explores in relation to gender, violence, and sexuality are the same themes interrogated by contemporaneous "bad girl" comics like *Ghost* and *Kabuki*, and even though *Strangers in Paradise* defined itself against the "bad girl" craze, both profited from the same hunger for narratives about queer, angry, violent young women like Katchoo. (Most readers whose letters were printed in the comic mentioned that Katchoo was their favorite character.) The comic itself clearly recognized this kinship, and twice featured dream sequences in which Katchoo appeared as a gun-toting "bad girl" superheroine (*Strangers in Paradise* vol. 3, no. 1, 33). In *Strangers in Paradise*, however, these "bad girl" elements were not permitted to dominate the narrative. The story oscillates between the perpetually enraged Katchoo and the thoroughly normal Francine, never allowing the thriller plotlines of the former to fully eclipse the slice-of-life storylines of the latter, with the love story between the two serving as the glue that holds the entire narrative together. As I have discussed, this pairing of a queer, butch, or trans "bad girl" heroine with a more traditionally feminine straight cis woman whom she loves recurs repeatedly in these comics: Selina and Maggie (*Catwoman*), Lukasz and Eden (*Mantra*), Elisa and Margot (*Ghost*), and Katchoo and Francine (*Strangers in Paradise*). However, in every other comic, the "bad girl" is clearly the main character, with the other woman relegated to supporting cast. Only *Strangers in Paradise* made a serious attempt to give them equal billing.

Strangers in Paradise thus serves to signpost the road not taken by the genre as a whole. As this chapter has shown, in 1989–1993 a whole range of comics responded to newly popular third-wave feminist discourses of "empowerment," sex positivity, and the importance of decoupling sex from gender, producing stories that explored what it might mean to be an "empowered woman" in a world dominated by institutionalized sexism and misogynistic violence. Over the years that followed, ideological shifts and commercial imperatives led most of them to lapse from social critique into soft-core pornography. *Strangers in Paradise* built and retained a substantial female audience simply by *not* doing this, by remaining in the same world of indie, feminist, alternative black-and-white comics where many of the rest began.

The fact that *Strangers in Paradise* was able to do this was a reflection not just of the ideological convictions of its creator but the economic conditions of its creation. Of the comic's 107 issues, three were published by Antarctic Press and eight by Image: The remaining ninety-six were published by Moore's own creator-owned Abstract Studios. They were virtually one-man productions, with Moore doing the writing, pencils, inks, lettering, and covers, the same model used by Gregory for *Naughty Bits*, and entirely different to the assembly-line production of monthly comics like *Mantra* and *Ghost*, which were usually produced by teams of five to ten. With full-color comics to produce, monthly deadlines to meet, and teams of artists, writers, letterers, and editors to pay, companies such as Malibu and Dark Horse had to follow market trends in order to remain profitable: Sales that sufficed for Moore's one-man studio would have been ruinous for a title like *Ghost*. When the tastes of their audience changed, they had no choice but to change with it, leaving *Strangers in Paradise* as an increasingly isolated example not only of what the "bad girl" genre once was but of what it might have remained had the demands of the market not led it in a different direction.

4

Girl Power

Postfeminist "Bad Girl" Comics

Frenzy Beast: "Bad Girl" Comics and Postfeminism, 1994–1996

The rise of the "bad girl" genre was extremely swift. In 1993, as Mike Barr noted, the received wisdom was that "women characters don't sell," and publishing a series about a solo heroine was seen as a major risk even for a medium-tier publisher like Malibu. By 1995 the situation had reversed, and "bad girl" titles had come to be seen as the *safest* commercial option for comics publishers, especially for small indie studios. Some of the resulting series, such as *Shi*, *Witchblade*, and *Lady Death*, became extremely popular. Many others—*Hammer Girl*, *Sinthia*, *Cynder*, *Ms. Cyanide*, *Hell's Maiden*, *Claire Voyant*, *Lionheart*, *Saffire*, and many, many more—appeared for just a few issues before vanishing without a trace.

So rapid a shift needs to be understood in relation to larger changes within the cultural landscape of the period, which moved swiftly to embrace the idea that female hypersexualization and sexual aggression could be read as markers of empowerment rather than degradation (Snyder 179, 189). As Susan Hopkins writes, these were years in which American pop culture rapidly absorbed these previously countercultural ideals regarding female empowerment, with the result that "what was once radical is now mainstream" (23). Both Naomi Wolf and Camille Paglia noted the rapid changes in attitudes to sex and gender that occurred between 1991 and 1994, with the latter attributing them, with characteristic lack of humility, largely to her own writings (Wolf, *Fire* xiv; Paglia, *Vamps* xiv–xv). A 1994 *Esquire* article described this new trend of feminist sex positivity as "do-me feminism": References to "babe feminism" and even "bimbo feminism" soon followed (Henry 111). That the term first appeared in a men's magazine is significant: Just as the 1980s antipornography campaigns led to surprising alliances between radical feminists and evangelical conservatives, so the "sex-positive" politics of the mid-1990s drew support both from third-wave "power feminists" and from purveyors of traditionally sexist men's media, even if they had rather different motives for encouraging women to feel empowered by taking their clothes off. Thus the years in which the "bad girl" trend peaked were also marked by the proliferation of men's magazines such as *Loaded* (1994), *FHM* (debuted in 1985, went monthly in 1994), *Maxim* (debuted in 1995), *Stuff* (1996), and *Front* (1998), all of which professed to celebrate female sexual power and agency while advancing an aggressively sanitized, airbrushed, pornified, and Eurocentric model of female beauty.

The same shift toward celebrating beauty and sex appeal as forms of female empowerment can be seen in many other areas of mid-1990s culture (Munford 274). These were the years which saw the popularization of the term "supermodel" by *Vogue* magazine, with models such as Cindy Crawford and Naomi Campbell achieving levels of fame previously reserved for movie stars. Susan Faludi and Wolf had both seen the fashion industry as a stronghold of sexism, but mid-1990s media increasingly depicted supermodels as icons of female power instead (Hopkins 75–84). (In this context, it is worth noting that one of Rob Liefeld's "bad girl" heroines was a model-turned-superheroine named "Vogue," and that *Wizard* magazine regularly suggested that supermodels would be the ideal people to play "bad girl" characters in film adaptations of comic books [*Wizard* no. 42, 42; *Wizard* no. 48, 88].) In early 1990s popular music, female-fronted bands such as Bikini Kill, Curve, Tori Amos, Jack Off Jill, and Garbage were heavily associated with socially oppositional subcultures such as Riot Grrrl, punk, and Goth, with female performers weaponizing sexual aggression as a form of cultural critique: Curve's 1991 single "Coast Is Clear" is typical of the period, with a snarling female vocalist articulating a history of mental illness and incestuous sexual abuse. However, 1994 saw the formation of the Spice Girls, whose breakout success in 1996 provided a model for the flood of subsequent girl bands who sanitized and popularized the formerly radical Riot Grrrl aesthetic (Hopkins 29–31).

It was the Spice Girls who popularized the phrase "girl power." Originating as a Riot Grrrl slogan, it soon became an affirmation of female empowerment that was depicted as compatible with sexualized, "girlie" femininity, rather than being opposed to it: Geri Halliwell's progress from nude model to Spice Girl superstar was particularly emblematic in this regard (Munford 269; Hopkins 19, 29–31, 36). 1994 saw Candace Bushnell begin her "Sex and the City" column for *The New York Observer*, while in 1995 Helen Fielding began her "Bridget Jones's Diary" column in *The Independent*: In 1996, both were developed into books, laying the foundations for the new and popular genre of "chick lit." "Girl power," men's magazines, supermodels, "chick lit," and *Sex and the City* could all be interpreted as "postfeminist" insofar as they depicted traditional forms of femininity and sex appeal not as incompatible with the pursuit of traditionally "masculine" forms of agency (money, power, status) but as tools that women might use to achieve them, and/or as enjoyable lifestyle choices that women might freely choose to adopt for their own pleasure without hampering their other opportunities (Snyder 189–190; Hopkins 2, 93). As Astrid Henry noted, "A new breed of sexual woman is being celebrated in our culture" (109). Its ethos was exemplified by the lesbian activist Linda Semple, who in 1992 complained about the judgmental attitudes of older lesbians: "They tell me I'm objectifying myself. They need to get over it. Fuck em" (Henry 124).

The "bad girl" genre thus arose within a very specific cultural-historical microclimate. Its target market was middle-class male comic collectors, who were rich with disposable income from the economic boom that began in 1994. This was an audience hungry for sexualized media, but not yet able to sate its lusts on internet pornography, as in 1994 only the unusually computer literate could source pornographic images from the bulletin boards that dominated the internet before the rise of the World Wide Web. Comics, of course, primarily dealt in action-adventure storytelling, but the mainstreaming of sex-positive feminist and postfeminist ideology in 1994–1996 offered a model for how pornographic levels of sexualization might be depicted as reinforcing, rather than detracting from, a character's action heroine credentials. Once it became clear that there was a market for such comics, the initial trickle rapidly broadened to a flood: In 1991, publishing a "bad girl" comic was still recognizably a countercultural gesture, but by 1995 it simply demonstrated a desire to follow the money. "Every month there seems to be a new crop of Bad Girl comic books featuring characters I've never heard of before," the *Vampirella* editor Meloney Chadwick remarked, "put out by companies I've never heard of before, produced by creators I've never heard of before" (*Wizard* no. 53, 134).

As a result, the genre came to be associated less with the world of alternative black-and-white indie comics and more with the visually lavish, full-color books produced by Image and its imitators. This transition to mass-market commercialism coincided with a shift in the genre's politics, as such books had higher overheads and could ill afford to adopt creative stances that might alienate major fractions of the comics-buying audience. One after another, mid-1990s "bad girl" heroines shifted from embittered feminist avengers to fun-loving, sex-positive adventuresses. They adopted less socially oppositional stances, often cooperating with the police or the security services. Their relationships with sex and sex work were radically simplified: Rather than seeing sex or prostitution as cultural battlegrounds, fraught with power imbalances and gendered violence, they were increasingly depicted as just good, bouncy fun for everyone involved. (In this they joined a broader media tendency to romanticize sex work following the surprise success of the 1990 rom-com *Pretty Woman* [Negra 99–100].) Their treatment of gender tended toward blunt assertions of equality: Women can do everything men can do, so if they end up as victims, it's probably their own fault. Their art styles became more exaggerated: Breasts became bigger, legs became longer, costumes became skimpier. Female readers abandoned them. Male readers bought them in heaps.

The "bad girl" trend was driven by demand from below, and seems to have initially been met with a certain nervousness by the comics industry. Early coverage in *Wizard* expressed alarm at the way that "astronomical anatomical attributes" and "scantily clad superheroines bending into all sorts of weird positions" had become "the current trend in comics." "More scantily clad women!" one article lamented. "I can't think of a better way to alienate our female readers than covering these books and sounding like a bunch of sexist slobs in the process!" (*Wizard* no. 36, 139). "No Psychology class can satisfactorily generalize the rationale behind the throngs of bad girl watchers," declared another. "The fascination with beautiful, but almost pathologically violent women . . . borders on a contagious neurotic complex" (*Wizard* no. 39, 135). By January 1995, however, rising sales led the magazine to identify "bad girls" as the "trend of the year" for 1994 (*Wizard* no. 41, 218–219). Thereafter *Wizard* became one of the main boosters of the fad, continuously featuring them in its monthly "Top Ten Comics" and "Top Ten Heroes" columns, and offering inflated estimates of the value of "bad girl" back issues such as *Shi* issue 1 and *Lady Death* issue 1. By 1996 it is hard to overstate just how omnipresent the pornographic "bad girl" aesthetic had become in *Wizard*, with images of huge-breasted, improbably posed women in skintight clothing appearing every few pages, giving the magazine an air of continuous, leering sexual aggression. When one female reader wrote in to ask why there weren't more women in comics (while adding, apologetically, "please don't take me as a feminist, as I'd really hate that"), her letter was printed immediately under a comics ad depicting an apparently nude golden-skinned woman twisting in midair to simultaneously display her breasts, thighs, and buttocks—an image which answered the letter writer's question rather better than the actual editor did (*Wizard* no. 55, 9).

Exactly how popular these comics were is difficult to gauge, because in July 1995 Marvel withdrew from Diamond distribution, meaning that Marvel comics were no longer included on Diamond's sales rankings. As a result, sales ranks from July 1995 to August 1996 are seriously distorted by the absence of Marvel titles, and comparing them with those appearing before or after is not comparing like with like. Even this imperfect data, however, makes clear that some of these titles were very successful indeed—most obviously *Lady Death*, which in 1995 routinely outsold everything except *Spawn*, *X-Men*, and *Gen13*, but also *Shi*, *Elektra*, *Catwoman*, *Angela*, *Vampirella*, *Glory*, *Witchblade*, and *Avengelyne*, all of which usually ranked in Diamond's top fifty. Exact sales figures are unavailable, but based on their positions in the sales ranks and the estimated market shares attributed to their publishers by Comichron, it seems plausible that at its height the "bad girl" genre may have accounted for as much as 10 percent of the entire American comics industry, as well as having major secondary consequences for how women were depicted in market-leading titles such as *X-Men* and *Gen13* (Comichron).

An insight into the genre's shifting status can be gained by comparing two multifranchise crossover comics published a year apart: *Shi/Cyblade* (1995) and *Gen13* issue 13 (1996). Both shared a similar premise: Comics are being destroyed by rampant consumerism, and quirky indie characters must band together to protect what is most valuable in the medium. In *Shi/Cyblade*, the threat came from the monopolistic power of Marvel Comics, depicted as a monster which uses creativity only "as grist for my ever-ravenous mill" (*Shi/Cyblade*). Ranged against it are a gathering of creator-owned indie comics heroes including Cerebus ("the one who showed us the way"), Bone, and the Tick, but also a large number of "bad girl" characters such as Shi, Cyblade, Glory, and Kabuki. (Katchoo from *Strangers in Paradise*, who appears here as a gun-wielding warrior, could plausibly be placed on either list.) A year later, in *Gen13*, the diagnosis had changed: What now threatened comics was "the Frenzy Beast," which embodied the blind pursuit of whichever comics are asserted to be the most valuable or collectible, regardless of their actual contents. The Beast was originally created by "the Wizard" (i.e., *Wizard* magazine), but now holds its creator captive: "Bad girl" heroines like Witchblade and Lady Death, who by 1996 had come to be seen as embodying the worst kind of trend- and gimmick-driven comics publishing, are depicted as minions of the Beast, while "real" indie heroes like Hellboy, Katchoo, Francine, and the Maxx stand against it. (As Katchoo asserts, facing off against a cavalcade of huge-breasted "Bad Girls," "a girl doesn't have to have *double-D* cups to make a difference" [*Gen13* vol. 2, no. 13C].) 1995 thus marks the last moment when "bad girl" indie comics could still semi-plausibly claim to be plucky outsiders. By 1996 they had, very clearly, become representatives of the industry's most dominant trends.

This was the era in which "bad girl" heroines were at their most culturally visible, and consequently at their most influential, contributing to a broader cultural shift away from the idea that action heroes had to be male. Eric Hammond, then–vice president of product development for Sega in America, cited "the 'bad' girl popular in comic books" as an inspiration for the character of Sarah Bryant in the popular *Virtua Fighter* games franchise (1993–present): *Virtua Fighter*, in turn, was cited by Toby Gard as a key influence on his most famous creation, Lara Croft, the star of the *Tomb Raider* series ("Sarah Bryant"; Gibbon). Cross-pollination between comics and video games in these years was intense: Popular mid-1990s video game heroines like Kitana (*Mortal Kombat*, 1993), Nina Williams (*Tekken*, 1994), and Sofia (*Toshinden*, 1995) had character designs inspired by "bad girl" comics, and both *Mortal Kombat* and *Tomb Raider* received 1990s comic book adaptations replete with "bad girl" art. The popularity of such characters subsequently gave rise to a wave of films based on comic book and video game heroines, including *Tomb Raider* (2001), *Resident*

Evil (2002), *Catwoman* (2004), and *Elektra* (2005). The *Catwoman* film was even advertised in comic books with the tagline, "Do you like bad girls?" (*Black Widow* vol. 3, no. 5). So strong did the link between comic books and action heroines become that when the female-led action movie *Ultraviolet* appeared in 2006, it opened with a montage that implied it had been adapted from a comic book, even though it was in fact an original production.

In this chapter, I shall survey some of the key titles to emerge from this period. Starting with the crucial transitional work *Sachs and Violens* (1993–1994), I shall go on to discuss Mike Deodato's infamous run on *Wonder Woman* (1994–1995) before returning to the titles discussed in chapters 1 and 2 to explore how they were rewritten to fit the changing demands of the market. Finally, I shall discuss Christina Z's run on *Witchblade*, one of the most successful "bad girl" titles and one of the very few to survive the genre's crash. Like the comics discussed in chapter 2, *Witchblade* initially dealt very directly with the relationships among gender, violence, beauty, and desire, and a comparison of its approach to theirs serves to demonstrate both the appeal and the limitations of the genre's postfeminist politics during its era of greatest commercial success.

"Violence Begets Sex": *Sachs and Violens*

Sachs and Violens was a four-issue miniseries released by Marvel in 1993–1994 and published, like *Elektra: Assassin*, under their non-code-approved "Epic" imprint. It was written by Peter David and drawn by George Pérez, who at the time was best known for his widely acclaimed reboot of *Wonder Woman*. In many respects it picked up where Mindy Newell's *Catwoman* had left off, and its heroine, J. J. Sachs, was clearly a rewrite of Newell's Selina: Both were female martial artists who worked in the sex industry, wore black leather, fought with whips, targeted men who preyed on women, and had sisters who were nuns. When Sachs buys her "Dominatrix X-10" bullwhip ("the knout with clout!!"), the storekeeper even mentions that sales of such whips had been boosted by *Batman Returns*, an acknowledgment of the role played by Catwoman in popularizing the figure of the female vigilante as avenging dominatrix (*Sachs and Violens* no. 2). Its plot, however, was much more lurid: Rather than the everyday cruelties of prostitution and police brutality, it deals with an organization of psychopathic child abductors and snuff film producers. Pitted against them are not just one vigilante hero but two: the whip-wielding martial artist J. J. Sachs, and the Vietnam veteran Ernie "Violens" Schultz.

The level of sexualized violence featured in *Sachs and Violens* was unusual by the standards of 1993, and David recalled being repeatedly asked by "troubled" interviewers: "Aren't you concerned that you're going to get into trouble over this?" He, and they, were concerned about two possible avenues of attack: one from the religious right ("some protector of public morals"), and one from anti-pornography feminists ("women have been complaining about violence against women in the media for some time now"). David's response was firstly to invoke free speech—issue 1 of the comic was literally dedicated to the First Amendment—and secondly to assert that he depicted the normalization of violence against women precisely so that he could critique it. As he wrote, "What I was endeavoring to put across was the way in which society has desensitized people to cruelty and depravity" (*Sachs and Violens* no. 2).

In issue 3 David printed a supportive letter from Avedon Carol, a member of Feminists Against Censorship and the co-editor of *Bad Girls and Dirty Pictures: The Challenge to Reclaim Feminism* (1993). In that book, Carol noted that feminist attitudes toward sex work and pornography had started to shift since the foundation of Feminists Against Censorship in 1989:

> Work on this book began at a time when discussion of the issues addressed herein seemed to be entirely one-sided, and all women were being represented as advocating even more strict censorship of pornography than we have now. . . . In the intervening period, things do seem to have changed somewhat. The feminist anticensorship arguments have begun to filter into the media, and many women's groups have re-evaluated their positions on these issues. (Assiter and Carol vii)

This reevaluation is clearly visible in much feminist writing of the period. Increasingly uncomfortable with what Kobena Mercer described as the "unhappy alliance" between antipornography feminists and Reaganite conservatives, many third-wave feminists began to view categorical denunciations of pornography as unhelpful: Thus Angela Bocage, writing her 1991 "feminist's case for pornography" in *The Comics Journal*, argued that "feminists who would disavow porn would deny themselves, and me, both a significant freedom and a potential educational device" (Mercer 93; Assiter and Carol 9–16; Snyder 189–190; Bocage 4). The phrase "bad girl" took on talismanic significance in these debates: Drawing on Lisa Orlando's 1982 article "Bad Girls and 'Good' Politics," in which she explained how important pornography had been to her in providing her with alternative models of female sexuality, writers such as Linda Williams and Loretta Loach began describing women who used pornography as "bad girls," and lesbian sadomasochism as a form of "'bad girl' sexuality" (Linda Williams 248; Loach 266). The "bad girl," here, is the woman who refuses to abide by conservative sexual norms, just like the protagonist of Madonna's 1992 single "Bad Girl." In fact, Madonna herself was frequently cited as a "bad girl" icon, whose vision of sexual empowerment feminists would do well to emulate: As Hopkins notes, "[She] offered white, middle-class academics an opportunity to play 'bad girl' and feminist at the same time" (6, 11, 46). In 1993, Paglia called Madonna "the future of feminism," praising her ability to demonstrate "the whore's ancient rule over men," while Wolf declared bluntly that "power feminism means learning from Madonna" (Paglia, *Sex* 4–5, 11; Wolf, *Fire* 108). As Lynne Segal lamented,

"While Madonna expresses [women's] desire, and rocks the masses, feminists are widely seen as anti-sex" (79). Henry notes that many third-wave feminists explicitly sought to depict themselves as "feminism's 'bad girls,'" and cites Merri Lisa Johnson, who summarized her desire for "a young feminism, a sexy feminism" by writing: "I wanted feminism to be *bad like me*" (Henry 96–97).

With this shift came a change in attitudes toward sex work and pornography. "Most sex workers are not looking for feminist salvation," Segal wrote in 1992, while Christobel Mackenzie mocked the idea that "being pushed around and demoralized for 40 hours a week is so much better than posing for pornography for a few hours and making a lot more money at it," and Anne McClintock argued that unionizing pornographers was more important than suppressing them (Segal 9; Mackenzie 148; McClintock 131). It also entailed a changing view of sadomasochistic sexualities. In 1989, Susan Cole argued, like Andrea Dworkin before her, that sadomasochism was inherently abusive even if all participants consented: "This is not consent, it is the internalized expression of sexual subordination" (124). Dworkin's *Mercy* included a spiteful parody of a lesbian sadomasochist, whom Dworkin depicted as a kind of moral idiot: "I like gagging her, I like dripping hot wax on her breasts. It is not the same as when a man does it. She and I are equals, the same. There is no moral atrocity or political big deal" (*Mercy* 340–341). By 1992, however, Loach noted that "what appears to be particularly disturbing to some feminists is that female sexuality, at least for some women, has now become much more associated with aggressive, tough, sometimes even violent behavior; it is the unacceptable face of female power" (273). Subsequent works such as the 1995 documentary *Bloodsisters* and the lesbian BDSM writings of Pat Califa (who in 1994 wrote, "I'd like to see more women become more phallic") insisted that there was no reason why sadomasochistic sexualities could not be compatible with feminist ideology (Henry 135; Assiter and Carol 15–16).

"Bad girl" comics like *Sachs and Violens* were one pop culture expression of this new "face of female power." Within the comics industry, the sex-positive stance adopted by David was still an outlier in 1993—thus all those "troubled" interviewers who worried that the comic had gone too far. Over the following years it became much more mainstream, and by 1996 no one was surprised by comic publishers filling their books with what Carol called "bad girls and dirty pictures," all while loudly claiming to support female empowerment. While a minor work in the overall history of comics, *Sachs and Violens* is thus of some value in demonstrating which way the cultural wind was blowing in 1993–1994.

Sachs and Violens is about the relationship between sex and violence, but it is also about the relationship between old and new traditions of action media. The Vietnam veteran Ernie "Violens" Schultz stands for the old tradition, in which the action hero is male, and emerges from a masculine world of war and violence: He fights with guns, and evokes older American media in which Vietnam veterans acted as vigilantes and action heroes, such as *Rambo, Missing in Action,* and *The Punisher*. By 1993, the Vietnam War was receding into history, and Schultz is aging, his hair graying: One villain describes him as "an overage Rambo," and Schultz himself laments that men like him have become a cliché (*Sachs and Violens* nos. 3–4). His partner, J. J. Sachs, stands for the new tradition, in which the action hero is young, hypersexualized, and female. She eschews guns for martial arts, as befits the Hong Kong–inflected action media of the 1990s, and whereas Schultz regards combat as a site of horror in which his Vietnam-era traumas are endlessly recapitulated, Sachs experiences it as erotic instead (*Sachs and Violens* nos. 3–4). In the comic they work together (and sleep together), but Schultz's time is clearly coming to an end. The genre's future, as the "bad girl" craze made clear, belonged to women like Sachs.

When they're not killing criminals, Sachs works as a glamor model, and Schultz is her photographer. Schultz thus enacts the traditional role of the action hero as the male *subject* of the gaze, wielding the phallic power of guns and cameras to control whatever he points at, whereas Sachs represents the new possibility that the action hero might instead be the female *object* of the gaze, someone whom the assumed male reader looks at rather than identifies with. Whereas Newell's Catwoman had raged against the exploitative cruelty of the sex industry, Sachs embraces her own objectification: In line with the arguments of writers like Carol and Loach, the comic insists that pornography is not bad in and of itself, and only *becomes* bad to the extent that it crosses moral lines through its use of underage participants and nonconsensual violence. Whereas Dworkin had seen pornography as inherently violent, *Sachs and Violens* maintains that sex and violence can and should be kept separate, in life and pornography alike: When they are mingled, it falls to Sachs and Violens to force them apart again. They thus act as ethical pornographers, shutting down those whose traffic in inherently nonconsensual material—snuff, pedophilia—brings their trade into disrepute.

Sachs's carefree attitude toward sex work (and sex) parallels her similarly carefree attitude toward violence. Held up at gunpoint by a man intent on robbery or rape, she casually disables him with her martial arts skills: As she tells Schultz, "It was more serious for *him* than it was for *me*. I kinda beat the *shit* out of him." Schultz is appalled—"Didn't you sign a formal *complaint* against him?"—but Sachs brushes him off: "He attacked me, I *clobbered* him. Aside from a busted nail, what's to *complain*?" (*Sachs and Violens* no. 1) The contrast with Newell's *Catwoman* here is telling: Sachs refuses to involve the police, not because she knows they are prejudiced against people like her but simply because she can't be bothered. David depicted law enforcement even more unsympathetically than Newell did, but Newell's political point that female sex workers cannot rely on police protection here gives way to an individualist fantasy that female sex workers who are tough enough don't *need* the police, because they're perfectly capable of taking care of themselves. A similar fantasy appeared in Miller's contemporaneous *Sin City*, where the sex industry is controlled and protected not by male pimps but by gun-wielding prostitutes in fetish gear.

Sachs and Violens thus marks the point at which the feminist avenger "bad girl" prototype of 1989–1993—still recognizably a version of Dworkin's "girls named courage who are ready to kill"—tips over into the postfeminist "bad girl" action heroine of 1994–1996, displacing the traditional male action hero in the process. Whereas Newell, Peter Milligan, Barr, and Eric Luke had explored the damaging ways in which sexual objectification is forced on women by society, Sachs happily embraces her role as a sex object. Comics like *Ghost* and *Mantra* had struggled (often unsuccessfully) to reconcile the feminist politics of their heroines with the hypersexualized costumes required to appeal to their target audiences, but Sachs, like Madonna, is depicted as a woman whose provocative dress is the *result* of her belief in female empowerment, not a betrayal of it. Her capabilities in sex and combat are depicted as going hand in hand, and there is no danger of a destructive rift opening up between her objectified image and her sense of self because, as her name implies, her sexual identity is the only identity she has.

There is a deep tension at the heart of *Sachs and Violens*. On one hand it insists that sex and violence should be opposites, and that those who combine the two should be (violently) punished: The proper attitude is shown by Schultz, the ethical pornographer, who keeps his war photos locked away from his pornographic work. He has retreated to a career of "*girlie* shots" precisely because he wants to "forget what happened over there," seeing his glamor photoshoots with Sachs as an antidote to the carnage he chronicled (and perpetrated) in Vietnam (*Sachs and Violens* no. 1). America's collective fascination with violence is depicted as a social sickness, in which a jaded audience has become bored with mere sex and now seeks a stronger thrill: "Madonna *wore out* the interest in sex pictures. But war? *Violence?* That's *happening!* That's *now!*" (*Sachs and Violens* no. 1). At the same time, however, the comic takes an obvious delight in sexualized depictions of Sachs inflicting violence on wrongdoers—a delight that Sachs herself clearly shares. Unlike Schultz, whose wartime experiences have left him tormented by nightmares, Sachs responds to violence with arousal, and while Schultz is initially disturbed by the fact that she finds it erotic when they kill people, his resistance soon crumbles when faced with her sexual invitations. Stripping off his clothes, he remarks, "*geez*, what am I . . . *nuts?!*" implying that the truly crazy thing to do would be to refuse such sexual opportunities (*Sachs and Violens* no. 3).

In the first issue, David explained that the series was intended to explore the relationship between sex and violence: It was "a series that attempts to draw a connection between the two, while at the same time exploring the fundamental hypocrisy in a society that, in casual parlance, has joined an act that ultimately leads to life with an act that ultimately leads to death" (*Sachs and Violens* no. 1).

It is this "hypocrisy" that Sachs and Schultz set out to combat, and yet, as David notes, "Violence begets sex": They do what they do because "they get an erotic charge from risking their lives" (*Sachs and Violens* no. 1). The distinction that the comic seeks to draw is between the "desensitized" sexual violence of the villains, for whom the murder of women and children is merely so much footage for their latest movie, and the arousal that Sachs feels after meting out righteous violence, which is depicted as natural and good: Experiencing it makes her feel that she's "thinking clearly for the *first time*" (*Sachs and Violens* nos. 2–3). The orgasmic violence of the "bad girl" vigilante is thus depicted not as equivalent to the misogynistic violence of her enemies but as its opposite and its cure, transforming both sex and violence into forces that empower women rather than debase them.

Unsurprisingly, not all the comic's readers were persuaded. "Aren't you a party to the desensitization just by your depictions of violence?" one asked. "Your comments in #1 suggest that you feel justified in your depiction of sado-masochistic torture because there are S&M magazines that show worse. I would have thought you could come up with a better argument" (*Sachs and Violens* no. 4). David's reply—"Those magazines present women in humiliating positions as entertainment, with no thought to how degrading it is. Whereas S&V portrays Wendy as a victim, and J.J. as angry and striking back on her behalf"—is somewhat naive: Both Wendy's death and J. J.'s revenge are presented by the comic in a highly sexualized fashion, and nothing prevents readers from using either or both as pornography if they wished to do so. Even though the comic presents the snuff filmmakers as villains, there are uncomfortable parallels between their work and that of David and Pérez: Both frame and storyboard scenes of sex, death, and violence in ways that make them enjoyable for their target audiences. The art makes abundantly clear how similar the cartoonist's frame is to

FIGURE 14 The cartoonist's frames replicate the pornographer's camera, while the porn director's voice echoes the comic writer's script, in *Sachs and Violens* issue 2 (1994). Written by Peter David, art by George Pérez, colors by John Stracuzzi, lettering by John Workman.

the pornographer's camera—indeed, there are some scenes in which Pérez's frames *are* the view through the pornographer's camera—and the snuff film director's instructions to his performers sound very much like the script that David must have given Pérez for the comic itself.

Whatever else it might have been, *Sachs and Violens* was not a cynical work. It came out *before* the cresting of the bad girl wave, at a moment when writing comic books full of sex and violence still looked like a creative risk rather than a cash grab. Acknowledging that it was not the kind of title readers expected from Pérez and himself, David wrote: "I've learned that when you restrict your creative activities to that which people expect, then they will stop expecting anything from you . . . or even caring about what you might do. Moreover, as a creator, one has an obligation to one's audience to try new and different things. To stretch. To grow" (*Sachs and Violens* no. 2).

Sachs and Violens thus needs to be understood in the context of the broader move in American comics away from mainstream superheroics and toward creator-owned titles dealing with adult subject matter "for mature readers"—the same move that gave rise to DC's Vertigo imprint and its imitators. Like them, *Sachs and Violens* was clearly animated by frustration with the convention that comic-book violence had to be kept completely walled off from sexuality, as though there was no possible erotic component to stories about gorgeous men and women doling out savage beatings while dressed in skintight costumes. But the *way* in which it explores these themes—by telling the story of a hypersexualized female martial artist who works as a porn model and fights in lingerie, depicted via male-gaze visuals very similar to those created by the evil pornographers she supposedly fights against—was very much in line with the early 1990s zeitgeist, which following the publication of Madonna's *Sex* was eager to equate female self-objectification with self-empowerment.

"You Were Just Entertainment": *Wonder Woman*

When George Pérez began work on *Sachs and Violens* he had just finished his hugely influential run on *Wonder Woman*, which lasted from 1987 to 1992. Pérez had reinvented its heroine, Diana, guided by his view that "what made Wonder Woman unique was both her feminism and the Amazon legends with their roots in Greek mythology": In his first issue he even personally thanked Gloria Steinem "for a feminist perspective that helped direct the series" (*Wonder Woman* vol. 2, no. 1; Cocca, *Superwomen* 37). In his account, the Amazons were created from the souls of women whose lives were "cut short by man's fear and ignorance," reborn as "a sacred sisterhood" to "lead humanity in the ways of *virtue*" (*Wonder Woman* vol. 2, no. 1). The editor Karen Berger hoped that the series "might bridge the gap between male and female readers" by means of an approach "that transcends the gap between the sexes" (*Wonder Woman* vol. 2, no. 2). By 1992 she had come to see the series as a job well done, in which Pérez had successfully depicted Wonder Woman as an "ambassador to Patriarch's world" who had "spread the message of the Amazonian ideals across the world—the message of peace, equality, humanity, and trust" (*Wonder Woman* vol. 2, no. 63).

After Pérez departed, the task of writing *Wonder Woman* passed to Bill Messner-Loebs, who wrote it until 1995. Changes began almost at once: Bondage imagery appeared with increasing frequency, with his fifth issue literally entitled "Wonder Woman in Chains!," and Diana was rewritten as a more warlike character, who maintained that "there is no greater pleasure than righteous battle." The "Amazonian ideals" praised by Pérez and Berger were depicted as weaknesses, ill suited to the violence of the modern world: As the editor explained, "Diana's viewpoint may be changing with the harsh realities she will be coming in contact with. Her Amazon ideals will not always be up to the task" (*Wonder Woman* vol. 2, nos. 66–67). She was seen as requiring updating to match the 1990s paradigm of the tough yet feminine action heroine—"Our current storyline calls for a Sigourney Weaver (with hair, please) or Linda Hamilton type"—leading some readers to worry she was being transformed into "a female Rambo," or that "Diana as the champion of victims has been cast aside in favor of gratuitous titillation" (*Wonder Woman* vol. 2, no. 67, 69, 71). Some feminist elements remained: Messner-Loebs's first major story depicted Diana leading a female rebellion against a misogynistic space empire "poisoned by its fear and loathing of the female," and when its emperor—biologically female, but trained to regard themselves as male—asks her "What does it feel like to be a woman?" she replies simply, "Good. It feels . . . good" (*Wonder Woman* vol. 2, no. 70) But the feminist cause was now clearly seen as one to be advanced through violence, preferably while wearing high-heeled boots. As one reader wrote incredulously: "I never thought I'd see [Diana] in black leather and heels" (*Wonder Woman* vol. 2, no. 73).

Penciling duties on *Wonder Woman* changed regularly, leading to frequent changes of visual style. It was finally assigned to the Brazilian artist Mike Deodato, who had already drawn action heroines for the martial arts comic *Samuree*, and in 1994–1995 Deodato worked with Messner-Loebs on a run that has since become infamous for definitively tipping *Wonder Woman* into "bad girl" territory (Cocca, *Superwomen* 39; Madrid 72–73). It became known among Messner-Loebs's friends as "porn Wonder Woman" because of the blatancy with which it traded on sex appeal: As Deodato remarked, "Every time the bikini was smaller, the sales got higher" (Cocca, "Negotiating" 99). Sales figures bear him out: *Wonder Woman* rose approximately 150 places in Diamond's monthly sales ranks over the course of Deodato's run (Comichron). *Wonder Woman* had not, historically, been a commercially successful title, and *Wizard* magazine observed its rapid rise with disbelief: "The current bad girl trend . . . is now making Wonder Woman popular. How the hell did *that* happen?" (*Wizard* no. 42, 117). Messner-Loebs and Deodato's comics told the story of how Diana is forced to compete for the title of "Wonder Woman" with a new challenger, Artemis, who

FIGURE 15 "Bad girl" heroine Artemis rescues "good girl" heroine Diana, who is held back by "the weight of [her] virtue," in *Wonder Woman* 2, no. 92 (1994). Written by Bill Messner-Loebs, drawn by Mike Deodato, colors by Trish Mulvihill, lettering by John Costanza. Nearly naked women with impossibly long legs and hair swiftly became Deodato's stylistic trademark.

was essentially the same character reimagined as a "bad girl" heroine: more violent, more aggressive, and more scantily dressed. In 1996, Artemis went on to star in her own series, in which she contrived to kill even more while wearing even less than she had during her time in *Wonder Woman*.

Messner-Loebs and Deodato's "porn Wonder Woman" entailed yet another reboot for the character, in which Diana was reset to her previous "good girl" status to heighten the contrast between her and Artemis. Its plot revolves around Hippolyta, Diana's mother and queen of the Amazons, who must decide which woman to send as her ambassador to "man's world": Diana, the liberal pacifist, or Artemis, the violent activist. As the ruler of an all-female (and implicitly all-lesbian) society, Hippolyta stands for old-style lesbian separatist radical feminism, which deals with the tensions between men and women by simply withdrawing from "Patriarch's world" entirely. Diana articulates a liberal reformist feminism, maintaining that equality can be achieved peacefully, through education, whereas Artemis takes a more uncompromising stance, insisting on the need for active resistance. The ways in which these different strands of feminist thought are (mis)represented by the comic provide important insights into their relationship with superhero comics at the start of the "bad girl" era, especially given Wonder Woman's long-standing status as a feminist icon and as the flagship female character for the entire American comic book industry.

As Henry has pointed out, the relationship between second- and third-wave feminism was frequently articulated in terms of an often-fractious relationship between mothers and daughters (42). This idea of feminism as a mother-daughter conflict was very much in the cultural zeitgeist in 1994, and may well have fed into the plot of Messner-Loebs and Deodato's *Wonder Woman*. In their first issue, Diana returns to her homeland, and Hippolyta asks about her progress: "So tell me . . . How does it go? Doubtless women have been freed from their oppression? Men and women enjoy equal respect and worth? You have founded *huge movements* of women and men to stop *violence*? Children are safe and free from poverty and coercion?" (*Wonder Woman* vol. 2, no. 90). When Diana admits that she has achieved none of these things because she has been working on a personal rather than political level—"I've made many friends, you see"—Hippolyta is "most disappointed": "When you could have been negotiating with statesmen to free whole *nations* of captive women, you have involved yourself in street brawls" (*Wonder Woman* vol. 2, no. 90). ("Negotiating with statesmen to free whole *nations*" was of course exactly what Diana had done back in her black-leather-wearing, proto-bad-girl space rebel days: Implicitly, all her subsequent human-scale adventures had been a waste of time.) Hippolyta's disappointment here is not just directed at Diana as a person but at the whole school of liberal feminism she stands for and its failure to achieve the kind of sweeping social changes demanded by radical feminists in the 1970s. She thus holds a contest to determine whether Artemis should replace Diana as Wonder Woman, and in this contest Artemis proves victorious.

Compelled to yield up her Wonder Woman uniform, Diana chooses a new costume: a black leather outfit strongly reminiscent of the one worn by the prototypical "bad girl" Goth vigilante Razor, who had shot to notoriety the year before. She forsakes Hippolyta's "Amazonian code"—"the code that keeps me from helping *anyone*, including *myself*!"—and becomes, like Artemis, a violent vigilante, using her powers to terrorize men who harm women (*Wonder Woman* vol. 2, nos. 93–94). Artemis, meanwhile, proves dismayingly unsympathetic to the plight of women who don't have superpowers: When a woman explains she endured an abusive marriage because otherwise "my babies would've *starved*," Artemis replies, "better they *starve* than that they have a mother who is a parasite and a *coward*!" (*Wonder Woman* vol. 2, no. 95). Artemis battles three sexist villains named "The Chauvinist," "The Exploiter," and "The Conqueror," respectively, and believes that by defeating them she has solved the world's problems (*Wonder Woman* vol. 2, nos. 95–98). However, Diana soon discovers that they were merely hired actors and mercenaries, paid to lose, telling her, "The media are lazy. Once you 'defeated' an evil *man*, the pressure went away. No one bothered to check to see if the underlying *problems* were still there. Nothing has changed. You were just entertainment" (*Wonder Woman* vol. 2, no. 98). More twists follow when it turns out that Hippolyta's original contest was rigged: She chose Artemis not because she believed in her ideology but because she foresaw the death of "Wonder Woman" at the hands of a demon and didn't want this fate to befall Diana. Horrified, Diana races to help Artemis battle the demon, but Artemis dies defeating it. Her last words, to Diana, are, "*You* are Wonder Woman" (*Wonder Woman* vol. 2, no. 100).

This is an extremely confusing story, but insofar as it has a central theme, it is about the conflict between a second-wave-coded feminist mother and her "bad girl" third-wave feminist daughters. Messner-Loebs and Deodato did not depict any of them as coming out of it very well. Hippolyta's isolationist lesbian separatism is judged the most harshly: The glorious Amazon history that she teaches Diana turns out to be mostly self-serving lies, and by the end she's reduced to a sad, broken figure, dressed in rags and flagellating herself in penance for her sins. Artemis's violent activism is presented as heartless, useless, and tragically easy to misdirect; she spends the series fighting meaningless battles while the world's real problems continue unabated, and dies believing that she has "dishonored" Wonder Woman's uniform through her "ambition" and "arrogance" (*Wonder Woman* vol. 2, no. 100). The story's judgment on Diana's liberal feminism is not quite so devastating, but Hippolyta's initial criticisms remain unanswered: She really *hasn't* achieved systemic change, and there's no indication that she ever will. She embodies a paradox that Henry observed in third-wave feminism: that while "younger women may have a strong sense of their own personal power," they were also "much less idealistic—and hopeful—about the possibility of revolutionary social change" (37). Even after Diana has renounced her pacifistic "Amazonian code," terrorizing individual men, one stalker at a time, seems to be the limit of her ambition.

While Messner-Loebs and Deodato were clearly much less sympathetic to feminism than Pérez had been, it would still not be quite fair to call this an entirely antifeminist story. "The Chauvinist" and "The Exploiter" may be fake villains, but the women's shelters they attack and the sweatshops they protect are symptomatic of real social problems, and the comic's succession of genuinely misogynistic antagonists makes clear why women still need feminist champions. The art, with its ludicrously exaggerated sexual dimorphism, makes the same point visually, often depicting huge, grotesquely muscular men looming like ogres over women. When one woman is foolish enough to tell her partner that she likes her men to be "*all* male"—"no whiny '*feminist men*' for *this* gal"—he immediately turns into a demonic monster devoted to "*iron power*" and offers her as a human sacrifice, which rather implies that feminist men might have been a better bet after all (*Wonder Woman* vol. 2, no. 99). It is even alert to the ease with which the then-fashionable language of kink-positive sexual liberation could act as a cover for genuine abuse. When Diana points out to a female hostage, "Your 'friend and partner' has you *chained* to the floor," she replies, "I like the chain. It's a nineties thing" (*Wonder Woman* vol. 2, no. 96).

However, the feminist idealism that had informed Pérez's run on the title is completely absent. Gone is any hope that the Amazons might offer an example of a better society to "Patriarch's world": Indeed, the portrayal of the Amazons is overwhelmingly negative, with most of them depicted not as exemplars of female empowerment but as sheltered children hiding from the world's complexities. The "virtue" that Pérez had depicted as their strength is depicted by Messner-Loebs as mere weakness: As Artemis tells Diana, "The weight of your *virtue* keeps holding you back" (*Wonder Woman* vol. 2, no. 92). The inspiring history of female independence created for the Amazons by Pérez is rewritten to be a tissue of fabrications, and Hippolyta, their feminist foremother, is presented as a mere fraud. Gone, too, is any suggestion that feminist superheroics can improve the world: Artemis's whole plotline mocks the idea that social change can come from tracking down bad men and beating them up. Collectively, these rewrites speak to a near-total loss of faith in the kind of feminist ideology that had informed Pérez's run. What remains is the "reformed" Diana, Wonder Woman as postfeminist "bad girl" superheroine: tough, streetwise, skeptical of grand ideals and gender essentialism, and fond of "kinky" costumes and black leather jackets. In all this, the comic reflected trends in much contemporaneous feminist writing, which defined itself against its second-wave foremothers, emphasized individualism and sexual self-expression, and was often reluctant to claim any ability to enact dramatic social change (Henry 36–44, 76, 126). As Kristyn Gorton noted, in media depictions of second- and third-wave feminism, "these two interpretations of feminism are set against each other, with an implication that women have either moved to a less politicised and less effective feminism; or, more generally, that there is no more need for feminism" (212).

Unsurprisingly, these developments proved controversial, and numerous female readers objected to the impossible proportions and skimpy costumes of Deodato's female characters (*Wonder Woman* vol. 2, no. 95). (In true postfeminist style, Messner-Loebs replied that the comics depicted men unrealistically as well, so there was really nothing to worry about.) Like Sue Storm, who was going through her own "bad girl" phase at the time, Wonder Woman was too iconic a character for her "bad girl" makeover to last, and when John Byrne took over the comic he reverted all of Messner-Loebs's changes, leaving the role of "bad girl" Wonder Woman to be taken up by a resurrected Artemis in her own title. But the fact that they happened at all testifies to the strength of the postfeminist "bad girl" wave in 1994–1995, and in many other comics such shifts proved much more lasting. It is to these titles that I will now turn.

"The Marketplace of Fevered Desires": Elektra, Catwoman, Vampirella, Mantra, and Ghost Revisited

Vampirella was first, as usual. Relaunched as a full-color title in 1992, it lasted six issues before being relaunched *again* as *Vengeance of Vampirella*, which ran from 1994 to 1996. A second series, *Vampirella Strikes*, ran alongside it from 1995 to 1996. The 1992 series changed Vampirella's appearance: Having previously been depicted as a rather slender woman, she now started to be drawn with huge breasts, which appeared to be constantly on the brink of falling out of her costume. It took only three issues for the inevitable bondage cover, which leeringly promised "Vampirella in chains!'" just five months after "Wonder Woman in chains!" had been published by DC. *Vampirella*'s editor, Meloney Chadwick, joked uncomfortably about losing her "feminist credentials" (*Vampirella: The Dracula War*). The 1994 series also changed Vampirella's politics: Having previously fought to defend democracy against secret influences, she now enlists in a secret government murder squad, in keeping with the fascination with secret agencies that swept popular culture in the wake of *The X-Files* (1993–2002). The three artists responsible for Vampirella's new look were Louis Small Jr., Jim Balent, and Adam Hughes, all of whom went on to have notable careers on subsequent "bad girl" titles.

Following his success drawing "Vampirella in chains," Balent was hired by DC for a new series of *Catwoman*, for which he drew all the art and covers from 1993 to 2000. Gone was the lithe gymnast of Newell's series: Balent's Catwoman was so busty as to make his Vampirella look relatively ordinary, with the art of almost every page organized around her balloon-like breasts. "I wanted to change Catwoman's look," Balent explained: "I wanted her to be a lot more sexy, to be very attractive-looking. Of course, she has a bigger figure than was depicted in the past . . . I'm not going to go back to her old look" (*Wizard* no. 33, 29–30). Not everyone approved of the shift, and Trina Robbins was swift to express her displeasure: "They're pushing it like it's some kind of feminist thing, with this strong woman. But then the art, the way she's draw, is unbelievably insulting. The thing that is stressed the most about her are these huge, improbable breasts. It's terribly insulting to women" (Cited in Voger 141). Like Vampirella, Catwoman was swiftly depoliticized, shifting from feminist vigilante to thrill-seeking cat burglar: In keeping with the postfeminist consumerism of the era, her only motives were pleasure and profit. As she remarked, "I'm not even registered to vote" (*Catwoman* vol. 2, no. 19).

Elektra came next, with a four-issue miniseries in 1995 followed by an ongoing series from 1996 to 1998. The latter was drawn by Deodato, who had just

FIGURE 16 Vampirella meets Catwoman, in a visual car crash of impossible poses, gigantic breasts, physics-defying hair, and thigh-high boots, in *Catwoman/Vampirella* (1997). Written by Chuck Dixon, pencils by Jim Balent, inks by Ray McCarthy, lettering by Kevin Cunningham.

finished his run on *Wonder Woman*, and he drew Elektra in the same hypersexualized style. Her character was greatly softened, made less ambiguous and more straightforwardly heroic—much to the dismay of some fans, who objected that she was meant to be "a withdrawn, brooding, cold, hard killer . . . a ninja assassin, not Pamela Anderson" (*Elektra* no. 7). Like Vampirella and Catwoman, Elektra was depoliticized in ways that seemed to miss the point of her character entirely, neutering the whole idea of Elektra as a commentary on Jung's Electra complex. *Catwoman* rewrote Selina's backstory so that the incident setting her on the path to crime was not the abuse of her (male) pimp but the abuse of her (female) school director (*Catwoman* vol. 2, no. 0). *Elektra* went even further: Her father was rewritten to have not been abusive after all, and sexual sin was displaced from him to her *mother*, whose murder was now depicted as righteous punishment for her wanton adultery (*Elektra: Root of Evil* no. 2). The exploits of both women were thus reframed as forms of self-expression rather than as deeds of vengeance against a patriarchal world that had wronged them. If anyone was now to blame for their excesses, it was other women, rather than men.

Mantra was also relaunched in 1995, with Lukasz passing on the mantle of Mantra to a new and much younger character, Lauren Sherwood.

Previously, Lukasz's tormented relationship with gender had been the main focus of the series: By replacing Lukasz with Lauren, a stereotypically "girlie" girl who was completely comfortable with her own femininity, the relaunch gutted the character's entire concept. Like Catwoman and Elektra, Mantra became a much softer and less confrontational character post-rewrite, and the comics themselves made little pretense of respecting Lauren as a character: She was constantly thrust into humiliating situations, and frequently required rescue from male allies. Finally, *Ghost* was relaunched in 1998. Gone were Elisa's Dworkinian sexual politics: Instead, she, like Vampirella before her, was rewritten as a black ops assassin. The plot turned its now-customary backflip, with Elisa's feminist friends and mentors all abruptly rewritten as treacherous villains. The art style became more pornographic. The emphasis on Elisa as an avenger of sexual exploitation vanished. Every female character suddenly had enormous breasts.

By mid-1990s standards there was nothing unusual about the gender politics of these five comics. I call attention to them here because, as I have discussed, each of them had previously been a self-consciously feminist work, engaged with themes of institutionalized sexism and gendered violence. Characters like Purgatori or Hari Kari were *created* as "bad girl" pinups, and were never meant to be anything else, but to turn Elektra or Catwoman into such a character entailed a deliberate rejection of that character's previous meanings, just as Messner-Loebs and Deodato deliberately rejected the optimistic feminism of Pérez in *Wonder Woman*. Carol lamented in 1994 that "feminism is represented as punitive, shrill, repressive, man-hating and anti-sex," with the result that "young women who believe in women's equality often shy away" (viii). This "shy[ing] away" is pretty much what these comics depict: Their heroines still "believe in women's equality," but reject overt feminism because, like Bridget in *Bridget Jones's Diary* (1996), they like men, they like sex, and they want to have fun. They are depicted as believing, in true postfeminist style, that sex appeal makes them powerful, not vulnerable. When a man suggests to Elektra that she should think about sex work, she replies: "Think about exploiting the dark, sensual fantasies that I inspire in men . . . ? Think about peddling my assets in the marketplace of fevered desires? Sure. I'll think about it" (*Elektra* no. 4).

I do not believe that there was anything particularly deliberate about this pattern of rewritings, or that these authors were even necessarily aware that they were inverting the meanings of the characters whose stories they were writing. 1990s comic book authors wrote under enormous pressure, often having to turn out more than one complete script per month. Under such conditions, few had the luxury of thinking about anything other than what might stave off cancellation for another few issues. Indeed, the pattern is significant precisely *because* it was almost certainly unconscious. One writer after another, grasping for ideas to keep their titles alive, seems to have separately and independently concluded that the safest option was to simultaneously sexualize and depoliticize their female protagonists. Collectively, these decisions thus provide a strong insight into the kind of heroines that the American comics industry believed their audience were interested in reading about in the mid-1990s.

As I have emphasized, in 1994–1995 it was still a novelty for this audience to be interested in reading about women at all, and the mere existence of so many ongoing female-led titles demonstrated that female characters had attained previously unprecedented levels of appeal among the comics-buying public. As *Wizard* noted, with evident surprise, "the hot babes of 1994 do something no female character besides *Wonder Woman* has ever been able to do: drive sales as the lead character of a successful title" (*Wizard* no. 38, 121). The standout title in this regard was *Catwoman*, which ran for ninety-four monthly issues plus numerous spin-offs, annuals, and crossovers: well over one hundred comics in all, in an era where even successful female-led titles were routinely canceled after twenty to thirty issues. *Catwoman* was also often written by women, at a time when this was still very rare in the industry: Jo Duffy wrote issues 1–14, Deborah Pomerantz wrote issues 22–24, and Devin Greyson wrote issues 54–71. Whereas previous female-led titles such as *Vampirella*, *Ms. Mystic*, *Samuree*, and *Silver Sable* had clustered in the lower half of Diamond's "Top 300" monthly sales charts, *Catwoman* generally held a rank of thirty to fifty, well above many long-established male-led titles such as *Hulk*, *Daredevil*, or *Fantastic Four* (Comichron). Its success and longevity indicate that its creators were more or less correct in gauging what their audience wanted from a superheroine comic, making *Catwoman* a much-imitated model for other titles in this period. Indeed, the pattern of changes discussed above was probably motivated largely by the belief that other female-led comics could be made more successful if only they were more like *Catwoman*. When *Wizard* devoted a special issue to women in comics in August 1995, its cover showed Balent's Catwoman leaping ahead of Wonder Woman and Supergirl, apparently having stolen their lasso and cape, respectively.

It is thus significant that *Catwoman* achieved success by leaning explicitly into the "bad girl" trend. "What appeals to me about Catwoman is that she's fun," Duffy explained in a 1994 interview with *Wizard* magazine. "Because she's not the heroine, she's allowed to be sexy and not apologize for it" (*Wizard* no. 33, 26). (Note here the assumption that a traditionally heroic female character *would* have to "apologize" for being "sexy": Duffy still clearly took for granted that unapologetic sex appeal was for "bad girls" only.) "When she's bad, she's very, very bad . . . ," declared the cover of the first issue, and its heroine was a self-described "very bad girl" who complained bitterly about men "trying to make a good girl out of me" (*Catwoman* vol. 2, no. 1, 3, 27). By 1996 readers were describing *Catwoman* as "the flagship in this new wave of 'bad girl' comics" (*Catwoman* vol. 2, no. 30). Teaming up with Huntress and Black Canary in the 1996 *Birds of Prey* miniseries, she gleefully sang her own version of the already iconic song from *Bad Boys* (1995): "Bad girls. Bad girls. What'cha gonna do when dey come for you?" (*Birds of Prey* no. 2).

Given the pornographic quality of Balent's art, it would be easy to assume that *Catwoman*'s success was straightforwardly due to its sex appeal, but in fact it was firmly at the soft-core end of the bad girl market. Many comics of the period offered more explicit sex and nudity: Balent even drew some of them, such as *Purgatori: The Vampire's Myth* (1996). In writing *Catwoman*, Duffy made clear that the one element of Miller's reimagining of Selina she completely rejected was "her past as a prostitute," which was entirely written out of Duffy and Balent's version of the character (*Wizard* no. 33, 26). Despite her appearance, Balent's *Catwoman* was a surprisingly chaste character: Whereas fellow bad girl Elektra engaged in casual sex, telling her lover "*I* don't want anything too *complicated*," Selina never had any sexual or romantic relationships at all, aside from occasional flirtatious kisses with Batman (*Elektra* no. 7). As Jeffrey Brown noted of 1990s action heroines more generally, "While the action heroine may look like the ultimate S/M fantasy figure, her sexual relations within the official narratives are usually depicted as very traditional." This wasn't true of Newell's queer version of *Catwoman*, but was very much true of Balent's (Brown, *Dangerous Curves* 189). Her unattached status is a sign of her freedom—when a prince tries to marry her, in supposed fulfillment of every girl's dream, she tears off her wedding dress and quips, "I'm staying single, baby!"—but it also suggests her immaturity, as someone who is seemingly unready for any kind of real relationship (*Catwoman* vol. 2, no. 18).

As the series continued, Selina appeared to age in reverse, with her demeanor growing more childish, and Balent drawing her with increasingly wide-eyed and childlike facial features. She came to exemplify "girl power," with the emphasis on *girl*: a major change from the furious *woman* that she had been in Newell's and Milligan's works. After fleeing a meeting with yet another man she's attracted to, apparently unready for any kind of physical or emotional intimacy, she even asks her pet cat: "Who am I? Tough as nails *feline fury*—or *little girl lost*?" (*Catwoman* vol. 2, no. 50). Discussing the action heroines of the period, Cristina Stasia has argued that the shift from the "hard-bodied" action heroines of the 1980s to the "girl power" heroines of the 1990s was associated with a depoliticization of female power:

> This new female action hero not only manifests anxieties about changing gender roles, but indicates a lack of anxiety as popular culture fulfils the prophecy of the term postfeminism: convincing women they live in a post-patriarchy. This model resonates with the female action film and the triumph of the fittest body/mind—a body which is almost exclusively white and middle-class and a mind which is free of political concerns. (238)

Selina isn't "white and middle-class"—the comic doesn't dwell on it much, but her background is clearly shown to be working-class and Hispanic—but she certainly has "a mind which is free of political concerns": At one point she even passes up a chance to become mayor of New York in order to continue her carefree life as a cat burglar in Gotham City (*Catwoman* vol. 2, no. 71). The comic's run from 1993 to 2000, during which Selina shifted from "*feline fury*" to "*little girl lost*," thus mirrored the transition Rikke Schubart noticed in the female action cinema of the same period, as "butch" action heroines gave way to what Schubart calls "high trash" characters defined by postfeminist politics, hypersexualized imagery, and moral weightlessness (298–300). It was because of tendencies such as these that, as Rebecca Munford noted in 2004, "many feminist critics have been quick to position 'girl power' and its 'bad girl' icons as a form of popularised post-feminism—a depoliticised product of 'backlash' rhetoric" (267).

I would thus suggest that *Catwoman* owed its success less to its straightforward sex appeal than to its ability to present female power and sexuality to male readers in a maximally unthreatening package. In contrast to her previous portrayal as a dominatrix who made a living by humiliating men for their sexual inadequacies, this version of Selina offered a sexual fantasy without any accompanying political or sexual challenge. In making this shift, *Catwoman* was very much in tune with the popular culture of the period: When Balent began the title in 1993, the pop-culture face of female empowerment was the thirty-five-year-old Madonna, but by the time he left in 2000 the mantle had passed first to the Spice Girls (whose average age in 1996 was twenty-two) and then to the eighteen-year-old Britney Spears, who performed dressed as a schoolgirl and attained fame as a child performer on *The Mickey Mouse Club*. Brown noted that action heroines grew progressively younger as the decade went on, and late 1990s "bad girl" titles like *Danger Girl* (1998–2001) increasingly featured teenage protagonists: As Hopkins wrote in 2003, "The cute but powerful girl-woman is now a dominant theme in mainstream popular culture" (Brown, *Bombshells* 11; Hopkins 1). Even Balent's obsessive focus on Selina's gravity-defying breasts ties in with this. As Wolf observed in *The Beauty Myth*, decrying the rising popularity of breast implants, "the Official Breast . . . best guarantees adolescence. . . . The breast that is high but also large and firm is most likely to belong to a teenager" (247–248).

The comic's male readers were vocal about how much they preferred this new, softer, sexier version of Selina. They wrote in to praise her bigger bust, her longer hair, and the skintight costume Balent designed for her, congratulating the artist on raising her to "megababe status" (*Catwoman* vol. 2, no. 4). Above all they praised the fact that she was "more likeable" than her previous, angrier incarnation: As one wrote, "This Catwoman is not the man-hating former hooker I've grown to dislike" (*Catwoman* vol. 2, no. 9, 17). One letter writer even admitted that he preferred Balent's cartoon women to real ones, writing: "My God—why can't real women rip these emotions out of me?" ("Ask Freud," the editor replied. "I just do comics" [*Catwoman* vol. 2, no. 13]). Female readers initially seem to have been entirely repelled by the comic, leading the editor to lament that "I would print letters from women if only they would write in!" (*Catwoman* vol. 2, no. 8). Over time, however, it does seem to have acquired a female audience, and while some female readers criticized its heroine as "Selina lite," others praised her for being "a strong, sexy, aggressive woman" (*Catwoman* vol. 2, no. 17, 22). Complaints about sexism continued—as one reader aggrieved by "the distortion of [Selina's] feminism" complained, "We don't need another bimbo"—but the editor held to the postfeminist line that strength and femininity were not incompatible, and that making Selina a "megababe" thus did nothing to undermine her status as a heroine (*Catwoman* vol. 2, no. 5, 16).

Easy though it is to mock Balent's *Catwoman*, it is important to recognize that its editor was not wrong to claim that "Catwoman has broken a lot of the stereotypes for female characters in comics" (*Catwoman* vol. 2, no. 18). It blazed a trail that other titles were swift to follow: In 1993 it was still unusual for female-led titles to appear in the top fifty monthly sales ranks, whereas by 1995 this record was routinely being broken, month by month, by bad girl titles such as *Angela*, *Shi*, *Vampirella*, *Glory*, and *Lady Death*. The secret to its success in marketing a comic written by women, about a woman, to an overwhelmingly male market was not *just* its pornographic character designs: After all, *every* "bad girl" heroine had a pornographic character design, and most of them lasted only a few issues. Instead, it lay in the presentation of a "bad girl" heroine whose "badness" did not reflect genuine wickedness, or ideological rebelliousness, or even queerness or sexual aggression, but instead was worn simply as a kind of fashion statement. In her hedonism, her girlishness, her political disengagement, and her playful self-objectification, Balent's run on Catwoman depicted the "bad girl" not as feminist avenger but as carefree postfeminist heroine: A version of empowered femininity that its target audience clearly found more appealing than the "man-hating former hooker" Selina had been depicted as only a few years before. Small wonder, then, that so many of its competitors raced to follow its example.

"Show Me *Your* Power": *Witchblade*

If the "bad girl" trend had a single standard-bearer, it would have to be Sara Pezzini, aka Witchblade. In her history of superheroines, Hope Nicholson picked Witchblade as the 1990s "icon of the decade," noting that "for a long period during the decade, Sara Pezzini was the most prominent female character in comics" (179–180). *Witchblade* was published by Top Cow, an offshoot of Image heavily associated with "bad girl" art: Its ads boasted that they were known for their "fabulous computer coloring," "cutting edge art," and "outrageously sexy women" (*Elektra* no. 3). First published in 1995, *Witchblade* quickly became one of the most popular "bad girl" titles, but unlike most of its competitors it survived the trend's decline: Whereas most "bad girl" comics were canceled in the late 1990s, *Witchblade* continued until 2015, marking it out as not just the most successful but also the most resilient example of the genre. *Witchblade* was also one of the very few "bad girl" franchises to find an audience outside comic shops, as it was adapted into a live-action TV show (2001–2002), an anime series (2006), and a manga version released in *tankōbon* form (2007–2008). Its success is doubly notable because it was one of the very few "bad girl" titles to be primarily written by a woman, Christina Z, who wrote *Witchblade* from 1995 to 2000. Her work on the title was initially characterized by intense engagement with themes of female empowerment: how to get it, how to keep it, and how to stop men from taking it from you.

From the very beginning, *Witchblade* was infamous for its sexually suggestive art and covers. "Yes, she's got big breasts" are literally the first words attributed to Marc Silvestri, who drew the initial art for *Witchblade*, in a 1995 interview on the comic (*Wizard* no. 51, 53). In a 2017 interview, the Top Cow editor Matt Hawkins described the social and economic context which led to the development of *Witchblade*'s art style:

> It was kinda the era, and that was kinda just the way it was, it was what was selling, and—we would take these sort of racier covers to conventions, and they would *always* outsell the non-racy covers. So, and I think, at the time—you've gotta keep in mind that at the time, especially in the '90s, that we were doing comics for . . . men. And boys! I mean that was the target audience, and there was not really even a thought—we never discussed that we're developing comics or writing comics or doing anything for women. . . . Every convention, every time you would do solicitations, because you'd list the book with two covers, and the racy ones would always sell more copies. And so it was sort of this self-fulfilling prophecy of chasing sales. (Napier, "Sexy to Sexual")

As I have emphasized, however, *Witchblade* was hardly alone in following this "self-fulfilling prophecy": Comic shops in 1995–1996 were crowded with "bad girl" titles drawn in similar styles. What allowed *Witchblade* to stand out, and even gather a modest female readership, was Christina Z's writing, which gave Sara a more developed inner life and a much more aggressive inner monologue than was standard for the genre. Wendy Browne, who was active in early *Witchblade* fandom, has written about how important it was to her that "one of the names on the cover belonged to a woman" (Browne). Other female fans spoke of their admiration for Sara as a "proactive heroine," even while complaining that "[her] costume left nothing to the imagination" (Napier, "Glove").

Christina Z's first *Witchblade* story arc told the story of an immortal billionaire and occultist, Kenneth Irons, who is obsessed with the power of a magical artifact, the Witchblade. Irons longs to wield it, but to no avail: The Witchblade accepts only female wielders, and Irons has turned his home into a shrine to the various women who have wielded it throughout history, including Joan of Arc. When the Witchblade accidentally bonds with a new wielder, the

New York detective Sara Pezzini, Irons tries to trick her into giving up its power to him. Initially horrified by her involuntary merger with the Witchblade, Sara almost yields to Irons but ultimately rejects him, defeating him and claiming the Witchblade's power for herself. The second story arc tells the story of Irons's wife, Dannette: Abjectly devoted to her husband, she submitted to magical experimentation to bond herself with the Witchblade on his behalf, only to find it still rejected her. Warped by Irons's experiments into a monster that must kill to live, she founds a modeling agency which funnels vulnerable girls to her so that she can murder them, believing the lives of such women to be of little account. Assigned to investigate these murders, Sara hunts down Dannette and ultimately uses the Witchblade to kill her, too.

These two stories are, very obviously, about female empowerment. Christina Z was very open about the way that she used *Witchblade* to imaginatively fill in the gaps of a female history that men had, historically, had no interest in recording, stating that "there are a lot of truly fantastic women in history who have done fantastic things . . . but a lot of these events in history were never really explained. My idea was that the Witchblade played a part in these historical events, and I wanted to tell those stories" (*Wizard* no. 63, 54). The Witchblade and its wielders stand for an entire suppressed history of female power, agency, and achievement, endlessly stigmatized and denied by the patriarchal authorities, and yet still somehow surviving to fight again in every generation. (Joss Whedon used a similar idea for his all-female lineage of "slayers" in *Buffy the Vampire Slayer*.) As a woman, Sara can tap into this power, while Irons, the patriarch-villain, wants to steal it from her.

The Witchblade eludes Irons because the more he forces women to serve him, the less capable of wielding it they become. Dannette, the submissive wife, cannot wield the Witchblade because she has submerged her own identity within the role demanded of her by her husband (an act symbolized by her magical mutilation), thus alienating herself from the heritage of female power and resistance that the Witchblade symbolizes in the first place. In line with Wolf's *Beauty Myth*, *Witchblade* identifies the fashion and beauty industries as key sites in which women are turned against each other, taught to despise and destroy one another just as Dannette despises and destroys the girls she recruits. By refusing to subordinate herself to Irons, despite the apparent safety that he offers her, Sara learns to channel the power of the Witchblade to destroy both Irons and Dannette, thus establishing herself as a worthy inheritor of its feminist legacy. "Unlike you, I'm not *stupid*," she tells Dannette: "I'm not going to *blame* my *plight* on some man who screwed me over. I refuse to let anyone, *man* or *woman* or *object*, decide *my* fate." Dannette, as she lies dying, replies brokenly: "I'm sorry, Sara. I wish I could have been as strong, as independent, as you" (*Witchblade* no. 14).

This story clearly demonstrates the influence of third-wave feminist ideology, with its emphasis on female *empowerment* as the necessary precondition for female liberation. More unapologetically than any previous "bad girl" title,

Witchblade depicted female power and aggression not as a tragic response to prior trauma—the standard explanation for why earlier "bad girl" characters such as Elektra, Razor, Shi, Kabuki, and Ghost were such violent, angry people—but simply as its heroine's natural and desirable state. Nicholson describes Sara as "the epitome of the 'strong female character' type," and cites Tini Howard's approving description of her: "She's not afraid of anything she can punch. She's pure '90s rock and roll, and that's a beautiful thing" (Nicholson 179–180). The comic invoked both Riot Grrrl iconography and BDSM imagery, both of which, as I have discussed, were associated with third-wave feminist empowerment politics at the time. Issue 24 sees Sara wearing a GRRRL T-shirt, and in a 1999 crossover with *The Darkness* (also written by Christina Z), she was, like Catwoman before her, depicted as a dominatrix, complete with whip.

In her 1993 book *Fire with Fire*, Wolf had enthused over the rising public profile of female boxers, athletes, and soldiers, which she saw as a promising sign of changing attitudes toward female empowerment. She praised women who owned guns and took self-defense classes, and imagined towns dotted with posters declaring "A hundred women in this town are trained in combat" (36, 51–52, 222, 230–232, 291, 329). In this regard, Sara is Wolf's ideal woman: someone who has taken heed of her call for girls to learn "power skills," and who has done so with such success that she can outfight and outshoot any man (272). She could almost have been written as a direct response to Califa's 1994 plea for women to become "more phallic": Even before acquiring the Witchblade she is shown firing her pistol from between her legs, emphasizing her status as phallic woman. A gangster tells her that "not too many chicks can pull the *trigger*"—but Sara can, because, like Wolf's bad girl power feminists, she refuses to accept that femininity (being a "chick") should be incompatible with exercising power and inflicting violence (*Witchblade* no. 1). It is this refusal that qualifies her to wield the Witchblade, which melds with her to become a kind of symbolic phallus, its spikes extending from her body to violently penetrate those who oppose her. As David Greven notes, this bracelet-that-becomes-a-blade combines yonic and phallic imagery, suggesting that Sara's power stems from her success in transcending traditional gender binaries in true third-wave feminist style (128).

The comic's title connects Sara to another key figure in the period's pop-culture feminist iconography: the witch. Long regarded as embodiments of evil, witches had been reappraised by feminist authors of the 1960s and '70s, who reinterpreted their practices as remnants of a peaceful, matriarchal, earth goddess–worshipping religion that had been suppressed by violent, sky god–worshipping Indo-Europeans in distant prehistory: The early modern witch hunts, in this interpretation, were merely the latest phase in a cultural battle between patriarchal oppression and matriarchal resistance that had been going on for thousands of years (Hutton 278–279). Works such as Starhawk's *Spiral Dance* (1979) and Zsuzsanna Budapest's *The Holy Book of Women's Mysteries* (1980) presented neopagan goddess worship as a form of feminist

FIGURE 17 Sara as phallic woman, in *Witchblade* issue 1 (1995). Note the visual mirroring of gun and high heels as emblems of masculine and feminine power, respectively. Written by Christina Z, David Wohl, and Brian Halberlin, pencils by Michael Turner, inks by D-Tron, lettered by Dennis Heisler.

spirituality, allowing modern women to position themselves as the spiritual inheritors of the ancient witches (344–346, 355–356). By the early 1990s, feminist witchcraft and "goddess spirituality" had become widespread, and Riot Grrrl musicians sometimes performed with the word "WITCH" written on their arms (Hopkins 30, 152–153). It was within this context that witches began to appear as sympathetic characters in popular media, with shows such as *Sabrina the Teenage Witch* (1996–2003) and *Buffy the Vampire Slayer* (1997–2003) depicting witches as young, beautiful, and heroic, rather than evil, ugly, and old. In comics this association of neopagan witchcraft with female empowerment and political resistance resulted in multiple titles starring witchy neopagan "bad girl" heroines, including *Dawn* (1995–2005), *Lady Pendragon* (1996–2000), *More Than Mortal* (1997–2000), and ultimately *Tarot* (2000–2023).

Witchblade draws on these ideas, and its secret all-female lineage of Witchblade wielders is clearly another version of the "hidden feminist witch tradition" trope that was popular in much of 1980s and 1990s feminist fantasy media. (As Ronald Hutton points out, the key work here was Marion Zimmer Bradley's 1982 fantasy novel *The Mists of Avalon*, which *Lady Pendragon* later cited as a direct inspiration [355].) The key difference between these works and *Witchblade* is that for once the patriarch-villain, Irons, does not hate or fear this secret female power: Instead, he craves it, and his craving is explicitly framed in terms of masochistic love. The Witchblade is what "he's devoted his *love* to": "This devotion is unrequited," and it maimed him "the one time he tried to *touch* it," but "like most bad relationships, the tortured partner keeps coming back" (*Witchblade* no. 1). Far from assuming, as Dworkin had done a decade earlier, that men would only ever regard female power with dread and loathing, Christina Z starts from the assumption that power makes women attractive, even irresistible: Sara is desired by almost every male character precisely because she is fully *empowered*, physically, sexually, and supernaturally. *Witchblade* thus articulates a classically third-wave view of female strength, aggression, and sex appeal as mutually reinforcing, rather than antagonistic, qualities. For all his power, Irons is a rather pitiable figure, helplessly attracted to the very forms of female independence that his patriarchal authority works to quell. The adoration of submissive, self-loathing women like Dannette can never compete with the longing he feels for the autonomous female power represented by the Witchblade.

However, *Witchblade* communicates very clearly that while empowerment might be compatible with sex appeal, it *isn't* compatible with any kind of traditional femininity, which the comic persistently associates with vulnerability and helplessness. Traditionally feminine women appear in the comic almost exclusively as victims, and Sara is a "strong female character" because, despite being female, she's able to perform normative masculinity better than any of the men around her, endlessly demonstrating that she's tougher, braver, and more aggressive than any of her male colleagues. Like the action heroines described by Schubart, Sara identifies with male culture (her dead father, male TV detectives, her male partners, her male boss), fights in defense of male-dominated institutions (the NYPD), and seems to have no female friends (Schubart 30, 33–36; Greven 149). When Irons attempts to steal the Witchblade's power from Sara, he dresses her in a white gown resembling a wedding dress: It is at this moment, when she appears at her most feminine, that she is also at her weakest, reduced to pleading with men for rescue like a damsel in distress. ("Don't hurt me. Please. I know you care—don't you?") When she reclaims the Witchblade, its spikes shred her dress, her aggressive, armored, and hypersexualized phallic femininity rising out of the ruins of her discarded "good girl" persona. Defeated, Irons grovels at her feet, masochistically begging her to kill him so that he can finally experience the feminine power that has eluded him for so long. ("*Kill me*. Show me the *essence* of the Witchblade. Show me *your* power.") Sara, domme that she is, responds by belittling and denying him, withholding the consummation that he craves. "No," she replies. "You don't deserve it" (*Witchblade* no. 8).

In visual terms, the Witchblade is the purest expression of the "sex equals power" equation that governs all "bad girl" comics. As the Witchblade activates its spines, Sara's clothes are torn away, so the more powerful she gets, the more naked she becomes: At full power she is usually nude apart from a kind of spiked thong bikini made from the Witchblade itself. As Schubart notes of 1990s action media, "Men have no problem identifying with men as victims and women as castrators if this happens in an erotic context where it is obvious that the women are there *to be looked at*" (228–229). The Witchblade guarantees that Sara exhibits exactly the right amount of to-be-looked-at-ness in every scene: The more Sara is empowered within the comic's narrative, the more she is objectified for the comic's readers, as though the comics were meting out the exact level of objectification necessary to make each level of empowerment read as "sexy" rather than "threatening" to its target audience. The hyperbolic masculinity of Sara's personality is thus counterbalanced by the hyperbolic femininity of her appearance. The fact that she is curvier and more naked than any other woman is what made it acceptable to such readers for her to also be tougher and angrier than any man.

Christina Z clearly approached *Witchblade* from a standpoint of sex-positive third-wave feminism. She insisted that she was never under pressure to increase the amount of sex and nudity in *Witchblade*: "In fact, I've received some to tone it down a bit. I hope it's not a strange thing for women to enjoy sex appeal as well?" (Browne). In a cultural context within which such unapologetic displays of female physical and sexual power were still relatively rare, and in which girls were, as Wolf lamented, routinely taught to repress their own power fantasies rather than express them, the comic understandably found a large and loyal audience (Wolf, *Fire* 276–277). However, *Witchblade* demonstrated the limits of such a stance as well as its strengths. Recalling her experiences as a teenage female *Witchblade* fan, Claire Napier wrote:

> *Witchblade* had the ongoing problem of making me feel over-visible as a young female reader. It was a woman-led title about a tough cop with a magic weapon, but it was also a comic with a premise—said magic weapon—designed to allow the artist to get that strong female protagonist at least partially, impractically, and unprofessionally naked with stunning regularity. It was a book about an individualistic, brawler heroine who wore her hair in her face and her shirts hemmed to rib level. Sara Pezini [*sic*] was designed to win, but she was also designed to be made (sexually) uncomfortable for the viewing pleasure of grotty nerds. I saw the grotty nerds when I was buying my books. I knew who was looking. I knew they had the option to also look at me.
>
> I could rely on Sara Pezini to make me feel capable, but I could also rely on her to make me feel pawed at. (Napier, "Crime")

In *Witchblade*, being looked at is a good thing, a source of power. People—even evil people, like Irons and his gorgeous, queer-coded bodyguard Ian Nottingham, a firm favorite with the comic's female fans—look at Sara, and they see how strong and fierce and beautiful she is, and they fall in love. But the reason they respond to her in this way is because she is a woman who inhabits her body *like a man*, always behaving as though her naked physicality is an emblem of strength rather than vulnerability. In this she is clearly in line with the "power feminism" argued for at the time by writers such as Wolf and Paglia, who diagnosed Western women as collectively suffering from "a fear of power" (Stasia 240). But within this paradigm, the kind of discomfort articulated by Napier could only be understood as weakness, proof that one had not yet sufficiently toughened up: not yet ready for empowerment, and hence not yet worthy to wield the Witchblade. Like so many other "bad girl" comics, *Witchblade*'s politics of empowerment ultimately amounted to a celebration of self-reliant postfeminist individualism that sometimes came perilously close to simple victim blaming. In Sara's world, if a woman isn't strong enough to be a "bad girl" heroine—with all the sex and violence and machismo and unflinching self-exposure that this entailed—then the only other option available was being weak enough to be a "good girl" victim instead. It is easy to understand why many female readers ultimately found this to be an unappealing choice.

"Sometimes the System Works": *Lady Justice* and Postfeminist Superheroics

In 1996, Tekno Comix published a fictional interview with their "bad girl" heroine Lady Justice—a vengeful spirit who visits wronged women, empowering them to take bloody revenge on their abusers. Her responses map out with some precision the cultural and ideological contexts within which the bad girl comics of 1994–1996 asked to be understood.

> HOBBIES Utterly wiping out those men who are the scourge of decent women from the plane of the living and sending them to their eternal damnation. Gun collecting. Bleaching my hair.
> FAVORITE MOVIES *Body Heat* and *Serial Mom*.
> FAVORITE AUTHORS Gloria Steinem, Ayn Rand, Mickey Spillane, and Joan of Arc (from her little known autobiography, *I'm Smoking More, But Enjoying It Less*).
> FAVORITE PERFORMERS Alanis Morissette certainly speaks to me.
> CAREER HIGHLIGHTS That Bobbitt thing was supposed to be a lark, but I'm pretty sure I made my point. (*Lady Justice* no. 8)

Like earlier "bad girl" heroines, Lady Justice is clearly depicted as a feminist avenger, whose role is to exterminate "men who are the scourge of decent women." But her feminism is of a very specific kind, in which traditional women's liberation (Gloria Steinem, Joan of Arc) has been combined with both radical individualism (Ayn Rand) and the kind of "hard-boiled" violence previously reserved for men (Mickey Spillane). She is proud both of her violence ("gun collecting") and her appearance ("bleaching my hair"), and she consequently views noirish femme fatales like the protagonist of the erotic thriller *Body Heat* (1981) as aspirational heroines rather than misogynistic stereotypes. She identifies with Alanis Morissette, who in 1996 was Anglophone pop culture's leading spokeswoman for female discontent, but at the same time she makes clear that her feminist anger isn't meant to be taken entirely seriously: She invokes the black comedy *Serial Mom* (1994), makes a joke about Joan of Arc's execution, and claims that Lorena Bobbitt's amputation of her husband's penis "was supposed to be a lark." She's angry, but she's not *that* angry, and her rampages are clearly meant to be enjoyable rather than terrifying to read about. All these traits—her individualism, her self-deprecating humor, her embrace of 1990s pop culture, and her combination of "masculine" violence and "feminine" sex appeal—serve to mark out Lady Justice, like so many of her "bad girl" contemporaries, as a distinctively postfeminist superheroine.

As a spectral female avenger who executed evil men with a pair of handguns, Lady Justice bore an obvious resemblance to *Ghost*, whom I discussed in the previous chapter. But whereas *Ghost* took (literal) aim at patriarchal institutions that preyed on women, such as the pornography industry, and explicitly justified her actions in terms of feminist ideology, *Lady Justice* battled the default villains of 1990s comics: street gangs, evil corporations, and organized crime. That these villains tended to be men and their victims tended to be women was noted but never explored: Unlike *Ghost*, it did not articulate any kind of explicit perspective on gender, though its claim that Lady Justice lives "cut off from the masculine world of clues and hard realities" suggests an essentializing, mystificatory view of femininity reminiscent of *Scimidar* (*Lady Justice* no. 1). Over the course of her adventures she empowered a range of different women—a mother, a child, a lawyer, a Latina gang member, a woman in a wheelchair—presumably to emphasize that female empowerment is not restricted to any one demographic: *Any* girl or woman can become "Lady Justice." But whomever she possesses takes on the exact same body and build: No matter who they were before, becoming "Lady Justice" transforms them, via a kind of supernatural makeover, into slender, nondisabled young women with big breasts (*Wheel of Worlds* no. 1). For *Lady Justice*, as for "bad girl" comics more generally, hypersexualization and conventional attractiveness are the necessary preconditions for empowerment.

As Robbins notes, there were a lot of ladies among the "bad girl" heroines of 1994–1996, including Lady Death, Lady Rawhide, Lady Justice, Lady Vampre, and Lady Pendragon (113). Brutally murdering people while nearly naked might seem like the antithesis of traditionally "ladylike" behavior, but the word suggests something of the importance that normative *femininity* has for these characters: No matter how violent they became, their artists continued to drape them in long hair and lipstick, lingerie and high heels. "Women's justice" evokes Catharine MacKinnon and Shulamith Firestone; "lady justice," no matter how gory, implies much less of a threat to the gendered status quo. (As if to exemplify this, when Lady Justice carries out her first vigilante killing, she stabs her victim to death by ballet dancing on his prone body in spiked high-heeled shoes, thus turning even murder into a performance of femininity: a true act of "lady justice.") Just as the mid-1990s popularity of Martha Stewart and Nigella Lawson expressed a postfeminist desire to demonstrate that female empowerment could be compatible with "ladylike" domesticity, so the "lady justice" of the "bad girls" found mainstream popularity among the comics-buying public by decoupling female power and violence from any broader critique of gender relations (Negra 130–132). The wrath of these postfeminist "bad girls" was increasingly directed *outward*, at a range of phantasmagorical Others: evil demons, power-mad scientists, murderous crime syndicates, cyborg ninjas. Targets closer to home—the abusive fathers, husbands, bosses, pimps, and policemen tackled by their feminist predecessors—steadily disappeared from their hit lists.

An excellent example of this transition can be seen in the Malibu Comics series *Elven* (1994–1995). Its protagonist, Elvia, is a Latina girl who gains the ability to transform into a monstrous alter ego, "Elven, the Avenger." In this form she initially preys on "male sex offenders and wife beaters," terrorizing and scarring them just as they have scarred and terrorized their victims. But Elven is swiftly reined by the appearance of the white male superhero Prime, who teaches her to moderate her violence and trust the system, telling her: "You made your point—you don't need to *carve* it into him! . . . Let the law punish him" (*Elven* no. 0). The series thus enacted the same swerve toward postfeminism that Schubart observed in the rape revenge films of the 1990s, in which hostility toward men in general was increasingly tempered by the inclusion of sympathetic male characters who supported the avenging heroine (103).

In subsequent issues Elven's monstrous, beast-like appearance was replaced with a more generically sexualized "bad girl" look, and each time she threatened to return to her vengeful ways Prime would stop her, sometimes by force. "Sometimes the system works," he tells her, after preventing her from attacking her mother's abusive boss: "And when it doesn't, *Elven* is waiting!" she replies (*Elven* no. 4). But in this series the system always *does* work: Rather than seeing the abuse of women as a cultural default, as *Ghost* and *Catwoman* had done, *Elven* depicts it as a swiftly corrected aberration from the norm, allowing Elven's superpowered violence to be reserved for supervillains rather than ordinary abusers. Like *Catwoman*, *Elektra*, and *Ghost*, *Elven* thus moved away from explicitly political, Riot Grrrl–style activism toward a more depoliticized, postfeminist "girl power." Like Vampirella and Witchblade, she learned to work with the authorities rather than against them; and like Lady Justice, she demonstrated that "lady justice" became much more acceptable to her target audience when delivered by someone who looks good in a bikini. These were years in which even the original "bad girl," Razor, started redirecting her attention from violent criminals to fantastical demon princes—with the result that, by 1996, the idea of the "bad girl" heroine as a vessel for potential cultural critique had become very attenuated indeed.

5

After the Fall

"Bad Girl" Comics Since 1997

The Downfall: Avatar Press

The heyday of the "bad girls" was very brief, lasting only from 1994 to 1996. By 1997 the genre was in serious trouble, and by 1998 it was in rapid and obvious decline (Madrid 97). Writing in 1997, Heidi Macdonald suggested that its adolescent readers had simply aged out of it: "Take the 'Bad Girls' craze. For a little while, these were the only comics that sold: Women with incredibly huge tits running around in submissive poses while pretending to save the world. Sure, it's titillating. But it's a particularly adolescent, immature kind of sexuality. It doesn't have anything to do with real sex" (92).

Of the scores of "bad girl" titles launched in 1994–1996, the vast majority had been canceled by 1998. Tekno Comix, which published *Lady Justice*, closed in 1997. Robert Liefeld's Maximum Press, which was primarily associated with the "bad girl" heroines Avengelyne, Glory, and Darkchylde, folded in 1997; its successor, Awesome Comics, opened in 1997 and by 1999 was already effectively defunct. In 1998, Lightning Comics, Brainstorm Comics, and Blackout Comics all ceased publication: All three had relied almost exclusively on "bad girl" comics for revenue. Crusade Comics canceled all their ongoing "bad girl" series in 1997–1998, though a handful of one-off comics continued to appear over the following years. London Night Studios, which had started the whole trend with *Razor* in 1992, canceled most of their titles during the same years, though the company staggered on into 1999 before closing entirely. *Ghost*, the last remnant of Dark Horse's hubristic attempt to create "Comics' Greatest World," was canceled in 1999. Chaos! Comics, which published *Lady Death* and her spin-offs, demonstrated unusual resilience by managing to stay in business until 2002.

The main cause for this rapid fall was the overall crisis in the comics market during 1996–1997, of which the most spectacular symptom was the bankruptcy of Marvel Comics in December 1996 (Gearino 149). The speculator bubble of the early 1990s, fueled by "The Death of Superman" and a hundred hype pieces in *Wizard* magazine, had burst, and by the end of 1996 the comics market was less than half the size it had been at its 1993 peak (Wright 283). Jean-Paul Gabilliet lays out the figures starkly: Between 1994 and 1996, the direct distribution comics industry lost two-thirds of its value, while the number of comic shops in America fell from 9,400 in 1993 to 4,500 in 1996 and 2,300 in 2002, obliterating the revenue base that companies like Lightning and Brainstorm relied on to stay in business (150–152). By 1999, comics sales were lower than they had been for fifty years (Robbins 140). Matt Hawkins, who was working for Image at the time, articulates the sense of bewilderment with which the indie comics industry responded to the crash: "We all were sorta young and brash and thought [the heyday of Image] was gonna last forever, and . . . it didn't. And so, the fall was kinda hard?" (Napier, "Lady Pendragon").

The crash hit all sectors of the comics industry, but it hit the bad girl titles harder than the rest. In its aftermath various attempts were made to restart the trend, but none prospered: The "bad girl" comics that were launched in the hostile environment of 1999–2000, such as *Lionheart* (1999), *Body Doubles* (1999), *Demonslayer* (1999–2003), *Exposure* (1999–2000), *Jade Warriors* (1999–2001), and *EVE Protomecha* (2000), mostly folded after a few issues. As I have discussed, the key selling point of the "bad girl" genre was that it supplied its readers with something that resembled both manga and pornography, in an environment where actual manga and pornography were not as easily accessible as they would later become. The foundation of Tokyopop in 1997 solved the first of these problems, bringing licensed, affordable manga translations to the U.S. market in *tankōbon* form (Brienza 50; Lopes 154–156). The rapid spread of the internet in 1996–1998 solved the second, heralding the arrival of a new age of internet pornography (Juffer 65).

In this new context, "bad girl" comics risked obsolescence, and by 1999 their speculative value on the secondary market had crashed. As female-led action media they were outclassed by manga such as *Battle Angel Alita*, while as erotica they could hardly compete with actual pornography, which the internet swiftly made ubiquitous. Even *Wizard* magazine, whose inflated valuations had done so much to stoke the trend, began to concede that comics such as *Razor* issue 1, *Lady Death* issue 1, *Shi: The Way of the Warrior* issue 1, and *Vengeance of Vampirella* issue 1 were not quite as valuable as they had seemed back in the heady days of 1995, slashing its assessment of their value by half or more. Under these circumstances, the only remaining reasons to continue buying such comics were if one had an enduring crush on a specific "bad girl" heroine or a persistent attachment (or fetish) for the genre's specific aesthetic. Every other economic, artistic, or erotic need they had previously met was, by this point, better catered to elsewhere.

Some titles survived the crash, though not unscathed. *Catwoman* seemed to lose all sense of its own identity after Jim Balent left the comic in 2000, with its writers subjecting its previously happy-go-lucky heroine first to a humiliating "women in prison" storyline and then to a literal identity crisis followed by a mental breakdown. By 2001 its authors were openly admitting that their plans for the title hadn't worked, and when it was canceled a few months later the last issue ended with the comatose Catwoman literally being thrown out with the trash (*Catwoman* vol. 2, no. 91, 94). Christina Z left *Witchblade* in 2000, after which the title suffered through years of increasingly incoherent writing and gratuitously pornographic artwork before finally being successfully rebooted by Ron Marz in 2004. In the interim, Top Cow repeatedly attempted to replicate their success by launching new "bad girl" titles like *Magdalena* (2000–2001, 2003) and *Aphrodite IX* (2000–2002), to little effect. *Warrior Nun Areala* rebooted itself in mid-storyline in a more explicitly manga style in 2000, in which form it survived until 2003. *Vengeance of Vampirella* and *Vampirella Strikes* were both canceled in 1996. Reimagined and resurrected in 1997 for a new series initially written by the star comics writer Grant Morrison, Vampirella lasted until 2000 before being reimagined *again* for a 2001 series initially written by Mark Millar, by the end of which her continuity had undergone four mutually contradictory reboots in ten years and no longer made any sense whatsoever. Like Areala, Vampirella was finally allowed to sink into merciful retirement in 2003.

Under these circumstances, it is dismaying but perhaps not surprising that the "bad girl" genre survived the decade mostly as a form of niche fetish pornography. The key company here was Avatar Press, which was launched in 1997 with the publication of an unremarkable "bad girl" title called *Pandora* (1997–1999). 1997 was an unpropitious time to be launching a new "bad girl" series, so Avatar moved swiftly to outflank what remained of their competition through the inclusion of more explicit nudity, in books like *Pandora Pinup* (1997) and *Pandora: Nudes* (1998). They also began aggressively acquiring the various "bad girl" characters orphaned by the closure of their original publishers: They acquired Nira X from Entity Comics, Widow from Ground Zero, and Donna Mia from Dark Fantasy in 1997, Razor from London Night in 1999, Avengelyne and *Coven* from Maximum Press in 2000–2001, *Exposure*, *Jade Warriors*, *Demonslayer*, and *10th Muse* from Image in 2000–2002, Shi from Crusade in 2002, Hellina from Lightning in 2003, Lady Death from Chaos! in 2004, and *More Than Mortal* from Liar Comics in 2006. Their use of these characters and series was incredibly cynical: Rather than being given ongoing series, each was featured only in a sequence of one-off specials and crossovers filled with extravagant quantities of sex, nudity, and violence, and usually featuring only the most rudimentary plot. Each issue was then published with a vast range of variant covers—topless covers, nude covers, foil covers, leather covers, and so on—in order to wring the maximum amount of money from each remaining member of each character's dwindling fan base.

Inapplicable though the term may be to fictional characters, it is hard not to think of the Avatar Press comics as a kind of prostitution. Characters like Nira X, Razor, and Widow may never have been perfect, but in 1993–1994 they had all represented genuine attempts to tell new kinds of stories about female power, whereas in the hands of Avatar Press they existed only to take their clothes off and have sex with each other. Lady Death always had an ultrasexualized character design, but under Chaos! Comics she had been part of an actual narrative, always fighting to control her destiny in defiance of the various demonic father-figures who sought to manipulate her. When Avatar Press obtained her they promptly gave her not just the customary "swimsuit special" but also a "bikini special," a "fetishes special," and a "leather and lace" special, each with at least fourteen variant covers. Customers were invited to purchase such sordid items as *Demonslayer Rave #1 Bad Schoolgirl Edition* (2001) or *Hellina #0 Adult Orgy Edition* (2003). The pretense that the heroines were being used as anything other than glorified fetish models became increasingly difficult to sustain.

An excellent example of the way that the genre devolved under Avatar can be found in the series *Webwitch*. Originally launched in 1997, it told the story of a female explorer, Nina Hoffman: When the (male) leader of her arctic expedition leads them into disaster, she takes shelter within a cave and discovers a hidden matriarchal "spider-nation" who welcome her as a daughter and transform her into one of their own. (Given that she refers to their leader as "Mother," it is noteworthy that the entrance to this womb-like cave rather resembles a vulva.) Returning to America, Nina begins to prey on men, impregnating them with monsters who devour them from the inside.

Much like the similarly spider-themed *Widow* five years earlier, *Webwitch* reads like a nightmare about the power of female sexuality, in which traditional gender roles are reversed and it is men rather than women who become the abject victims of their reproductive biology. As the narrator describes, "A *monster* grows within the pitiful shell that was once Fred Robinson . . . It keeps him alive . . . as it *consumes* his flesh. He is now close to *death* as his belly begins to swell and swirl with alien life" (*Webwitch* no. 2). Caught up in the "bad girl" crash of 1997, *Webwitch* lasted only three issues before breaking off mid-story. When Avatar Press relaunched it in 2002, they subjected it to a vicious rewriting, even more extreme than those imposed on *Catwoman*, *Elektra*, *Mantra*, and *Ghost* in the mid-1990s.

In the original, Nina was a scientist who *posed* as a stripper to entrap men; in the 2002 rewrite, she was only ever a stripper, her professional past having been entirely written out. In the original, there was a strong implication that Nina's loyalty to her new mother was genuine: After all, the spider-nation saved her from the male ego and incompetence that would otherwise have cost her her life. In the rewrite, the spider-nation is purely evil, and Nina's loyalty is compelled by crude mind control: As one character explains, "She *wants* to help us eliminate the hive of the spidernation and kill the queen that has been using her as a puppet" (*Tim Vigil's Webwitch* no. 1). Most significantly of all, in the rewrite Nina no longer fatally impregnates men: Instead she creates new monsters by impregnating *herself*, which she does by having sex with as many men as possible. The 1997 story imagined new forms of female power and solidarity, capable of unsettling existing gender hierarchies; the 2002 version reduces Nina to little more than an abject walking womb, totally defined by sex, who secretly resents her mother and would much rather be on the boys' side instead. In all these respects it exemplifies the Avatar Press approach to "bad girl" comics, in which everything that had previously made the genre genuinely challenging or political was stripped out in favor of mere pornography. *Tim Vigil's Webwitch* issue 1 may not have had a very interesting story, but it did have lots of nudity and fourteen variant covers, and by 2002 these had become much more important commercial assets for an Avatar "bad girl" comic to possess.

Self-Destruction: *Magical Drama Queen Roxy*

Gen13 was never quite a "bad girl" comic, although its hypersexualized heroines contributed to the trends that made the "bad girl" genre possible. In 1998, however, Image published an experimental three-issue spin-off miniseries entitled *Magical Drama Queen Roxy*, which provided a window into the fantasy life of one of the *Gen13* superheroines, written and drawn by *Dirty Pair* artist Adam Warren. Unpopular in its own day and utterly forgotten since, it nonetheless provides an intriguing glimpse into the genre in the midst of its own self-destruction.

The protagonist of the series, Roxy, was the least sexualized female member of the *Gen13* super-team, and the one that its editor noted their female readers most frequently identified with (*Gen13* vol. 2, no. 2). But her superheroic status brings her no happiness: As the series begins, Roxy is consumed by self-loathing, and everyone around her considers her a failure. Her boyfriend criticizes her looks, and her female friends are unimpressed by the fact that she has "never heard of the term '*patriarchy*.'" "Everybody wishes I was someone else . . . someone *better* . . . ," Roxy laments: "Someone smarter or more responsible or *bigger-breasted* . . ." She falls asleep, and her anime-filled imagination plunges her into a dream in which she is a *Sailor Moon*–style magical girl. In this form she wins the heart of "the Prince" (an idealized version of her boyfriend), only to be confronted by "the P.C. Queen," a nightmare version of her "politically correct" friend Sarah. The queen critiques Roxy's heteronormative princess fantasy for its ideological failings, and splits the Prince into two: a crude, "id-driven" caveman, and a "new age man" who is "superego incarnate" (*Magical Drama Queen Roxy* no. 1).

Roxy's two boyfriends represent, fairly explicitly, the two factors that fed into the creation of "bad girl" comics. The "superego" boyfriend loves superheroines because he "really admire[s] empowered women": For him they are continuous with other forms of feminist media, and he invites Roxy to "cuddle up and read the latest issue of *Strangers in Paradise* together." The "id" boyfriend loves them simply because of their sex appeal: As he explains, while drooling, "me *like* lesbos! Ughh! Hot *two-girl* action!" Roxy struggles to live up to both ideals simultaneously, but the P.C. Queen mocks her fantasies of superheroism for being racist and antifeminist, and her self-esteem is further undermined when she encounters the "unnaturally proportioned" living doll "Bobbi" (i.e., Barbie), who explains that she exists "to reinforce your entirely *valid* feelings of physical *and* intellectual inferiority!" Reeling, Roxy tries to draw inspiration from pop-culture expressions of female power, such as the music of Alanis Morissette, only to find herself being criticized for "the pathetic way you lapped up every *chick act* the big record companies *manufactured*": What she took to be her own rebellion turns out to just be someone else's product. Witheringly, her friend even accuses her of liking those most mainstream of pop feminists, the Spice Girls, saying: "Maybe you're a closet *spice fan*, after all" (*Magical Drama Queen Roxy* no. 2).

As her dream disintegrates into a nightmare, Roxy finds that the constituent parts of the mid-1990s superheroine ideal simply don't add up to a coherent whole. She can't be an empowering feminist role model *and* an objectified sex fantasy; she can't be a rebel outsider if she's also a commercialized cog in the capitalist machine; and from the perspective of the Native American lesbian P.C. Queen, even Roxy's triumphs as the "great white princess" still remain oppressively heteronormative and Eurocentric. Rather than inspiring Roxy, the idealized superheroine Bobbi just makes her feel inadequate: Ultimately, in a send-up of comic-book breast fetishism, Bobbi ends up self-destructing after her bosom becomes so massive that it creates a localized singularity. ("Goodness! My enormous breasts are undergoing gravitational *collapse*[!]") Roxy longs to impress her boyfriend, hoping that this will make her feel better about herself, but as the series continues she is forced to admit that she doesn't even like him very much: The only point in his favor is that her exes were even worse. The things that are meant to make her feel powerful and desirable just make her feel miserable, leaving her to seek comfort in cigarettes, ice cream, and *Sailor Moon* (*Magical Drama Queen Roxy* no. 2).

Finally the P.C. Queen summons a giant robot in a maid costume to destroy Roxy. "Relish her inherent *contradictions*," she says: "A product of *white male* technology, garbed in a sexist, fetishistic, *degrading* costume . . . but *summoned* here, in a spirit of progressive ardor, to shake up the white man's capitalistic, exploitative, overclass-nurturing, resource-overconsuming *pseudo-cyberpunk metropolis*!" (This entire description could be applied to quite a lot of 1990s "bad girl" heroines, from Vampirella onward.) According to the queen, who is clearly fluent in late 1990s postmodernist theory, the robot "disturbs the semiotic fault lines of the white man's *oppressive megalopolis*," forcing the comic to regress through the stages of its own construction: first to the color guide stage, then to inks, then pencils, then layouts, and finally all the way back to the script, which turns out to be full of notes from the writers complaining about their sales figures and plotting how many panels they can copy from manga. ("Use some rips from *AKIRA* volume 3 here; odds are, no-one will notice.") Roxy finally taps into her "*womynpower*" to save the day—"I'm *magical*, damn it"—but as everyone praises her she realizes that she must be dreaming, because "nothing this *nice* could possibly happen to me in *real life*!" Shortly afterward she wakes up, still miserable, having solved nothing. The series concludes with the words "THE END (*sob*)," as though the comic itself is crying over its inability to offer her more meaningful help (*Magical Drama Queen Roxy* no. 3).

As the example of Avatar Press showed, in the post-crash market the only way to reliably sell "bad girl" comics was by doubling down on male-gaze sex appeal. *Magical Drama Queen Roxy* shows a bitter awareness of this, and when the comic collapses down to its script, the page is shown to be covered in red annotations (implicitly from the editor) bemoaning its poor sales:

> Damn. This miniseries' sales figures are just *sad*, aren't they? Maybe we could *Spice Them Up* by working, say, more '*Panty Shots*' into the story? (Hey, it works for *Danger Girl*, man.)
>
> . . .
>
> Or Maybe we could make roxy's *breasts* a great deal larger? (Hey, it works for *Battle Chasers*, man.) (*Magical Drama Queen Roxy* no. 3).

However, as the series itself had shown, the more comics relied on such devices to drive sales, the more they alienated potential readers like Roxy, locking the genre into a spiral of diminishing returns. Even *Danger Girl*, a rare example of a relatively successful post-crash "bad girl" series, lasted only six issues before shifting to irregular publication.

Magical Drama Queen Roxy was certainly not guiltless of the failings it pointed out in others, but in its own way, it offered a rather perceptive diagnosis of where the hypersexualized superheroines of the mid-1990s had gone wrong. Even when animated by genuine "progressive ardor," their vision of "female empowerment" was too narrow to appeal to more than a small minority of female readers: It was too white, too straight, too commercialized, too fetishistic, too wedded to standards of attainment and attractiveness that most women knew they would never be able to achieve. Roxy does not experience these archetypes as empowering: They just make her feel bad about herself, and they offer her nothing that she can usefully apply to her actual life. Had the "bad girl" comics of 1994–1996 succeeded in their initial ambitions to attract a female readership then this might have helped to shield them from the downturn of 1996–1997, just as the sales of Vertigo's graphic novels held steady while the rest of the comics market crashed around them (Savlov; Licari-Guillaume, *Vertigo* 59). But in 1997–1998, Roxy's real-world counterparts—and there were many of them—flocked, like Roxy, not to *Shi* but to *Sailor Moon*, which offered its readers a version of "female empowerment" that wasn't premised on giant breasts, male-gaze visuals, and gory violence. The jokes in *Magical Drama Queen Roxy* about the extent of the comic's borrowings from manga attest to its recognition that, by 1998, most of the crucial battles had already been lost.

"Something Uglier": The Post-Bad-Girl Wave

In 1997, the soon-to-be-defunct Amazing Comics Group published a comic entitled *Angel Heat*. In an interview with the consulting editor, the writer David Campiti and the managing editor Howard Feltman explained their concept for the comic:

DAVID I tried to come up with a creative slant that nobody else was taking. I certainly didn't want the sword-and-leather "bitch girl" route.
AMAZING That's "bad girl," isn't it?
DAVID Not the way it's been portrayed as of late! Don't get me started . . .
HOWARD Yeah, the "good girls with attitude" approach has mutated into something uglier, more violent, and we didn't want that here. (*Angel Heat* no. 1)

Angel Heat was clearly conceived as an anti-bad-girl book. Its amnesiac angelic heroine is a "good girl" without any kind of "attitude": She literally falls from heaven onto the bed of the teenage male protagonist, announces that "I must learn to be your *perfect girlfriend*," and promptly submits to all his requests, from taking his virginity to allowing herself to be dressed in revealing outfits and high heels (*Angel Heat* no. 1). She is supernaturally powerful, but despite being stronger than him she remains entirely submissive, a blank slate for him to inscribe with his own desires. She is unambiguously white, heterosexual, and normatively feminine: She is literally named "Angel White," and the comic makes clear how much she enjoys dressing in lingerie and providing the protagonist with sexual favors. In all these respects she acts as the antitype of the aggressive, assertive, queer "bad girl" heroines that Campiti and Feltman clearly disliked so much: characters like the nun-turned-biker Shotgun Mary, who in the same year "outed" herself as a lesbian in *Shotgun Mary: Blood Lore* (1997).

Angel Heat lasted only a single issue, but its very existence calls attention to just how disruptive the "bad girl" trend was within its original context. Angel White highlights why it was once possible to read characters like Shi and Lady Death as progressive: They possess power, agency, and sexual autonomy, pursue their own objectives, and hint at queer desires. They scorn submission to patriarchal authorities: Lady Death literally leads a rebellion against her own father. While "bad girl" comics certainly pandered to sexist assumptions, it is also important to recognize the ways that they often disturbed them, just as the admixture of influences from manga, neopaganism, and Riot Grrrl feminism allowed them to include alternate gender norms and value systems that threatened the hegemony of Angel White's "good girl" Christianity.

Following the 1996–1997 crash, all that was worst about the "bad girl" trend survived in the comics published by Avatar Press—but much of what was best about it passed on into the mainstream of American comics, where the "bad girl" wave had shattered forever the assumption that "girl books don't sell." The same years which saw the trend's decline witnessed the appearance of a new wave of female-led superhero comics from Marvel and DC, including *Black Widow* (1999, 2001, 2004–2006), *Birds of Prey* (1999–2009), *Batgirl* (2000–2006), *Harley Quinn* (2000–2004), *Bloodstone* (2001–2002), *Elektra* (2001–2004), *Catwoman* (2002–2010), *Emma Frost* (2003–2005), *Fallen Angel* (2003–2008), *X-23* (2005, 2007), and *Supergirl* (2005–2011). Similarly, the short-lived Crossgen Comics briefly enjoyed success with female-led titles such as *Meridian* (2000–2004), *Mystic* (2000–2004), and *Sojourn* (2001–2004). The overlap between this new wave and the fading "bad girl" trend was symbolized by the four-issue *Ghost/Batgirl* crossover published in 2000, the first year of *Batgirl*'s regular series and the last year of *Ghost*'s.

These titles were strongly influenced by their "bad girl" predecessors, and many featured morally ambiguous heroines with backgrounds as criminals, assassins, or supervillains. For Batgirl to be reimagined as a teenaged Asian ex-assassin, as she was in the 2000–2006 series, would have been inconceivable before the "bad girl" wave, but was unremarkable after it: The same could be said of X-23, a murderous teenage female clone of Wolverine with a traumatic history of sex work, violence, and abuse. The 2004–2005 *Black Widow* series depicted its heroine as both a ruthless killer and an outspoken feminist, who objected bitterly to sexual double-standards and deliberately broke the spines of would-be rapists. Most significant of all was Harley Quinn, an amoral, bisexual female supervillain who from 2000 on increasingly shifted from antagonist to protagonist of the stories in which she appeared. These characters swiftly acquired strong fan followings: Harley Quinn, in particular, steadily eclipsed Wonder Woman as DC's highest-profile female character over the course of the 2010s (Burke 1.3, 4.5). Their success demonstrated that it was no longer necessary for mainstream superheroines to restrict themselves to being "good girls with attitude," and that being "something uglier [and] more violent" had become not just permissible but positively advantageous.

It was in these titles that the lessons of the "bad girl" wave were put to use. In their fondness for telling stories about violent women in formfitting black outfits, these comics clearly borrowed heavily from their "bad girl" predecessors while simultaneously moderating their excesses. The "bad girl" trend had shown that audiences would accept comics about queer, morally ambiguous heroines, but their gore and nudity were increasingly discarded, allowing the development of narratives with much wider potential appeal. As Neal Curtis and Valentina Cardo argue, titles such as *Birds of Prey* and *Harley Quinn* allowed female writers to redeploy "bad girl" iconography in new ways, strengthening their "feminist credentials" (384–386). Cocca notes that they rejected the idea that female-led superhero comics had to be "something close to costumed porn": Compared to the glut of mass-murdering women in lingerie who filled the genre in the mid-1990s, their heroines had more plausible costumes, less improbable proportions, and—in most cases—stronger moral codes (*Superwomen* 67). In 1999 Chuck Dixon described the new *Birds of Prey* as a response to changing reader demands, declaring, "An ongoing book about two mature, independent, intelligent, resourceful women who actually manage to keep their clothes on is a reality. All because you demanded it" (*Birds of Prey* 2, no. 1). The very first issue of the 2002 *Catwoman* series depicted her throwing away the skintight purple

FIGURES 18A AND 18B Left, the improbably dressed and proportioned "bad girl" Catwoman from *Catwoman* 2, no. 69 (1999). Pencils by Jim Balent, inks by Marlo Alquiza, colors by Roberta Tewes. Right, the reimagined Catwoman from *Catwoman* 3, no. 1 (2002). Art by Darwyn Cooke and Mike Allred, colors by Matt Hollingsworth.

costume and thigh-high boots of her "bad girl" days, replacing them with a looser black catsuit. "It looks . . . *practical*," Batman tells Catwoman upon seeing her new costume. "That's what *I* thought, too," she replies (*Catwoman* vol. 3, no. 1).

1999 also saw the publication of Gail Simone's famous "Women in Refrigerators" letter objecting to violence against women in superhero comics. Several of the responses to Simone identified what she called "the seemingly-dying bad girl comics trend" as part of the problem: Thus the Marvel editor Joe Quesada wrote that "too many creators got on the 'Bad Girl' bandwagon and did nothing but pander and exploit their own creations . . . many creators that I've talked to solely created those characters to be exploited and exploitative" (Simone, "Fan"; Quesada). Ron Marz acknowledged that "half-naked women on covers spike sales," and that "publishers are unfortunately more concerned with survival than with sensitivity to women," but suggested that the time for such short-sighted publishing tactics was now past: "If we want to save our industry, maybe we should stop ignoring half the population as possible readers" (Marz). Reading through the responses, the sense of collective embarrassment about the then-recent trend is palpable, and many creators ended their letters to Simone by resolving to do better in future. Simone herself concluded that "I actually think things are improving . . . comics simply aren't as grim anymore" ("Fan").

In retrospect, the "bad girl" trend can be seen as a transitional phase. The giant breasts and ultraviolence proved transitory: The more basic recognition that modern superheroines no longer had to conform to the archetype of the straight white "good girl" has been much more lasting. "As soon as my makeup and my wig is on I'm no longer me, I'm Harley," explains one of the Harley Quinn cosplayers quoted by Liam Burke. "I'm more confident, I'm more crazy" (Burke 4:10). The pairing of "confident" and "crazy" here is significant: Harley's "bad girl" identity confers confidence precisely because it grants implicit permission to reject restrictive social norms, whereas older "good girl" heroines like Supergirl could confer only heightened expectations of moral conformity. But as Burke's interviewees make clear, Harley's identity is available and appealing to them precisely because her repeated redesigns have made her look "achievable," unlike older superheroine costume designs that only the "super confident" would consider wearing in real life (Burke 4.6–4.7).

Tellingly, the single creator most associated with modern Harley Quinn comics, both as a writer and as an artist, is Amanda Conner. As I have discussed, Conner was involved with the "bad girl" genre from the beginning: modeling for *Elektra*, drawing *Vampirella*, working for Crusade Comics. In *Harley Quinn* she reused many classic "bad girl" traits—the crazed, violent heroines, the rejection of traditional superhero morality, the visual storytelling built around bright colors and dynamically posed female figures who refuse to be contained within the layout of a regular grid—but reconfigured them to no longer exist solely for the male gaze. "How *cool* would it be to have my own comic book?" Harley enthuses in the first issue of Conner's 2014 series. "Men and boys admiring my good looks, young girls wanting to be just like me when they grow up. Women wanting the chance to act like me any time it pleases them." "Whatta role model you are," says a nearby stuffed beaver, its voice presumably a figment of Harley's delusional imagination, to which she replies: "Yeah—I *am*, right?" (*Harley Quinn* vol. 2, no. 0). The exchange recalls 1990s controversies over whether "bad girl" heroines were bad role models—debates played out, for example, in the letter pages of *Silver Sable*—but it also lays out the logic behind the comic (*Silver Sable* no. 18). Harley exists for "men and boys" to admire, but unlike earlier "bad girls," this is not her *only* purpose: She also functions as a "role model," an aspirational figure of social rebellion and queer liberation for girls and women to "act like . . . any time it pleases them." (Not *all* the time, as an enforced social performance, but *any time it pleases them*.) The same issue brings the whole genre full circle by depicting Harley happily "driving in a hot car with my even hotter girlfriend," in what quickly turns into an homage to one of the original inspirations for the whole "bad girl" genre, *Thelma and Louise* (*Harley Quinn* vol. 2, no. 0). But as her car goes over a cliff, Harley begins arguing with her writer, demanding that this time she and her girlfriend should be given a happy ending.

By the mid-2000s, post–"bad girl" comics of the *Batgirl* and *Harley Quinn* kind were clearly ascendant. The pinup covers that marked early issues of *Emma Frost* and the 2001 *Elektra* series gradually disappeared, and by 2007, "bad girl" art had fallen so far out of favor that when Sana Takeda drew a bondage-themed cover for *Heroes for Hire* issue 13, in apparent homage to Deodato's infamous cover for *Jade Warriors* issue 1 (1999), it sparked an instant backlash online. Even some of the original "bad girl" heroines were ultimately rebooted in post–"bad girl" form: Examples include *Ghost* (2013–2015), *Aphrodite IX / IXth Generation* (2013–2016), *Witchblade* (2017–2020), and *Warrior Nun Dora* (2019), each of which saw a classic 1990s "bad girl" reimagined with clearer feminist politics and a more practical costume. Similarly, when the "bad girl" comics *Van Helsing* and *Warrior Nun* were adapted to television as *Van Helsing* (2016–2021) and *Warrior Nun* (2020–2022), their heroines were heavily rewritten and redesigned, with their original costumes consigned to history. Still, the "bad girl" genre did not entirely disappear. In some forms, it endures even today, and its last survivals may provide some hints as to the trend's long-term legacies.

Survivals and Mutations: Twenty-First-Century "Bad Girl" Comics

In 2000, the famous horror mangaka Junji Ito published the final chapter of his *shoujo* manga serial *Tomie*, which he had been writing and drawing since 1987. *Tomie* tells the story of a girl whose beauty leads men to obsess over her, first devoting themselves to her and then murdering her, usually destroying their own lives in the process. Each part of the butchered Tomie then grows into a new version of her, beginning the cycle anew. Written during the same years that saw the rise and fall of the "bad girl" genre in America, *Tomie* articulated the basic truth that the "bad girl" comics collectively refused to face: that the urge to exalt and venerate women as idealized objects of desire often grows from the same soil as the urge to degrade and destroy them. The beautiful, unstoppable, and self-sufficient "girl power" goddess-heroine of 1990s pop-culture mythology, whom all men desire but who will never need or desire any man, inspired feelings of both reverence and rage in heterosexual male audiences: thus the characteristic double motion of "bad girl" narratives, within which heroines are alternately celebrated and humiliated, depicted in bondage on one page and in triumph on the next. Many female readers clearly recognized the hostility in these comics, the resentment of women that often radiated from their pages, but their authors and publishers tended to simply deny that any such hostility existed. They consequently found themselves unable to expand beyond their original target market, leading to their rapid demise once that market melted away.

By the time Ito finished *Tomie*, the "bad girl" genre was in clear retreat. *Witchblade* endured; so did *Tomb Raider*, which lasted until 2005, buoyed by the popularity of the video game franchise it was based on. Perhaps the most striking survival was *Tarot: Witch of the Black Rose* (2000–2023), a creator-owned series written and drawn by Balent after he left *Catwoman* in 2000. Trading on his existing fan base and staggering levels of breast fetishism, the series ran for an astonishing 141 bimonthly issues—but *Tarot* was virtually a one-man production, with Balent doing the scripts, pencils, colors, and covers. Like the similarly personal *Strangers in Paradise*, it was thus insulated from the broader trends that saw most other "bad girl" titles either fall into the hands of Avatar Press or disappear entirely.

However, a subsection of the comics-buying audience clearly never stopped hungering for "bad girl" material: Indeed, like Tomie, the genre has demonstrated a surprising ability to resurrect itself following each apparent demise. In 2005, Zenescope launched *Grimm's Fairy Tales*, which retold classic fairy tales in a horror-fantasy vein comparable to *Sandman* or *Fables* (2002–2015), while also trading on pinup covers and female character designs drawn by the veteran "bad girl" artist Al Rio. Initially written as an anthology of disconnected stories, *Grimm's Fairy Tales* ultimately developed a metanarrative starring its heroine, Sela Mathers, and became the foundation for a multi-title Zenescope extended universe that still exists today. Their titles were based on well-known public domain sources (e.g., Robin Hood, *Alice in Wonderland*), and all had highly sexualized female protagonists. When Zenescope published a multi-universe crossover event in 2012, it was called, appropriately enough, *Grimm Fairy Tales Presents Bad Girls*. Zenescope is also noteworthy as the only major comics company to still publish an annual "Swimsuit Special," a tradition that most publishers abandoned in the early 2000s.

Similarly, Dynamite Comics began a new series of *Red Sonja* in 2005. It swiftly proved successful—so much so that Dynamite began acquiring and publishing comics starring other "bad girl" characters, including Vampirella (2010), Lady Rawhide (2013), Chastity and Purgatori (2014), the 1960s erotic sci-fi heroine Barbarella (2017), and even the 1940s jungle heroine Sheena (2017). In 2010, Dynamite also began publishing adaptations of Edgar Rice Burroughs's science fiction stories starring John Carter of Mars. However, Carter was rapidly upstaged by the nearly naked Martian heroine Dejah Thoris, who soon came to dominate the comic. She was given her own series in 2011, and has since joined Red Sonja and Vampirella as one of Dynamite's least clothed and most bankable heroines.

These titles never regained the prominence such comics enjoyed in the mid-1990s, but Zenescope's and Dynamite's titles have maintained a ghettoized but persistent presence in comic shops up to the present day (Gearino 77). Unlike the pornographic and largely plotless "bad girl" comics produced by Avatar from 1998 to 2006, Zenescope and Dynamite mostly publish action-adventure narratives similar to those of other publishers, except that they still use "bad girl" art styles and their heroines wear skimpier costumes. For some years they were joined in this by Aspen Comics, whose *Executive Assistant* franchise (2009–2014, 2018) was a true 1990s throwback, filled with beautiful but ruthless female Asian assassins in skintight outfits. Interestingly, Dynamite's efforts to launch their own original "bad girl" heroines in titles like *Blood Queen* (2014), *Cherish* (2022–2023), and *Siren's Gate* (2022–2024) have been less successful, suggesting that much of their market is based on nostalgia and enduring loyalty to the characters themselves.

The most spectacular survival of "bad girl" comics has been online. In 2014, the Chaos! Comics "bad girls" were acquired by Dynamite—all except Lady Death, the rights to whom remained with Avatar. Avatar published one final *Lady Death* series in 2015, and to raise funds for it they turned to the then-novel expedient of online crowdfunding, running a 2014 Kickstarter campaign because, they explained, "It's a tough time to launch a book with a strong female protagonist" ("Lady Death Lives at Boundless"). The campaign was not a success, raising only $12,995 for the whole series, and in 2015 the rights to the character reverted to her original author, Brian Pulido. Pulido then ran a much more successful Kickstarter campaign to raise funds for his own *Lady Death* comic, raising $76,553 for a single issue. Since then Pulido has run a separate Kickstarter for every single issue of each comic produced by his new company, Coffin Comics. The most successful of these, *Lady Death: Necrotic Genesis* (2022), raised $532,722 for a single comic—more than forty times what Avatar had managed eight years earlier, and one of the highest sums ever raised for a comic on Kickstarter.

Pulido's success did not go unnoticed. Over the last decade many other "bad girl" titles, long since rendered commercially unviable as regular comic books, have been resurrected via online crowdfunding campaigns, including *Nira X*, *Warrior Nun*, *Shi*, *Jade Warriors*, and *Double Impact*. Others, including *Razor*, *Witchblade*, and *Avengelyne*, have used Kickstarter campaigns to raise funds for new prestige editions of comics long out of print. Kickstarter has also proved fertile ground for the creation of new "bad girl" comics, such as

Patriotika (2017–2022), *White Widow* (2018–2021), and *Sister Mercy* (2019–2025). Supported, like *Lady Death*, by separate Kickstarters for every issue, they have flourished while traditionally published modern bad girl titles like *Shinku* (2011), *Arhian* (2015), and *Astria* (2016) failed. As with internet fan fiction and pornography, the anonymity of online commerce allows unfashionable, low-status material to be created and consumed without fear of judgment: Customers who might feel uncomfortable buying such works in an actual comic shop can support them on Kickstarter, safe in the knowledge that no one else needs to know about their reading habits. In these online spaces, in almost complete isolation from mainstream American comics culture, sex-and-violence-fueled "bad girl" comics have been quietly enjoying something of a renaissance.

These Kickstarters are noteworthy for the amount of money pledged by each supporter. *Necrotic Genesis* had just 3,418 backers, meaning that they pledged an average of $155 for a single comic book, and this figure is not unusual: Pledges of $100 or more per issue are commonplace, meaning that an audience of just a few hundred readers can make a comic commercially viable. What such backers want is not just the comic itself, which they can usually obtain for a few dollars by backing at the "pdf only" level, but the vast range of alternate cover editions, which have been taken further on Kickstarter than they ever were by the 1990s comics industry. Topless covers, nude covers, foil covers, holographic covers, lenticular covers, metal covers, glow-in-the-dark covers, and similar gimmicks proliferate, allowing the most dedicated backers to spend several hundred dollars buying multiple versions of a single comic. In the 1990s, variant covers were used as a marketing tactic, trading on the promise that they might one day be valuable and collectible. But no one buying thirty variant editions of an original 2020s "bad girl" comic can truly believe that they will one day become sought-after collector's items: Instead they trade on pure 1990s nostalgia, on the remembered pleasures of hoarding "bad girl" comic variants and being the only person in one's friendship group to own the special holofoil edition. Many middle-class teenagers from 1995 are now fortysomething professionals with copious disposable incomes, and thousands of them evidently remember their adolescent comic-collecting days with sufficient fondness to want to reenact them online.

It is thus noteworthy that the variant cover market is the one place where "bad girl" art has regained a foothold at both Marvel and DC. Having acquired a bad reputation during the speculator boom of the 1990s, variant covers began creeping back in the 2010s, and it is now common for a single issue of a mainstream superhero comic to have five or more variant covers. Frequently, some will be "pinup" covers, featuring suggestively posed female characters and sold at higher prices: Some artists, including Stanley Lau ("Artgerm"), Shikarii, Nathan Szerdy, and Lesley Li, have built whole careers by drawing "bad girl"–style variant covers for comics that would never use such styles in their interior art. Collectively, these survivals—the Kickstarters, the variant covers, the Dynamite and Zenescope titles—clearly demonstrate that the impulses behind the "bad girl" trend did not simply vanish in 1997–1998. Indeed, as recently as 2021, Titan Comics enjoyed a surprise breakout hit with *Gun Honey* (2021–2025), a hard-boiled crime thriller about a busty Asian woman with a gun, who appears topless in just about every issue and nude on many of its numerous variant covers.

The most self-conscious example of "bad girl" revivalism was Jason Martin's *Vampblade* (2016–2021). Its heroine is a comic shop employee who unexpectedly acquires the powers of an obscure "bad girl" heroine whose comic she read as a girl—powers that, to her irritation, also compel her to *behave* like a "bad girl" heroine, complete with frenzied bloodlust and frequent nudity. The comic is littered with visual quotations from 1990s "bad girl" comics like *Ghost* and *Elektra*, presumably intended as "Easter eggs" for fans of the genre. As Martin explained in the first issue:

> Vampblade is a bit of an odd duck, in that her design is very much tied to that 90s sensibility, yet her story takes place in today's world. A world that now frowns upon ass-kicking half naked leather clad ladies in entertainment. But that's okay, because not everyone wants their entertainment sanitized and squeaky clean, or all their heroines to be idyllic role models fit for little girls!
>
> Sometimes you just want black latex, chains, blades, blood, and goo . . . well if so, Vampblade's here for you! (*Vampblade* vol. 1, no. 1)

The key issue here is whom the "you" in the last sentence refers to. Martin notes that the aspiration of modern comics to tell socially conscious stories for diverse audiences (what he dismissively refers to as "idyllic role models fit for little girls") is in tension with the ongoing appetite of some readers for '90s-style "blades, blood, and goo": What he doesn't explicitly acknowledge is that this split runs along demographic lines, and that the "you" who wants more black latex and chains in comics is disproportionately likely to be straight, white, and male. Later the comic stages a debate between two comics fans: one Black, who complains about "the objectification of women in comics" and declares that "comics are more inclusive now, and this kind of immature misogyny has no place anymore!" and one white, who replies that "it's fine if *you* want to see more diverse and empowering books. But there's a whole shit ton of people who don't . . . or you know, still want the stupid stuff too" (*Vampblade* vol. 1, no. 5). The continuance of "immature misogyny" in comics is thus reframed as a defense of pluralism: Everyone should be allowed to read what they want and ignore what they don't. From this perspective, the *real* bigots are the ones who try to impose their preferences on others rather than allowing impersonal market forces to determine what is and is not published—a position very much in line with the kind of anticensorship 1990s liberalism that helped give rise to the "bad girl" wave in the first place. *Vampblade* also acknowledges the importance of online

Kickstarters for modern "bad girl" comics. When its heroine meets the artist who created the comics her powers come from, a comic which (like many real "bad girl" comics) was canceled after just four issues in 1998, he explains its discontinuation by saying: "weren't no damn kickstarters to fund this shit back then!" (*Vampblade* vol. 1, no. 10).

To be a "bad girl" comics fan in the 2020s, part of Martin's "shit ton of people who . . . still want the stupid stuff," may well imply unreconstructed sexism, but can hardly be reducible to it. In a world awash with sexually explicit manga, anime, and online pornography, there are much easier ways to gratify a desire for hypersexualized action media than by spending $100 on a "heavy metal edition" of *Necrotic Genesis* issue 1. It implies an ongoing loyalty to a very specific comic-book aesthetic, one which is as retro now as the Silver Age art of Kirby and Ditko was in 1992. Buyers of these works are vocal about their nostalgic appeal, and remarks such as, "It really takes me back to being a teenager in the 1990s," "I remember (too many years ago) buying the very first issue of Shi when it first came out at my local comic book shop," "Exhited [*sic*]! I was a teenager back in the 90s when I discovered Lady Death!!," and "[I've] been a fan of Lady Death since I was a kid in the 90s" abound on their Kickstarter comment pages (*Necrotic Genesis* comments; *Shi Omnibus* comments). The audience for titles like *Gun Honey* is harder to discern, but its emphasis on highly priced variant covers implies that it, too, is aimed at older collectors. At the time of writing, the most recent *Gun Honey* issue has *thirty-five* variant covers, including multiple nude covers—a number that would have startled even Avatar Press at their most desperate.

Of course, people in all times and places commonly feel nostalgic for the era of their youth, but to express such feelings in this particular way implies nostalgia for certain specific aspects of the period: for "raunch culture," sex-positive feminism, and old-style Clintonian liberal politics, all of which have been scathingly reappraised since the #MeToo movement in works such as Alison Yarrow's *90s Bitch* (2018). Modern fans of 1990s culture commonly stress their view of it as a less censorious age, when people freely "tried and did different things" without fear of "judgement from social media" (Lawton). As *Vampblade* puts it in the shamelessly nostalgic *Vampblade '98*, "We didn't give a fuck about society and normal life. It was the 90s" (*Vampblade '98* no. 1). In this sense, the very knowledge of how much mainstream 2020s comics culture would disapprove of comics like the Nude Copper Holofoil edition of *Syn Machina #1* (2023) may well be a key element of their appeal.

For all their adult pretentions and deliberate "political incorrectness," there is something oddly innocent about most modern "bad girl" titles. Everette Hartsoe runs some of his "bad girl" Kickstarters under the name "Red Pill Publishing," which implies a desire to appeal to the online antifeminist "manosphere," but most of these comics contain little of the aggressive misogyny of the early Avatar Press era, and none of the poisonous incel revenge fantasies that mark some modern manga such as *Redo of Healer* (2017–present).

Instead, many of them read like attempts to evoke an earlier, less politically fraught era, before the War on Terror and the financial crisis and the socially shattering effects of the internet. Theirs is a world where it is always 1994, where *Fire with Fire* is still the last word in feminist thought, where censorship is the greatest of evils, and "female empowerment" means getting naked and beating people up. It is a world where supporting women's rights is *easy*, because women want exactly what men want and thus demand only access to male institutions, rather than for those institutions to undergo any kind of change or reform. In these comics, as in idealized childhood memories, it is always summer, always swimsuit season. They make no attempt to appeal to, or even acknowledge, female readers, but for their target market, who as straight male "kid[s] in the 90s" were ideally placed to benefit from the decade's permissiveness and prosperity, they clearly act as comforting reminders of an era before the world darkened, and grew cold.

Conclusion

How Bad Were the "Bad Girls"?

Over the course of this book, I have mapped out the rise and fall of the "bad girl" genre, from its origins in the martial arts heroines of 1980s comic books to its twenty-first-century decline. As I have discussed, the trend arose out of a very specific confluence of cultural forces: the ideologies of "sex-positive" third-wave feminism and postfeminism, the mainstreaming of "raunch culture" and pornography, the overlapping rise of Image Comics and Vertigo's "mature readers" imprint, and the stylistic influences of manga, all coupled with the economic realities of the 1990s boom economy, which gave its target audience the disposable income they needed to buy the variant covers and trading cards on which the genre's business model relied. For a few years, these factors combined to make comic-book stories about violent, hypersexualized women seem desirable, relevant, and even progressive—but once these circumstances no longer applied, the genre withered. The American comics industry did eventually recover from the crash of 1996–1997, but the "bad girl" genre never regained the level of prominence that it enjoyed in the mid-1990s, and today it survives primarily as a nostalgia-driven ghost of its former self.

Recent years have seen numerous "bad girl" relaunches, including a new reimagining of *Witchblade* (2024–2025), the release of *Shi: Return of the Warrior* (graphic novel 2020, comic book 2024–2025), and even the publication of *Jade Warriors: Zettai No Edition* (2023), which finally completed a storyline left unfinished by the comic's cancellation in 2001. But as their price points demonstrate, these works, like the Kickstarter campaigns discussed in chapter 5, are firmly targeted at older collectors looking to extend collections begun in the heyday of the genre, a quarter century ago. Within Western comics, collecting modern "bad girl" titles has become an expensive niche hobby, as the endless stream of highly priced, limited-edition "collectibles" advertised on the Zenescope website suggests. Adolescent male audiences hungry for male-gaze fan service in comics still exist, but today they primarily gravitate to Japanese manga series such as *Highschool of the Dead* (2006–2013), *Fairy Tale* (2006–2017), *Freezing* (2007–2015), *High School DxD* (2010–2018), *Seven Deadly Sins* (2012–2020), and *Edens Zero* (2018–2024), where prices are lower and ultrasexualized action heroines remain commonplace.

Ideologically, the gender politics which gave rise to the "bad girl" genre have come to seem increasingly antiquated, especially since the mainstreaming of the #MeToo movement in 2017. Just as the antipornography feminism of the 1980s critiqued the sexual revolution of the 1960s and 1970s, arguing that sexual permissiveness within a context of entrenched gender inequality was more likely to lead to abuse than liberation, so the liberal sexual politics of the 1990s and 2000s have come to be heavily criticized in post–#MeToo feminist writing as exploitative rather than empowering, giving rise to cultures characterized by the normalization of sexual violence (Yarrow). The gender politics of "bad girl" comics, as of 1990s "raunch culture" more broadly, relied on the notion that women might *freely choose* to objectify themselves, as a form of self-empowerment and self-expression. But much modern intersectional feminist writing has critiqued the idea of the autonomous liberal subject on which such "choice" feminism and postfeminism relied, drawing attention to the networks of power and inequality within which such subjects are always enmeshed, and questioning whether such individuals might not "freely choose" something very different if only other options were made available to them.

The reputation of 1990s pop feminism has been further dented by a series of damaging revelations over the last decade. In 2014, the pioneering neopagan feminist author Marion Zimmer Bradley, whose work was so influential on "bad girl" fantasy comics, was posthumously accused by her daughter, Moira Greyland, of abusing her children and enabling the pedophilia of her husband, Walter Breen (Flood). In the same year, Pamela Anderson, who in the 1990s was widely hailed as a symbol of unrestrained female sexuality, revealed her traumatic history of childhood sexual abuse, and in 2016 she spoke out against the dangers of online pornography, remarking that she no longer saw "this kind of objectification [as] a compliment" (Bruton; Kurson). In 2004, Britney Spears was cited by Susan Hopkins as an icon of female empowerment, but in 2019 information emerged about the abusive and exploitative conditions of the conservatorship under which her career had been managed, leading to the #FreeBritney social media campaign of 2020 (Hopkins 60–61; Anguiano). In 2020–2021, Joss Whedon, whose show *Buffy the Vampire Slayer* (1997–2003) provided the 1990s with one of its key pop-feminist icons, was accused by multiple women of abusive and inappropriate behavior (Shapiro). In 2024, Neil Gaiman, whose works had been so beloved by feminist comic readers in the 1990s, was accused by five women of sexual assault (Pustz 86; Creamer).

Collectively, such cases have made grimly clear how often the "pro-sex" liberal feminism of the period provided a cover for predatory, exploitative, and abusive behavior, and how easily the victims of such abuse could be hidden in plain sight, their inappropriate sexualization and trauma-induced mental health issues willfully misread as proof of how free and empowered and sexually liberated they were. With such cases in mind, it is hard to read the male-authored "bad girl" comics of the 1990s without remembering all the real women who were forced or manipulated into performing other people's fantasies of "bad girl" sexuality, on their screens and in their bedrooms, and the psychological toll that such performances often took on them. Meanwhile Naomi Wolf, who in the mid-1990s was America's foremost spokeswoman for "power feminism," has become an anti-vaccination conspiracy theorist apparently convinced that Covid-era public health measures are being used as cover for a totalitarian takeover by the state (Klein).

As this book has stressed, the "bad girl" genre was never *just* about exploitation. In the early 1990s these comics were in serious dialogue with third-wave feminist social critique, forming part of the same cultural conversation about the legitimacy of female power, violence, and vengeance that gave rise to works such as *Thelma and Louise* and *Dirty Weekend*. Comics such as *Ghost*, *Mantra*, and *Catwoman* may never have been perfect, but they drew heavily upon the then-recent works of feminist writers like Wolf and Judith Butler, using queer, aggressive, gender-fluid heroines to actively challenge heteronormative patriarchal assumptions about society and the place of women within it. But this moment of ideological engagement proved extremely brief, and by the mid-1990s these three titles, and many others like them, were tilting rapidly toward depoliticized postfeminist superheroics. This shift bears witness to the power of market forces in the brutally competitive and crisis-ridden comics market of the period, whose economic incentives encouraged forms of short-term trend chasing that ultimately proved disastrous. Only idiosyncratic, one-person productions such as Roberta Gregory's *Naughty Bits* or Terry Moore's *Strangers in Paradise* were sufficiently insulated from such forces to retain their initial ideological focus, holding themselves mostly aloof from the doomed "bad girl" gold rush of 1994–1996.

In this respect, the "bad girl" craze surely represents one of the great missed opportunities in American comics history. In 1991–1993 the comics industry was collectively grappling with issues of power and gender, spurred on by the renewed feminist activism that arose out of the Anita Hill hearings of 1991 and the 1992 "Year of the Woman." The appearance of works such as *Catwoman: Defiant* or *Her Sister's Keeper* shows that all the conceptual materials needed for superhero comics to address these topics lay ready to hand. America had once had a thriving tradition of girl's comics, and in retrospect it seems clear that the time must surely have been ripe for someone to build on the foundations of DC's *Amethyst: Princess of Gemworld* and create an American equivalent to *Sailor Moon* capable of appealing to audiences far beyond the traditional adolescent male comic shop demographic. But instead the industry doubled down on its existing audience, with results that ultimately proved catastrophic, especially for the many indie publishers that staked everything on the success of their "bad girl" titles.

As I have discussed, such decisions are easy enough to understand in context. They formed part of the larger boom-and-bust narrative of the 1990s American comics market, in which a multitude of small publishers, spooked by the instability of the comics market, attempted to imitate the initial success of Image Comics, not realizing how fragile and temporary it would turn out to be. The "bad girls" represent only the extreme edge of the industry's general rush toward sex and violence, which flooded '90s comics with the muscle-bound cyborgs and ninja girls in swimsuits for which the era remains infamous today.

In this case, however, there was another factor in play: what psychologists refer to as "in-group bias." Few readers or creators in the period seem to have actively *wanted* to exclude women from comics—most, in fact, seem to have wanted the reverse—but they favored solutions that did not disrupt their own established practices and preferences, with results that ultimately proved largely counterproductive. As I have discussed, many of the people involved in the "bad girl" craze frequently expressed their desire to appeal to female audiences, and many of the comics themselves made earnest (if often clumsy) attempts to address feminist issues through their storytelling. But their sense of what female readers might want to read was skewed by their ideologically convenient commitment to "sex-positive" postfeminist gender politics, which would not allow them to acknowledge that few women would ever voluntarily read comics starring huge-breasted swordswomen wearing high heels and bikinis, regardless of what stories they told. When female readers tried to explain how uncomfortable such imagery made them, they were generally told that it *shouldn't*—because it was intended to celebrate women rather than exploit them, and because being sexy made women powerful rather than vulnerable, and because after all their male characters were drawn in equally unrealistic ways. Women consequently came to shun comic shops, and the prediction that only male-gaze sex appeal translated into higher sales became a self-fulfilling prophecy. When the comics retailer Joe Field was asked in 2001 how to make comics shops "less intimidating for female customers," he advised retailers to "be aware of the environment you create," especially "what display posters you put up that might be potentially offensive": an acknowledgment of just how thoroughly the omnipresent "bad girl" iconography of the 1990s had alienated potential female readers (ICv2).

The consequences extended well beyond the mid-1990s. Having missed their moment of reckoning with their own inherited sexism, American comics largely ceded the female audience for sequential art to manga instead: Thus Field noted that when women *did* come to his shop, it was mostly because they were looking for *shoujo* manga like *Sailor Moon* and *Ranma 1/2* (ICv2). Even after the success of the Marvel Cinematic Universe made superhero media mainstream in the 2010s, the market for American comic books remained heavily male dominated, with predictable consequences for the designs of its female characters (Beaty and Woo 98). The excesses of "bad girl" character design have faded, but skintight costumes and idealized supermodel bodies remain the norm: As Jill Lepore bluntly pointed out in 2015, most comic book superheroines still "look like porn stars," demonstrating what Bart Beaty and Benjamin Woo describe as the persistent "parallax between what is seen within the comics world as a relatively progressive (to some, even radical) superhero comic and its reception outside the comics world" (Lepore; Beaty and Woo 98). Even in film, the superheroines who appeared in early 2010s superhero movies were mostly angry, violent, and highly sexualized characters such as Catwoman (2012), Black Widow (2012), Gamora (2014), Scarlet Witch (2015), and Harley Quinn (2016), a trend that only started to shift with the #MeToo-era releases of *Wonder Woman* (2017) and *Captain Marvel* (2019). Furthermore, as I have discussed, during the 1990s these "bad girl" aesthetics spilled out into the then-nascent and similarly male-dominated American computer game industry, leaving a legacy of sexist character design that went largely unchallenged until the Gamergate controversy of 2014—a moment that has subsequently taken on outsized significance in the rise of the online alt-right.

It is easy, then, to condemn the badness of the "bad girls," and to hold them up as an example of what *not* to do for an industry currently wrestling with issues around the inclusion and representation of LGBTQIA+ people and people of color. Certainly this was my own initial reaction to the genre, as I started reading my way through the comics that comprised it. At the same time, however, it is worth recognizing that the genre also provided an important stepping stone to other things: It provided opportunities for female comics writers such as Christina Z, Jo Duffy, and Devin Greyson, it demonstrated decisively that a market existed for female-led comics, and it contributed to the normalization of queer characters, who appeared frequently in "bad girl" titles at a time when they were still largely invisible in more mainstream superhero media. 1990s Marvel comics did not usually feature characters like Konrad, a queer-coded male dancer who is magically transformed into a woman in *Elektra*, decides (s)he's happy to stay that way, and begins a relationship with a bisexual Asian man, but *Elektra*'s status as Marvel's "bad girl" book gave it a level of license to explore nonnormative sexualities and gender identities in a way that, say, *Spider-Man* could not. Embarrassing though such debts may be, modern comics like *Harley Quinn* may owe more to their "bad girl" predecessors than they generally like to admit.

In 2007–2008, the *Witchblade* writer Christina Z returned to comics to write *Shadow Hunter*, a series ostensibly created by the 1990s porn star Jenna

Jameson, and starring her superheroic alter ego "Jezzerie Jaden" as a sword-wielding supernatural warrior. In true "bad girl" style, the series was a commercial failure, running for only three issues, one of which consisted mostly of plot summaries of its never-to-be-written sequels. But in her introduction, Christina Z explained what had drawn her to what, at that stage, she must surely have known was likely to be a doomed project. "[I] love creating stories about women in power," she wrote. "Lilith is the ultimate rebel . . . She is the one who stood up to the Almighty. She has no fear" (*Shadow Hunter* no. 0).

And they never *did* have any fear, the bad girls. They were children of a fearless age. They were not afraid of men, or the church, or the state. Not of God, or Satan, or the inevitable armies of cyborg vampire ninjas. Not of sex, or nudity, or political incorrectness. Not absurdity, or incoherence, or bad taste. Not of feminist criticism. Not of the religious right.

Not even of things they really *should* have been afraid of.
Not even of things that we should *still* be afraid of.
They never had any fear.

Let that be their epitaph.

Works Cited

Secondary Scholarship

Alexander, Ella. "Wonder Woman." *British Vogue*, 31 March 2011, https://www.vogue.co.uk/article/eva-herzigova-has-a-baby-boy. Accessed 22 May 2024.

Anguiano, Dani. "The #FreeBritney Movement Finds Its Moment." *The Guardian*, 14 November 2021, https://www.theguardian.com/music/2021/nov/14/freebritney-movement-britney-spears-conservatorship. Accessed 27 October 2024.

Arons, Wendy. "'If Her Stunning Beauty Doesn't Bring You to Your Knees, Her Deadly Drop Kick Will': Violent Women in the Hong Kong Kung Fu Film." *Reel Knockouts: Violent Women in the Movies*, edited by Martha McCaughey and Neal King, U of Texas P, 2001, pp. 27–51.

Assiter, Alison, and Avedon Carol. *Bad Girls and Dirty Pictures: The Challenge to Reclaim Feminism*. Pluto, 1993.

Beaty, Bart. *Comics Versus Art*. U of Toronto P, 2012.

Beaty, Bart, and Benjamin Woo. *The Greatest Comic Book of All Time: Symbolic Capital and the Field of American Comic Books*. Palgrave Macmillan, 2016.

Beckman, Frida. "Good Girl Art—Facing Images of Women in David Mack's *Kabuki*." *Journal of Graphic Novels and Comics*, vol. 2, no. 1, 2011, pp. 39–54.

Bocage, Angela. "Define the Terms, Dismiss the Dregs, and Enjoy the Results." *Comics Journal*, vol. 143, 1991, pp. 3–4.

Boom, Richard. "Everette Hartsoe's Razor FAQ's Up At 600%." *Comics for Sinners*, 7 June 2013, https://www.comicsforsinners.com/everette-hartsoes-razor-faqs-up-at-600/. Accessed 11 May 2023.

Brienza, Casey. *Manga in America: Transnational Book Publishing and the Domestication of Japanese Comics*. Bloomsbury, 2016.

Brookner, Jackie. "Feminism and Students of the '80s and '90s: The Lady and the Raging Bitch; Or, How Feminism Got a Bad Name." *Art Journal*, vol. 50, no. 2, 1991, pp. 11–13.

Brown, Jeffrey. *Beyond Bombshells: The New Action Heroine in Popular Culture*. UP of Mississippi, 2015.

———. *Dangerous Curves: Action Heroines, Gender, Fetishism, and Popular Culture*. UP of Mississippi, 2011.

———. "If Looks Could Kill: Power, Revenge, and Stripper Movies." *Reel Knockouts: Violent Women in the Movies*, edited by Martha McCaughey and Neal King, U of Texas P, 2001, pp. 52–77.

Browne, Wendy. "Disciple of the Witchblade." *Women Write About Comics*, 31 July 2015, https://womenwriteaboutcomics.com/2015/07/disciple-of-the-witchblade/. Accessed 18 March 2024.

Bruton, F. Brinley. "Pamela Anderson: I Was Gang Raped in High School." *NBC News*, 19 May 2014, https://www.nbcnews.com/pop-culture/celebrity/pamela-anderson-i-was-gang-raped-high-school-abused-kid-n108786. Accessed 27 October 2024.

Bukatman, Scott. "X-Bodies." *Uncontrollable Bodies: Testaments of Identity and Culture*, edited by Rodney Sappington and Tyler Stallings, Bay Press, 1994, pp. 92–129.

Burke, Liam. "Harley Quinn and the Carnivalesque Transformation of Comic Book Fandom." *Transformative Works and Cultures*, vol. 35, 2021, https://journal.transformativeworks.org/index.php/twc/article/view/2015. Accessed 13 June 2024.

Busiek, Kurt. Foreword. *Vampirella Masters Series 5*. Dynamite, 2011.

Butler, Judith. *Gender Trouble*. 10th Anniversary ed., Routledge, 2006.

Canadian Federation of Students. "Sexualised and Gender Violence." https://www.cfsmb.ca/campaigns/sexualised-and-gender-violence. Accessed 21 February 2024.

Carol, Avedon. *Nudes, Prudes, and Attitudes*. New Clarion, 1994.

CBLDF Case Files. "Oklahoma v. Planet Comics." https://cbldf.org/about-us/case-files/cbldf-case-files/planet-comics/. Accessed 24 May 2024.

Cocca, Carolyn. "The 'Broke Back Test': A Quantitative and Qualitative Analysis of Portrayals of Women in Mainstream Superhero Comics, 1993–2013." *Journal of Graphic Novels and Comics*, vol. 5, no. 4, 2014, pp. 411–428.

———. "Negotiating the Third Wave of Feminism in *Wonder Woman*." *PS: Political Science and Politics*, vol. 47, no. 1, 2014, pp. 98–103.

———. "Reproducing Inequality and Representing Diversity: The Politics of Gender in Superhero Comics." *Spaces Between: Gender, Diversity, and Identity in Comics*, edited by Nina Eckhoff-Heindl and Veronique Sina, Springer, 2020, pp. 1–15.

———. *Superwomen: Gender, Power, and Representation*. Bloomsbury, 2016.

Cole, Susan. *Pornography and the Sex Crisis*. Amanita, 1989.

Comichron. "Comic Book Sales by Month." https://www.comichron.com/monthlycomicssales.html. Accessed 21 February 2024.

Costello, Brannon, and Brian Cremins. "Introduction—'Avenues of Free Thought and Fellow Feeling': US Comic Books in the 1980s." *The Other 1980s: Reframing Comics' Crucial Decade*, edited by Brannon Costello and Brian Cremins, Louisiana State UP, 2021, pp. 1–20.

Creamer, Ella. "Neil Gaiman Screen Adaptations Halted After Allegations of Sexual Misconduct." *The Guardian*, 13 September 2024, https://www.theguardian.com/books/2024/sep/13/neil-gaiman-screen-adaptations-halted-after-allegations-of-sexual-misconduct. Accessed 27 October 2024.

Cremins, Brian. "'Entertainment Should Be an Adventure': Reggie Byers, *Shuriken*, and the Black-and-White Boom." *The Other 1980s: Reframing Comics' Crucial Decade*, edited by Brannon Costello and Brian Cremins, Louisiana State UP, 2021, pp. 105–119.

Curtis, Neal, and Valentia Cardo. "Superheroes and Third-Wave Feminism." *Feminist Media Studies*, vol. 18, no. 3, 2018, pp. 381–396.

Diamond, Sara. "Pornography: Image and reality." *Women Against Censorship*, edited by Varda Burstyn, Douglas & McIntyr, 1985, pp. 40–57.

Dole, Carol. "The Gun and the Badge: Hollywood and the Female Lawman." *Reel Knockouts: Violent Women in the Movies*, edited by Martha McCaughey and Neal King, U of Texas P, 2001, pp. 78–105.

Dworkin, Andrea. *Mercy*. Four Walls Eight Windows, 1991.

———. *Pornography: Men Possessing Women*. Women's Press, 1981.

Elfring, Mat. "See Every Costume Invisible Woman Wore While in Fantastic Four." *Comic Vine*, 3 August 2015, https://comicvine.gamespot.com/articles/see-every-costume-invisible-woman-wore-while-in-fa/1100-153109/. Accessed 11 May 2023.

Faludi, Susan. *Backlash: The Undeclared War Against Women*. Vintage, 1992.

Fielding, Helen. *Bridget Jones's Diary*. Picador, 2014.

Firestone, Shulamith. *The Dialectic of Sex: The Case for Feminist Revolution*. Jonathan Cape, 1971.

Flood, Alison. "SFF Community Reeling After Marion Zimmer Bradley's Daughter Accuses Her of Abuse." *The Guardian*, 27 June 2014, https://www.theguardian.com/books/2014/jun/27/sff-community-marion-zimmer-bradley-daughter-accuses-abuse. Accessed 27 October 2024.

Gabilliet, Jean-Paul. *Of Comics and Men: A Cultural History of American Comic Books*. Translated by Bart Beaty and Nick Nguyen, UP of Mississippi, 2010.

Galvan, Margaret. *In Visible Archives: Queer and Feminist Visual Culture in the 1980s*. U of Minnesota P, 2023.

Gamble, Sarah. "Postfeminism." *The Routledge Companion to Feminism and Postfeminism*, edited by Sarah Gamble, Routledge, 2001, pp. 36–45.

Gearino, Dan. *Comic Shop: The Retail Mavericks Who Gave Us a New Geek Culture*. Ohio UP, 2017.

Gibbon, Dave. "Q&A: The Man Who Made Lara." *BBC News Online*, 28 June 2001, https://web.archive.org/web/20021215074846/http:/news.bbc.co.uk/2/hi/entertainment/1410480.stm. Accessed 21 February 2024.

Glazer, Sarah. "Manga for Girls." *New York Times*, 18 September 2005, https://www.nytimes.com/2005/09/18/books/review/manga-for-girls.html. Accessed 27 October 2024.

Gorton, Kristyn. "(Un)fashionable Feminists: The Media and Ally McBeal." *Third Wave Feminism: A Critical Exploration*, edited by Stacy Gillis, Gillian Howie, and Rebecca Munford, Palgrave Macmillan, 2007, pp. 212–223.

Greven, David. "Throwing Down the Gauntlet: Defiant Women, Decadent Men, Objects of Power, and *Witchblade*." *Action Chicks: New Images of Tough Women in Popular Culture*, edited by Sherrie Inness, Palgrave Macmillan, 2004, pp. 123–152.

Groth, Gary. "Confessions of a Smut Peddler." *Comics Journal*, vol. 143, 1991, pp. 5–7.

———. "Todd McFarlane Interview." *Comics Journal*, vol. 152, 1992, pp. 45–70.

———. "Vertigo Roundtable." *Comics Journal*, vol. 163, 1993, pp. 46–58.

Hayton, Christopher. "Evolving Sub-Texts in the Visual Exploitation of the Female Form: Good Girl and Bad Girl Comic Art Pre- and Post-Second Wave Feminism." *ImageText*, vol. 7, no. 4, 2014.

Healey, Emma. *Lesbian Sex Wars*. Virago, 1996.

Henry, Astrid. *Not My Mother's Sister: Generational Conflict and Third-Wave Feminism*. Indiana UP, 2004.

Herbst, Claudia. "Lara's Lethal and Loaded Mission: Transposing Reproduction and Destruction." *Action Chicks: New Images of Tough Women in Popular Culture*, edited by Sherrie Inness, Palgrave Macmillan, 2004, pp. 21–46.

Hernandez, Lea. "Lea Hernandez Responds." *Women in Refrigerators*, https://lby3.com/wir/c-lhern.html. Accessed 16 June 2024.

Hills, Elizabeth. "From Figurative Males to Action Heroines." *Screen*, vol. 40, no. 1, 1999, pp. 38–50.

Hills, Matt. *Fan Cultures*. Routledge, 2002.

Hopkins, Susan. *Girl Heroes: The New Force in Popular Culture*. Pluto Press, 2002.

Hutton, Ronald. *The Triumph of the Moon*. Oxford UP, 1999.

ICv2. "How to Sell Shojo." 5 August 2001, https://icv2.com/articles/comics/view/607/how-to-sell-shojo. Accessed 29 October 2024.

Inness, Sherrie. *Tough Girls: Women Warriors and Wonder Women in Popular Culture*. U of Pennsylvania P, 1999.

"International History of TBTN." *Take Back the Night*, https://takebackthenight.org/history/. Accessed 21 February 2024.

Johnson, Brian. "Dazzler, Melodrama, and Shame: Mutant Allegory, Closeted Readers." *Supersex: Sexuality, Fantasy, and the Superhero*, edited by Anna Peppard, U of Texas P, 2020, pp. 103–128.

Juffer, Jane. *At Home with Pornography: Women, Sex, and Everyday Life*. New York UP, 1998.

Jung, Carl. *The Theory of Psychoanalysis*. Nervous and Mental Disease Publishing Co., 1915.

Kashtan, Aaron. "*Amethyst, Meet Misty,* and *Angel Love*: Historical Footnotes or Paths Not Taken." *The Other 1980s: Reframing Comics' Crucial Decade*, edited by Brannon Costello and Brian Cremins, Louisiana State UP, 2021, pp. 318–334.

Klein, Naomi. *Doppelganger: A Trip into the Mirror World*. Allen Lane, 2023.

Kurson, Ken. "Talking Porn with Pamela Anderson and Rabbi Shmuley." *Observer*, 20 September 2016, https://observer.com/2016/09/talking-porn-with-pamela-anderson-and-rabbi-shmuley/. Accessed 27 October 2024.

"Lady Death Lives at Boundless." *Kickstarter*, https://www.kickstarter.com/projects/boundless/lady-death-lives-at-boundless/description. Accessed 5 June 2024.

Lawton, Megan. "Why the 90s and Noughties Are Having Such a Moment." *BBC News*, 17 July 2023, https://www.bbc.co.uk/news/newsbeat-66199129. Accessed 14 June 2024.

Lepore, Jill. "Looking at Female Superheroes with Ten-Year-Old Boys." *New Yorker*, 7 May 2015, https://www.newyorker.com/culture/cultural-comment/marvel-a-force-female-superheroes. Accessed 14 June 2024.

Levy, Ariel. *Female Chauvinist Pigs*. Free Press, 2005.

Licari-Guillaume, Isabelle. "Delayed Recognition: Wendy and Richard Pini's Elfquest." *The Other 1980s: Reframing Comics' Crucial Decade*, edited by Brannon Costello and Brian Cremins, Louisiana State UP, 2021, pp. 23–38.

———. *Vertigo Comics: British Creators, US Editors, and the Making of a Transformational Imprint*. Routledge, 2023.

Loach, Loretta. "Bad Girls: Women Who Use Pornography." *Sex Exposed*, edited by Lynne Segal and Mary McIntosh, Rutgers UP, 1992, pp. 280–294.

Lopes, Paul. *Demanding Respect: The Evolution of the American Comic Book*. Temple UP, 2009.

Lotz, Amanda. "Theorising the Intermezzo: The Contributions of Postfeminism and Third Wave Feminism." *Third Wave Feminism: A Critical Exploration*, edited by Stacy Gillis, Gillian Howie, and Rebecca Munford, Palgrave Macmillan, 2007, pp. 71–85.

Macdonald, Heidi. "You Guys Need to Get Laid." *Comics Journal*, vol. 200, 1997, pp. 92–99.

Mackenzie, Christobel. "The Anti-sexism Campaign Invites You to Fight Sexism, Not Sex." *Bad Girls and Dirty Pictures: The Challenge to Reclaim Feminism*, edited by Alison Assiter and Avedon Carol, Pluto, 1993, pp. 139–145.

Madrid, Mike. *The Supergirls: Fashion, Feminism, Fantasy, and the History of Comic Book Heroines*. Exterminating Angel Press, 2009.

Marcus, Sara. *Girls to the Front: The True Story of the Riot Grrrl Revolution*. Harper Perennial, 2010.

Marz, Ron. "Ron Marz Responds." *Women in Refrigerators*, https://lby3.com/wir/c-rmar.html. Accessed 16 June 2024.

McCaughey, Martha, and Neal King. "What's a Mean Woman Like You Doing in a Movie Like This?" *Reel Knockouts: Violent Women in the Movies*, edited by Martha McCaughey and Neal King, U of Texas P, 2001, pp. 1–24.

McClintock, Anne. "Gonad the Barbarian and the Venus Flytrap." *Sex Exposed*, edited by Lynne Segal and Mary McIntosh, Rutgers UP, 1992, pp. 111–131.

Mercer, Kobena. "Just Looking for Trouble: Robert Mapplethorpe and Fantasies of Race." *Sex Exposed*, edited by Lynne Segal and Mary McIntosh, Rutgers UP, 1992, pp. 92–110.

Misemer, Leah. "Serial Critique: The Counterpublic of *Wimmin's Comix*." *Journal of the Comics Studies Society*, vol. 3, no. 1, 2019, pp. 6–26.

Modleski, Tania. *Feminism Without Women: Culture and Criticism in a "Postfeminist" Age*. Routledge, 1991.

Moretti, Franco. "Conjectures on World Literature." *New Left Review*, vol. 1, 2000, pp. 54–68.

———. "The Slaughterhouse of Literature." *Modern Language Quarterly*, vol. 61, no. 1, 2000, pp. 207–228.

Munford, Rebecca. "'Wake Up and Smell the Lipgloss': Gender, Generation, and the (A)politics of Girl Power." *Third Wave Feminism: A Critical Exploration*, edited by Stacy Gillis, Gillian Howie, and Rebecca Munford, Palgrave Macmillan, 2007, pp. 266–279.

Napier, Claire. "Crime and Patience." *Women Write About Comics*, 24 February 2017, https://womenwriteaboutcomics.com/2017/02/crime-and-patience-witchblade-animated/. Accessed 18 March 2024.

———. "From Sexy to Sexual." *Women Write About Comics*, 19 September 2017, https://womenwriteaboutcomics.com/2017/09/sexy-sexual-witchblades-return-top-cows-maturing-eroticism/. Accessed 18 March 2024.

———. "Glove, Bracelet, Bikini, Halberd." *Women Write About Comics*, 17 July 2015, https://womenwriteaboutcomics.com/2015/07/glove-bracelet-bikini-halberd-exit-the-witchblade-for-good/. Accessed 18 March 2024.

———. "Lady Pendragon." *Women Write About Comics*, 29 May 2017, https://womenwriteaboutcomics.com/2017/05/lady-pendragon-what-you-want-to-know/. Accessed 18 March 2024.

Necrotic Genesis comments. *Kickstarter*, https://www.kickstarter.com/projects/coffincomics/coffin-comics-all-new-lady-death-necrotic-genesis-1/comments. Accessed 14 June 2024.

Negra, Diane. *What a Girl Wants? Fantasizing the Reclamation of Self in Postfeminism*. Routledge, 2009.

Nicholson, Hope. *The Spectacular Sisterhood of Superwomen: Awesome Female Characters from Comic Book History*. Quirk Books, 2017.

North, Jenny. *Mantraverse*. https://www.mantraverse.com/. Accessed 21 February 2024.

Owen, A. Susan, Sarah Stein, and Leah Vande Berg. *Bad Girls: Cultural Politics and Media Representations of Transgressive Women*. P. Lang, 2007.

Paglia, Camille. *Sex, Art, and American Culture*. Penguin, 1993.

———. *Sexual Personae*. Yale UP, 1990.

———. *Vamps and Tramps*. Viking, 1994.

Peppard, Anna. "'This Female Fights Back!' A Feminist History of Marvel Comics." *Make Ours Marvel: Media Convergence and a Comics Universe*, edited by Matt Yockey, U of Texas P, 2017, pp. 105–137.

———. "'Is That a Monster Between Your Legs or Are Ya Just Happy to See Me?': Sex, Subjectivity, and the Superbody in the *Marvel Swimsuit Special*." *The Routledge Companion to Gender and Sexuality in Comic Book Studies*, edited by Frederick Luis Aldama, Routledge, 2021, pp. 90–105.

———. "Presence and Absence in Theory and Practice: Locating Supersex." *Supersex: Sexuality, Fantasy, and the Superhero*, edited by Anna Peppard, U of Texas P, 2020, pp. 1–29.

Pustz, Matthew. *Comic Book Culture: Fanboys and True Believers*. U of Mississippi P, 1999.

Quesada, Joe. "Joe Quesada Responds." *Women in Refrigerators*, https://lby3.com/wir/c-jques.html. Accessed 16 June 2024.

Ray, Steve. "Meet the Comics Creators #1." *DC World*, 9 November 2018, https://dcworld.org.uk/breaking/2018/11/09/meet-comics-creators-1-amanda-conner-jimmy-palmiotti/. Accessed 12 June 2024.

Robbins, Trina. *From Girls to Grrrlz: A History of Women's Comics from Teens to Zines*. Chronicle, 1999.

Rogers, Mark. "Political Economy: Manipulating Demand and 'The Death of Superman.'" *Critical Approaches to Comics*, edited by Matthew Smith and Randy Duncan, Routledge, 2012, pp. 145–156.

Rosenfeld, Stephanie. "Looking for Girls in All the Boys' Places: An Unlikely Feminist Film Fest." *Bitch Media*, 29 February 1996, https://www.bitchmedia.org/article/looking-for-girls-all-boys-places. Accessed 11 May 2023.

Rubenstein, Anne. "Some Notes on the Difficulties Inherent in Writing Seriously About Graphic Narrative." *Comics Journal*, vol. 200, 1997, pp. 98–99.

"Sarah Bryant." *NEXT Generation*, vol. 4, no. 46, Imagine Media, October 1998, p. 83.

Savlov, Marc. "A Sort of Legend: Neil Gaiman, Storyteller." *Austin Chronicle*, 10 September 1999, https://www.austinchronicle.com/books/1999-09-10/73755/. Accessed 26 June 2024.

Schubart, Rikke. *Super Bitches and Action Babes: The Female Hero in Popular Cinema*. McFarland, 2007.

Segal, Lynne. "Sweet Sorrows, Painful Pleasures." *Sex Exposed*, edited by Lynne Segal and Mary McIntosh, Rutgers UP, 1992, pp. 65–91.

Sewer Mutant. "Inside the Rise and Fall of Cry for Dawn," 3 October 2022, https://sewermutant.com/inside-the-rise-and-fall-of-cry-for-dawn-deb790133ae1. Accessed 11 May 2023.

Shapiro, Lila. "The Undoing of Joss Whedon." *Vulture*, 17 January 2022, https://www.vulture.com/article/joss-whedon-allegations.html. Accessed 27 October 2024.

Shi Omnibus comments. *Kickstarter*, https://www.kickstarter.com/projects/shiomniv1/shi-omnibus-edition-vol-1-kickstarter-exclusive/comments. Accessed 14 June 2024.

Simone, Gail. "Fan GAIL SIMONE Responds." *Women in Refrigerators*, https://lby3.com/wir/r-gsimone.html. Accessed 16 June 2024.

———. "Five Questions with Mindy Newell." https://fivequestionswith.wordpress.com/mindy-newell/. Accessed 21 February 2024.

Snyder, R. Claire. "What Is Third-Wave Feminism? A New Directions Essay." *Signs*, vol. 34, no. 1, 2008, pp. 175–196.

Stasia, Cristina. "'My Guns Are in the Fendi!' The Postfeminist Female Action Hero." *Third Wave Feminism: A Critical Exploration*, edited by Stacy Gillis, Gillian Howie, and Rebecca Munford, Palgrave Macmillan, 2007, pp. 237–249.

Tasker, Yvonne. *Spectacular Bodies: Gender, Genre, and the Action Cinema*. Routledge, 1993.

Tasker, Yvonne, and Diane Negra, eds. *Interrogating Postfeminism: Gender and the Politics of Popular Culture*. Duke UP, 2007.

Tung, Charlene. "Embodying an Image: Gender, Race, and Sexuality in *La Femme Nikita*." *Action Chicks: New Images of Tough Women in Popular Culture*, edited by Sherrie Inness, Palgrave Macmillan, 2004, pp. 95–122.

Uslan, Michael. Introduction. *Batman in the Fifties*, edited by Bill Finger et al., DC Comics, 2021, pp. 5–9.

Vares, Tiina. "Action Heroines and Female Viewers: What Women Have to Say," *Reel Knockouts: Violent Women in the Movies*, edited by Martha McCaughey and Neal King, U of Texas P, 2001, pp. 219–243.

Voger, Mark. *The Dark Age: Grim, Great, and Gimmicky Post-modern Comics*. TwoMorrows Publishing, 2006.

Walters, Suzanna. "Caged Heat: The (R)evolution of Women-in-Prison Films." *Reel Knockouts: Violent Women in the Movies*, edited by Martha McCaughey and Neal King, U of Texas P, 2001, pp. 106–123.

Wertham, Frederic. *Seduction of the Innocent*. Rinehart, 1954.

Whelehan, Imelda. *Modern Feminist Thought: From the Second Wave to "Post-Feminism."* Edinburgh UP, 1995.

Williams, Linda. "Pornographies On/scene, or Diff'rent Strokes for Diff'rent Folks." *Sex Exposed*, edited by Lynne Segal and Mary McIntosh, Rutgers UP, 1992, pp. 233–265.

Williams, Paul. "Questions of 'Contemporary Women's Comics.'" *The Rise of the American Comics Artist: Creators and Contexts*, edited by Paul Williams and James Lyons, UP of Mississippi, 2010, pp. 135–149.

Williams, Paul, and James Lyons, eds. *The Rise of the American Comics Artist: Creators and Contexts*. UP of Mississippi, 2010.

Wilson, Elizabeth, and Gillian Rodgerson. *Pornography and Feminism: The Case Against Censorship*. Lawrence and Wishart, 1991.

Wolf, Naomi. *The Beauty Myth*. Vintage, 1990.

———. *Fire with Fire*. Chatto and Windus, 1993.

Wright, Bradford. *Comic Book Nation: The Transformation of Youth Culture in America*. Johns Hopkins UP, 2003.

Yarrow, Alison. *90s Bitch: Media, Culture, and the Failed Promise of Gender Equality*. Harper Perennial, 2018.

Young, Paul. *Frank Miller's Daredevil and the Ends of Heroism*. Rutgers UP, 2016.

Zahavi, Helen. "Dirty Weekend—Reviews." https://www.helenzahavi.com/dirty-weekend-reviews. Accessed 21 February 2024.

Zeisler, Andi. *We Were Feminists Once: From Riot Grrrl to Covergirl: The Buying and Selling of a Political Movement*. Public Affairs, 2017.

Comics

Action Comics. Vol. 1. DC Comics, 1938–2011, 904 issues plus issue 1,000,000.

Akemi. Brainstorm Comics, 1997, 1 issue.

Allegra. Image, 1996, 4 issues.

Alley Cat. Silverhawk Productions, 1999–2000, 6 issues.

Angel Heat. Amazing Comics, 1997, 1 issue.
Bad Girl Backlash. AC Comics, 1995, 1 issue.
Batman. Vol. 1. DC Comics, 1940–2011, 713 issues plus issue 0 and issue 1,000,000.
Birds of Prey. Vol. 1. DC Comics, 1996, 4 issues.
Birds of Prey. Vol. 2. DC Comics, 1999–2009, 127 issues.
Bitchy Butch. Fantagraphics, 1999, 1 issue.
Black Widow. Vol. 3. Marvel, 2004–2005, 6 issues.
Blade of Shuriken. Eternity, 1987–1988, 5 issues.
Camelot 3000. DC Comics, 1982–1985, 12 issues.
Captain America. Vol. 1. Marvel Comics, 1968–1996, 454 issues.
Catwoman. Vol. 1. DC Comics, 1989, 4 issues.
Catwoman. Vol. 2. DC Comics, 1993–2001, 94 issues plus issue 0 and issue 1,000,000.
Catwoman. Vol. 3. DC Comics, 2002–2010, 83 issues.
Catwoman: Defiant. DC Comics, 1992, 1 issue.
Claire Voyant. Lightning Comics, 1996, 1 issue.
The Crow. Written and drawn by James O'Barr. Trade paperback edition from Kitchen Sink Press, 1993.
Cry for Dawn. Cry for Dawn Productions, 1989–1993, 9 issues.
Cyberforce. Vol. 2. Image, 1993–1997, 35 issues.
Cybernary. Wildstorm, 1995–1996, 5 issues.
Cynder Nira X. Immortelle Studios, 1996, 2 issues.
Daredevil. Vol. 1. Marvel, 1964–1998, 380 issues.
Dejah Thoris and the Green Men of Mars. Dynamite, 2013–2014, 12 issues.
Demonslayer. Next Entertainment, 1999–2000, 3 issues plus issue 0.
Dirty Plotte. Drawn and Quarterly, 1991–1998, 12 issues.
Elektra. Marvel, 1996–1998, 19 issues plus one flashback issue.
Elektra: Assassin. Epic, 1986–1987, 8 issues.
Elektra Lives Again. Epic, 1990, 1 issue.
Elektra: Root of Evil. Marvel, 1995, 4 issues.
Exposure. Image, 1999–2000, 4 issues.
Fangs of the Widow. London Night Studios (issues 1–4) and Ground Zero Comics (issues 5–14), 1995–1997, 14 issues.
Fantastic Four. Vol. 1. Marvel, 1961–1996, 416 issues.
La Femme Vampirique. Brainstorm, 1997, 1 issue.
Flesh and Blood. Brainstorm Comics (issue 1) and Blindwolf Comics (issues 2–3), 1995–1996, 3 issues.
Gen13. Vol. 2. Wildstorm, 1994–2002, 77 issues plus issue -1, issue 13B, and issue 13C.
Gen13 Bootleg. Image, 1996–1998, 20 issues.
Ghost. Vol. 1. Dark Horse, 1995–1998, 36 issues.
Ghost Special. Dark Horse, 1994–1998, 3 issues.
Harley Quinn. Vol. 2. DC Comics, 2014–2016, 30 issues plus issue 0.
Immortal II. Image, 1997–1998, 5 issues.
Jade Warriors. Vol. 1. Image, 1999–2000, 3 issues.
Lady Death/Shi. Avatar Press, 2006, 2 issues plus preview and issue 0.
Lady Justice. Vol. 1. Tekno Comix, 1995–1996, 11 issues.
Lois Lane. DC Comics, 1986, 2 issues.
Manga Shi. Crusade, 1996–1997, 3 issues plus issue ½.
Mantra. Vol. 1. Malibu Press, 1993–1995, 24 issues.
The Maxx. Image, 1993–1998, 35 issues.

Naughty Bits. Fantagraphics, 1991–2004, 40 issues.
New Talent Showcase. DC Comics, 1984–1985, 15 issues.
Nira X. Vol. 2. Entity Comics, 1995, 4 issues.
Nira X. Vol. 3. Entity Comics, 1995–1996, 3 issues.
Nira X Soul Skurge. Entity Comics, 1996–1997, 3 issues.
Pandora. Avatar Press, 1997, 2 issues plus issue 0.
Penthouse Comix. Penthouse Comics, 1994–1998, 33 issues.
Purgatori: The Vampire's Myth. Chaos! Comics, 1996, 3 issues plus issue 0.
Razor and Shi Special. London Night Studios, 1994, 1 issue.
Razor Annual. London Night Studios, 1993–1995, 2 issues.
Razor: Cry No More. London Night Studios, 1995, 1 issue.
Razor: Uncut. London Night Studios, 1995–1999, 39 issues, numbered 13–51.
Sachs and Violens. Epic, 1993–1994, 4 issues.
Scimidar. Vol. 1. Eternity, 1988–1989, 4 issues.
Scimidar. Vol. 2. Eternity, 1989, 4 issues.
Scimidar. Vol. 3. Eternity, 1990, 4 issues.
Shadow Hunter. Virgin Comics. 2007–2008, 3 issues plus issue 0.
Sheena: Queen of the Jungle. London Night Studios, 1998–1989, 3 issues plus issue 0.
Shi: Art of War 1998 Tourbook. Crusade, 1998, 1 issue.
Shi / Cyblade. Image, Crusade, 1995, 2 issues.
Shi: The Series. Crusade, 1997–1998, 13 issues.
Shi: The Way of the Warrior. Crusade, 1994–1997, 12 issues.
Shuriken. Vol. 1. Victory Productions, 1985–1987, 9 issues.
Shuriken. Vol. 2. Eternity, 1991, 6 issues.
Shuriken: Cold Steel. Eternity, 1989–1990, 6 issues.
Shuriken: Hellbender. Eternity, 1990, 1 issue.
Silver Sable. Marvel, 1992–1995, 35 issues.
Spider-Woman. Vol. 1. Marvel, 1978–1983, 50 issues.
Strangers in Paradise. Vol. 1, reprint edition. Abstract Studios, 1997, 3 issues.
Strangers in Paradise. Vol. 2. Abstract Studios, 1994–1996, 14 issues.
Strangers in Paradise. Vol. 3. Image, Abstract Studios, 1996–2007, 90 issues.
The Tenth. Vol. 2. Image, 1997–1998, 14 issues plus issue ½.
Tim Vigil's Webwitch. Avatar Press, 2002, 3 issues plus issue 0.
Vampblade, Vol. 1. Action Lab, 2016–2017, 12 issues.
Vampblade '98. Action Lab, 2017, 1 issue.
Vampirella: Death and Destruction. Harris, 1996, 3 issues.
Vampirella: The Dracula War. Harris, 1992–1994, 5 issues plus issue 0.
Vampirella: Morning in America. Harris, 1991, 4 issues.
Vamps. Vertigo, 1994–1995, 6 issues.
Vogue. Image, 1995, 3 issues.
Warrior Nun Areala. Vol. 3. Antarctic Press, 1999–2001, 19 issues.
Warrior Nun Areala: Resurrection. Antarctic Press, 1998–1999, 3 issues.
Webwitch. Avatar Press, 1997, 2 issues plus issue 0.
Wheel of Worlds. Tekno Comix, 1995–1996, 1 issue plus issue 0.
Whisper. Vol. 1. Capital Comics, 1983–1984, 2 issues.
Widow: Flesh and Blood. Ground Zero Comics, 1992–1993, 3 issues.
Widow/Luxura: Blood Lust. Ground Zero Comics, 1996, 1 issue.
WildCATS. Image, 1992–1998, 50 issues plus issue 0.
Witchblade. Top Cow, 1995–2015, 185 issues plus issue ½ and issue 500.

Witchblade Takeru Manga. Vol. 1. Art by Kazasa Sumita, script by Yasuko Kobayashi, translated by Shoko Oono. Top Cow Productions, 2006.
Wizard: The Guide to Comics. Wizard, 1991–2011, 235 issues plus issue 0 and issue 2000.
Wonder Woman. Vol. 2. DC Comics, 1987–2006, 226 issues plus issue 0 and issue 1,000,000.
X/1999. Vol. 1. Story and art by CLAMP, translated by Lillian Olsen. Viz, 2003.
X-Men. Vol. 1. Marvel, 1963–1981, 141 issues. Published as *Uncanny X-Men* from issue 114.

Index

Note: Page numbers in italics refer to illustrations.

About the Author

JOSEPH CRAWFORD is an associate professor of English literature at the University of Exeter. His academic research explores the history of popular culture from the eighteenth century to the present day. He is the author of four previous academic monographs: *Raising Milton's Ghost*, *Gothic Fiction and the Invention of Terrorism*, *The Twilight of the Gothic*, and *Inspiration and Insanity in British Poetry*.